TAKE THAT HILL!

Pergamon Titles of Related Interest

Alsudairy *et al.*   FIVE WAR ZONES: THE VIEWS OF LOCAL
                     MILITARY LEADERS

Collins   GREEN BERETS, SEALS & SPETSNAZ: US &
          SOVIET SPECIAL MILITARY OPERATIONS

Godden   HARRIER: SKI-JUMP TO VICTORY

Hunt & Blair   LEADERSHIP ON THE FUTURE BATTLEFIELD

Myles   JUMP JET: THE REVOLUTIONARY V/STOL
        FIGHTER

Related Journals*

DEFENSE ANALYSIS

DEFENCE ATTACHE

*Free specimen copies available upon request.

TAKE THAT HILL!

Royal Marines
in the Falklands War

Nick Vaux
Major-General Royal Marines
Commando Forces

Forewords by
General P. X. Kelley & Max Hastings

PERGAMON-BRASSEY'S
INTERNATIONAL DEFENSE PUBLISHERS, INC.
(a member of the Pergamon Group)

WASHINGTON · NEW YORK · LONDON · OXFORD
BEIJING · FRANKFURT · SÃO PAULO · SYDNEY · TOKYO · TORONTO

U.S.A. (Editorial)	Pergamon-Brassey's International Defense Publishers, 8000 Westpark Drive, Fourth Floor, McLean, Virginia 22102, U.S.A.
(Orders)	Pergamon Press, Maxwell House, Fairview Park, Elmsford, New York 10523, U.S.A.
U.K. (Editorial)	Brassey's Defence Publishers, 24 Gray's Inn Road, London WC1X 8HR
(Orders)	Brassey's Defence Publishers, Headington Hill Hall, Oxford OX3 0BW, England
PEOPLE'S REPUBLIC OF CHINA	Pergamon Press, Room 4037, Qianmen Hotel, Beijing, People's Republic of China
FEDERAL REPUBLIC OF GERMANY	Pergamon Press, Hammerweg 6, D-6242 Kronberg, Federal Republic of Germany
BRAZIL	Pergamon Editora, Rua Eça de Queiros, 346, CEP 04011, Paraiso, São Paulo, Brazil
AUSTRALIA	Pergamon-Brassey's Defence Publishers, P.O. Box 544, Potts Point, N.S.W. 2011, Australia
JAPAN	Pergamon Press, 8th Floor, Matsuoka Central Building, 1–7–1 Nishishinjuku, Shinjuku-ku, Tokyo 160, Japan
CANADA	Pergamon Press Canada, Suite No. 271, 253 College Street, Toronto, Ontario, Canada M5T 1R5

F3031.5
.V38
1986

First edition 1986

Published in United Kingdom by
Buchan & Enright, Publishers Ltd
53 Fleet Street, London EC4Y 1BF

Library of Congress Cataloging in Publication Data
Vaux, Nick.
Take that hill!
Includes index.
1. Falkland Islands War, 1982—Commando operations.
2. Great Britain. Royal Marines. Commando, 42—
History—Falkland Islands War, 1982. 3. Falkland
Islands War, 1982—Regimental histories—Great Britain.
F3031.5.V38   1987   982'.064   87–13532
ISBN 0–08–035548–X

Photoset in North Wales by
Derek Doyle and Associates, Mold, Clwyd

*Reproduced, printed and bound in Great Britain by
Hazell Watson & Viney Limited,
Member of the BPCC Group,
Aylesbury, Bucks*

CONTENTS

ILLUSTRATIONS

Harassing the fleeing enemy (*Ryan*)
'L' Company resting on the outskirts of Stanley (*Ryan*)
' "Argies" are tragic!' (*Corporal Alan Sharpe*)
The RSM, 2/IC and Sergeant Harradine, Stanley airfield (*Ryan*)
Lance-Corporal Cuthell with General Menendez (*Ryan*)
Sergeant Napier on the glacier, Southern Thule (*Sergeant J. Napier*)
'The ragged cliff-top dwellers' (*Sharpe*)
'Is Daddy really back?' (*Western Evening Herald*)
Presenting Mike Norman with his Mention in Despatches (*Ryan*)
At the first Mount Harriet Day Parade, 1983 (*Ryan*)
The RSM reads the lesson (*Ryan*)
Police Constable Adams in Stanley (*Senior Aircraftman [Phot.]
    Johnson*)
Laying a wreath on Lieutenant Nunn's grave, 1986 (*Johnson*)

MAPS

Drawn by Neil Hyslop

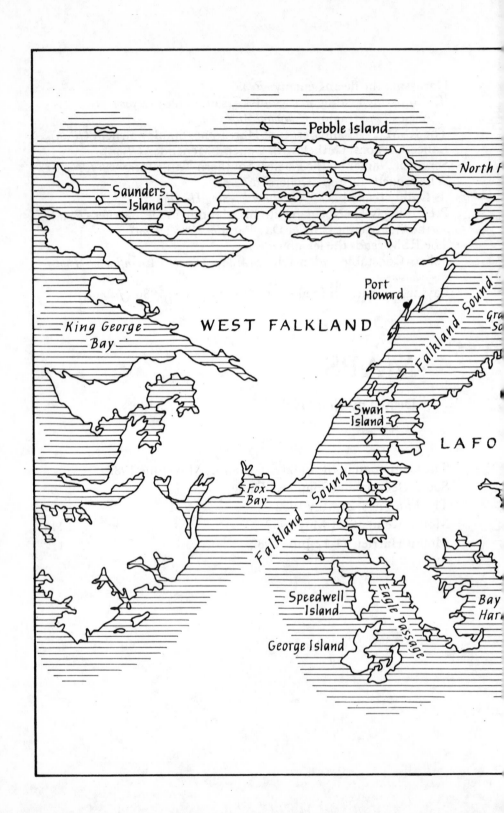

Sound

Douglas
Settlement

Teal

Inlet

ing Head

Port San Carlos

△ Cerro Montevido

San Carlos
River

Cow Bay

Berkeley Sound

Teal Inlet
Settlement

Top Malo
House

Mt Low
△

Wireless Ridge

San Carlos

Estancia
House △ Mt Longdon

Mt Kent △

EAST FALKLAND

STANLEY

ex Mts

Two Sisters △
Mt Harriet △

△ Sapper Hill

Camilla Creek House

Fitzroy
Settlement

Bluff Cove
Settlement

Darwin

een
ent

Choiseul Sound

Swan Inlet

Lively Island

Low Bay

Wireless Ridge

Tumbledown

Moody Brook

Sapper Hill

Stanley Harbour

Airport

Mt William

STANLEY

Sea Lion Islands

Port Harriet

0   5   10   15 km

This book is dedicated to Royal
Marines with nicknames like 'Smudge',
'Taff', 'Chalky', and 'Sticks', who have
enriched my career with challenge and
humour. In this short war they
displayed the legendary courage,
endurance and discipline that have so
often made the British invincible. It was
my exceptional fortune to command 42
Commando when they proved this once
again.

AMERICAN FOREWORD
by P. X. Kelley

This is not a book on grand strategy. Lord knows, there are more than enough of those. This is a book about professionalism, courage, determination, and selfless dedication in battle. Specifically, it is an intimate story of the 650 gallant "Green Berets" of 42 Commando, Royal Marines, during the Falklands Campaign in 1982 — a campaign which added yet another chapter to their illustrious history.

For his inscription in my copy of his book, the author wrote: "To General 'P.X.' — Who commanded his own company of Royal Marines on operations in another far flung outpost." Indeed I did, and by coincidence it was with 42 Commando, Royal Marines. I joined "42" aboard HMS Bulwark off the coast of Aden Protectorate in early 1961, and served as Commanding Officer, "C" Troop, in Singapore, Malaya, and Borneo. This was my final assignment during a tour as the U.S. Marine Corps Exchange Officer with the Royal Marines, a tour which included, among other things, five weeks of indescribable agony during the celebrated Commando Course at the Infantry Training Center, Lympstone. Upon successful completion of this course, and only upon successful completion of this course, a graduate was authorized to wear the coveted Green Beret. As I reflect back upon the "tortures of Dartmoor," I still recall by fellow squad members — young 18 year old Royal Marine recruits who had a difficult time understanding why a 32 year old "Yankee Marine" Captain had volunteered for such human misery. Was it worth it? Damned right it was! It taught each of us that after the human body has reached the limits of physical endurance, it can still go on "guts and heart." This was a lesson which served me well for the rest of my career as a U.S. Marine, and one which helps explain the extraordinary physical accomplishments of 42 Commando during the Falklands Campaign.

Lieutenant Colonel (now Major-General) Nick Vaux is a "Marine's Marine" in the truest meaning of the phrase. Having spent two years as the Royal Marine Representative at our Marine Corps Development and Education Command at Quantico, Virginia, he is no stranger to the "Yankee Marines." To the contrary, he is a well known and respected leader — one who tells a spellbinding story of men in combat. Nick's professionalism and sense of humor are captured in the order he gave to his Marines on the parade ground at Bickleigh Barracks as they prepared to embark aboard Canberra: "42 Commando, to the South Atlantic – Quick March." To the professional military man, that says it all!

Nick Vaux makes a point that the Falklands Campaign was an, "almost chivalrous conflict." More often that not, that's the way it is with the Marines — as strange as that may seem to the uneducated reader. Marines are a paradox. On the one hand they are "tough as nails" on the battlefield, but, on the other, they are human and compassionate. This is highlighted in a message handed to the Regimental Sergeant Major of "42", as he re-embarked in Canberra, by four Argentine soldiers: "To all the military forces and crew aboard this ship. We are sorry for all of the troubles we may have caused you during this trip, and we are greatly grateful to you for your kind treatment of us. Thank you."

To the warriors of 42 Commando, Royal Marines, who performed so magnificently during the Falklands Campaign: — WELL DONE — PER MARE PER TERRAM — CARRY ON!

July 1987
Washington, D.C.

P. X. KELLEY
General, U.S. Marine Corps (Ret.)
Former Commandant

BRITISH FOREWORD

by Max Hastings

At the beginning of 1982, more than a quarter of a century after Suez, a post-imperial generation of British citizens and British soldiers had adapted ourselves to a world in which the idea of participating in a conventional war seemed impossibly remote. When the news came that Argentina had invaded the Falkland Islands, most of us were bewildered: a civilized Latin-American state valued so highly a possession which we valued so little, that it was prepared to go to war for it. When the British government announced the mobilization of a task force to the South Atlantic, the sense of unreality heightened. Whatever the moral, political, military logic of the government's action, it was hard to believe that Britain's armed forces were to be deployed – perhaps committed to fight, to inflict and accept loss. The image accorded so ill with the vision of modern, passive, declining Britain to which our generation was resigned.

Thus, in a kind of uncertain haze, some thousands of officers and men of the Army and Navy, together with a handful of correspondents, embarked for the South Atlantic. Aboard the great hulk of *Canberra*, stripped of all the comforts and cuisine that entitled her to be called a 'luxury' liner, we met each other warily for the first time, exchanged drinks at the bar, waved farewell to those left behind on the quayside as the lines were cast off. We deepened our acquaintance as we ploughed south through the Bay of Biscay, towards the warm sunshine of mid-Atlantic, and thence onward into the great seas and deadly earnest of the southern ocean. We drank with each other in the Crow's Nest bar, amid the scaffolding supporting the flight deck above our heads. We ate amid the dubious comforts and congealing gravy of the

1

dining-room deep in the bowels of the ship. We chatted on the upper decks through the long mornings, as men drilled again, and again, and again with weapons and equipment: 'cock gun, mag off; check gun, mag on'. We sat crowded together in the cinema for briefings on Argentina, her army, the Falklands, the climate. After a month at sea, we began to know each other quite well; after a second month afloat and ashore, many of us had become friends; by the coming of peace, bonds had been forged by common experience that would last a lifetime.

I set off from Southampton with the advantage of a deep-rooted liking and affection for servicemen. In the previous fifteen years or so, I had done my share of war reporting in Africa, Indochina, the Middle East and some lesser trouble spots. I had become well-accustomed to the ways of the US Army, full of admiration for the expertise of the Israeli, nostalgically fond of the Indian. But, because I am English and steeped in the history of the British Army, I had always deeply regretted missing the opportunity to be with them at war. This was not, I hope, because I was particularly eager to see Britain fight or British servicemen die; but out of pure sentiment. Having been passionately fond of Winston Churchill's *The River War* since my teens, I had been dogged all my life by regret that I could not hope to sit stirrup to stirrup with a lancer line, or file a despatch from the field of Omdurman. Many modern British journalists, of course, have reported on the British Army's experience in Northern Ireland. But there, where we spent only an hour or two with a unit before returning to civilian company in our offices and hotels, none of us achieved really close relationships with the military. Perhaps it would have made us less sceptical, less effective reporters, had we done so. But, now that the generation who did National Service has almost faded into retirement, there are few active reporters with an intimate acquaintance with, or understanding of, the services and their ways.

Thus, for most of us on *Canberra*, the long voyage into the South Atlantic provided a completely new experience. It was fascinating to watch the relationship develop between reporters and service officers. Our dealings with the Navy were seldom very happy. Most naval officers are bluff men, accustomed to speaking their minds. The senior naval officers of the Task Force made clear, from Southampton to San Carlos, their lack of enthusiasm for the press, and its presence with the fleet. With a few enchanting exceptions such as Captain Jeremy Larken and his officers on *Fearless*, press relations with the Navy were strained. It was made clear that we were lucky not to be chained in the bilges. In contrast, from the beginning, the Army and Royal Marines delighted and impressed even the most radical and sceptical of the correspondents. Their natural good manners, their evident professionalism, their witty scepticism about the task upon which they were embarked, were hard to resist. We became fond of almost all of them, from Colonel Tom Seccombe – the senior officer on *Canberra* – through 'H' Jones and Hew Pike of 2 and 3 Para, Malcolm Hunt of 40 Commando, their officers and NCOs, their other ranks – and, of course, Nick Vaux of 'Four-Two'.

My six feet five inches of gangling journalist might reasonably have irked Nick – a slightly built five feet nothing, as it seemed to me. But the quick, modest, disarming grin, founded upon great and justified self-confidence, never left him for long. I was delighted to discover that his wife bred Connemara ponies, and that he himself had ridden in steeplechases, just as I relished the preoccupation of one of the young Blues and Royals troop commanders with his polo ponies. It seemed immensely pleasing, in 1982, to find service officers still possessed of such sensible rural passions. And with the passing weeks, I also began to understand how much Nick was liked and respected by his Commando. He possessed great endurance and determination, professionalism and common sense. The longer one studies military history, the more sharply one perceives that men often dislike being led in battle by bombastic heroes. They fear them too much. Men like to be commanded by those they believe will do their utmost to bring them back alive when the job is done. Vaux, I began to perceive on *Canberra* and saw in full measure on East Falkland, is one of those. He was the same man in the Crow's Nest bar as on the side of Mount Kent, as when he took that charming gnome's grin onto the summit of Mount Harriet: cool, committed, understated, utterly dependable.

On the morning we landed at San Carlos, 21 May, Nick was charmingly forgiving (indeed, probably much relieved, though he was too polite to show it) by my absence from the ranks of his Commando. I had very much wanted to go to war with 'Four-Two', until I learned at the eleventh hour that for the first day, they were to remain in reserve aboard *Canberra*. I went ashore instead with 40 Commando, who proved delightful hosts. In the first days that followed, through the air battles around the anchorage, I was shuttling hither and thither between the ships and shore, watching the action and filing despatches. I did not see Nick again until one memorable night in his room in the settlement at Port San Carlos, as we prepared for the landing on Mount Kent. Nick's version of events in these pages suggests even more deplorable chicanery on my part, to get aboard one of his helicopters for the night landing, than I would admit to myself. But my best moment of the night, after furious protests from some officers and NCOs that I should be stealing space from a useful marine to take my useless limbs up the mountain, came when Nick took me aside and muttered: 'Look, Max. I'm not going to give you permission to come with us. But if we get up there and I find you with us, then let's just say that I won't make any fuss.' I loved him for that. And so it came to pass. After a nerve-racking night contour flight to the mountain, I tumbled out of a Sea King alongside Colonel Michael Rose, a dozen marines and Nick himself.

I spent only twenty-four hours on that unspeakably bleak summit, where I shivered through the night in my sleeping-bag, when none of Nick's assault team possessed any such refinements of comfort. All through the days that followed, while correspondents and commanders shuttled to and fro between the hills and the ships – with the live-saving chance to thaw out between sorties – 42 Commando stuck it out on Mount Kent, in conditions that defied reason. They held the vital jumping-off ground for the final, decisive battle for Stanley. There was constant debate whether, as conditions worsened and men deteriorated, they should be brought down off the hill to recover. But the Argentines could not be permitted to reoccupy the ground Vaux's men held, and the helicopter assets needed to move men down the hill and up again were in desperately short supply. 'Four-Two' stayed on Mount Kent and Wall Mountain beyond, until on the evening of 11 June, the moment came for them to launch their battle.

This time, to my immense delight, I was with them again. I listened to Nick Vaux's calm, forceful exposition of the plan – his own, strikingly imaginative plan – at the Commando briefing. Men hugged themselves in the wind while he traced his intention to push the Commando round in a long hooking movement, to hit the objective from the rear. 'Four-Two' were to seize Harriet, while 45 Commando and 3 Para assaulted the heights to the north. All that afternoon, we stamped our feet in the powdery dust of snow, chatted over our brews, and peered through binoculars at that impossibly remote alien land across the valley – the enemy's positions. My own worst moment of the day came when the dauntless Kim Sabido of Independent Radio News suddenly demanded of the CO: 'Nick, please may I go with "L" Company?' 'L' Company would assault after surprise had been lost and enemy resistance was at its height. My heart sank. For a moment, I thought: 'Oh God, now I shall have to ask to go with them, too.' But one of the advantages of being thirty-six rather than twenty-six is that one is no longer afraid to admit the limits of one's own courage. I was content to follow Nick's Tac HQ, and watch the assault from a reasonably safe distance. But I could not help remembering the days, light years ago, on the voyage south, when I feared so much that when the battle began, the land force commanders would deny us the chance to see the action. Nick just said cheerfully: 'Well, Kim, if you're sure you want to. Go ahead.' And so Kim Sabido put himself further forward in the Mount Harriet battle than any correspondent at any other moment in the Falklands War, and got the marvellous radio despatch that he deserved.

Nick tells the story of the Harriet battle too well in these pages to need repetition. We endured an interminable and frightened night – fearful, above all, of mines underfoot as we stumbled forward, freezing in the glare of the spasmodic Argentine flares. From time to time I caught Nick's quiet, unhurried voice talking decisively into a radio handset, pushing men on or holding them back. Then, at last, as dawn came up, we stood atop the mountain. His plan had triumphantly succeeded. At tiny cost to his Commando, he had led them to the objective. As the light grew, we gazed pityingly upon the distant dots of fleeing Argentines, pursued by shellfire called down on them by the Battery Commander alongside us. We rejoiced in our own survival, and in the Commando's marvellous success: a success for absolute professionalism, determination, unit spirit – and leadership, leadership at troop and company level, but above all by the unit CO. It was Nick Vaux's performance on Mount Harriet, as much as anything else that he did in the war, which was recognized in the subsequent Honours List by the award of the Distinguished Service Order.

3 Commando Brigade's hard-won victories on the night of 11/12 June exhilarated the entire landing force. Once the Argentines had been dislodged from their strongest positions at such relatively tolerable cost, it was evident that final victory was only a matter of time. Yet even the most optimistic never imagined for a moment that only two days later, Port Stanley would fall, and the Argentines offer their capitulation. The sense of relief was overwhelming. It would be foolish to pretend that, as an enemy, they had possessed the courage or technical competence of, say, the Germans or Japanese. But, with even a slender ration of determination, they might have protracted the battle for the Falklands through the winter weeks, at terrible cost to the British landing force exposed on the mountains. When Nick Vaux and 42 Commando at last tramped into Stanley, they knew they had shared in a small military miracle. Amid the acute discomforts and cold of the sheds in which they were housed, a mile or so outside the town, they savoured the end of the battle.

Nick never lost his sense of fun. Two days after the war ended, I went to visit him in the hut he was using as a headquarters. Once peace returns, so too does the most enjoyable aspect of war, that you can get away with doing almost anything without anybody asking questions or quoting regulations. I told the Colonel I was sorry I had missed the chance to try firing a 60-mm 'bunker buster', which had been used to such effect on the battlefield. 'Regimental Sergeant-Major!' called the Colonel obligingly. 'Take Mr Hastings outside and let him fire a sixty-six at the hill!' So I did, and the bang was most gratifying. But by that stage, all of us felt that we had heard enough bangs to last us our lifetimes. Even the most ardent spirits of the Royal Marines and the Parachute Regiment, men who had been so impatient to test themselves on the battlefield back on the ships a few weeks before, were visibly, movingly, grateful that it was all over, that no more men need die, that we could all go home.

When I came back from the South Atlantic, like so many others I cherished above all the memory of the men I had met and learned to know there, and my admiration for what they had done. Each of us has his own list of companions who, if we did not see them again for years, we should never forget. Foremost on my own was Vaux, who had made me laugh so often, who had shown such exemplary patience and kindness to me, who had done so much that I appreciated so much. I am delighted that he has written this book. It is too modest, and says too little about what he and those around him achieved. But it gives the authentic tone, the flavour, of a summer in the South Atlantic in which a few thousand British servicemen did something which, however eccentric the cause of the war, was still wholly fit to be admired and honoured.

MAX HASTINGS
July 1986

PROLOGUE

The wind whistled eerily amongst the crags, buffeting malevolently every now and again, sometimes causing the swirling mist suddenly to envelop us. With the increasing light of dawn we could discern the silhouette of a small gap in the rocks, towards which we squelched up the peaty slope. In the gloom I could read the map contours only with difficulty, but this distraction seemed justified while my companion acted as lookout. The rain spattered across our waterproof smocks, and fighting-order straps squeaked and rasped under their burdens.

We were almost at the summit, breathing more heavily, straining up the last gradient, as vulnerable as we could be, when the chilling, unmistakable clash of an automatic weapon being cocked electrified the senses. Who knows how one will react at such a moment? Freeze? Run? Attack in desperation?

I never had time to find out, because a swift push sprawled me down, and at the same time our saviour shouted urgently, but clearly, 'British Commandos! Royal Marines! British … '. The balance of our lives tilted back an age, or an instant, later with the soft 'snick' of a compressed action being released. Our war would continue.

For once, this was no training exercise on Dartmoor. The scene was Mount Kent, and the ambushers were men of the Special Air Service. I was commanding 42 Commando Royal Marines, and the Regimental Sergeant-Major had just averted disaster – as RSMs so often do.

1

THE CALL TO ARMS

The shrill insistence of the telephone dragged me bemusedly from the deep sleep that settles in the early hours. I was not expecting to be rung. After thirty years in the Service reaction to calls in the night is instinctive, however exhausted or over-indulged one's system may have been. But my reflexes were switched off. I was on leave; someone else was safeguarding my responsibilities. I would be flying to America in a few hours. It was about 0400 hours on Friday, 2 April 1982 ...

'Nick, I am glad to have caught you before you flew', said Colonel Ian Baxter, who directed the administrative and logistic organizations within Commando Forces Royal Marines. 'That trip is out now. Your unit is recalled forthwith and we would like you back there as soon as possible. The Argentines are expected to invade the Falklands within the next twelve hours.' He rang off briskly, after confirming that the duty personnel had been alerted to implement the well-practised contingency system for Recall. It would be more difficult than usual this time, because most of us had begun three weeks' leave after our winter training deployment to North Norway. I tried to remember how many officers were abroad; realizing that, for a start, the Second-in-Command and Operations Officer were among them.

As I attempted to reassure an anxious voice from the bed that this was just a precautionary recall, I must confess that my initial reactions were of frustration and cynicism, rather than conviction and enthusiasm. Even if the Argentines did invade, would Britain really retaliate? If so, how? And with what? Air strikes or naval blockades seemed two possibilities, with an amphibious operation a rather distant third. Of course, if there was such an operation then the Royal Marines would have to do it, but surely this was all weeks, if not months away, by which time the United Nations, or someone else, would have negotiated a settlement? In the meantime I was losing out on a long-planned reunion with old friends in Norfolk, Virginia. We had expected to meet this very evening at The Raven bar, for Brandy Alexanders and spare ribs. I had been away from America for a long time, and certainly did not fancy a trip to the Falklands.

As the car hurtled through the dark Devon lanes towards Bickleigh Camp, home of 42 Commando Royal Marines, I tried to remember whether it would be winter in the South Atlantic ...

When I walked into the outer office my morale was partially restored by the reassuring sight of the Adjutant and Regimental Sergeant-Major already galvanizing the Commando into action. How they had got there before me I did not even bother to ask; effective Adjutants and RSMs somehow always know. I was fortunate in both. The Adjutant, Phil Wilson, an enormous, forceful officer with a devastating wit, was liked and trusted at every level within the Commando. His colleague, Warrant Officer First Class Dave Chisnall, BEM, epitomized the example and experience essential to maintaining respect and confidence among the 650 or so highly trained men who comprise a Royal Marines Commando.

The problem for the moment was to ensure that all of these 'Royals' were alerted, directly or through the police, to return from leave at once. This was a daunting task, which would occupy all that day and most of the next, with marines hastening back from leave at home or abroad almost everywhere in the world. As I wrestled with other problems next door I became occasionally aware of Phil's inimitable approach to various individuals:

'Yes, lad, I *do* know where Marrakesh is, but I still expect you back here by 1200 hours tomorrow. No, Her Majesty does not pick up the tab for your bird ...'

'OK, well *don't* tell him before the service, but make sure he hoists it in *before* he's had a drink at the reception. Otherwise he'll think it's another of your pathetic jokes ...'

It was to be the first of many great points of pride for me that almost everyone in the unit was back within three days. We eventually embarked with only one NCO missing, and even he managed to reach the ship from the West Coast of America before we actually sailed.

Meanwhile planning, administration and resupply proceeded at breakneck speed, while I desperately attempted to supervise, advise or support the subordinate commanders in their labours. Hardest pressed at this stage was Captain Dennis Sparks, the Quarter-master. The 'QM' is a legendary figure in the military hierarchy. Traditionally, and sensibly, he is promoted through the ranks to this crucial appointment, for reasons of experience, initiative, and an acquisitive nature. Dennis was no exception. He combined the parsimony of a squirrel with the predatory instinct of a fox. The Commando lacked for nothing that was available; often seeming to have more than its share. He was the second oldest officer in the Commando after myself, which made for a special understanding between us, despite the frustrating regularity with which he carried off the veteran's prize in so many unit competitions. Normally he was responsible for controlling over £7 million of weapons, stores, vehicles and equipment. An arctic warfare unit must hold duplicate issues of kit and equipment for winter or conventional operations, which complicates logistics and increases expense. Now we were being inundated with additional war stores, notably ammunition, which rolled through the camp gates in chartered juggernauts with inexorable efficiency. On top of all this, we had only partially unpacked from Norway; most of the arctic clothing was still being cleaned, and some of the weapons were being overhauled. 'Not to worry, Colonel, you just leave me to sort it out and all will be well,' said Dennis. I did.

Someone else with a crucial role to play at any time, but now under special pressure, was my 'understudy', Major Guy Sheridan, the unit second-in-command. Inevitably this is a delicate relationship, as I suppose it must be for principal player and understudy in the theatre. But on military operations never more so. For then the 2/IC must ensure he can take over instantly, if necessary, without encroaching prematurely upon the authority of the Commanding Officer. Many a peacetime partnership has unexpectedly foundered after the bugle blew, but Guy and I had been close friends for many years and there was never to be that problem. A lean, uncompromising, sometimes shy individual, Guy Sheridan positively glowed with vitality in the face of physical challenge. As a Royal Marine, he had specialized for many years in the demanding skills of Mountain Leadership, acquiring wide experience climbing in the United Kingdom, Europe and the Himalayas. In between times he had represented Great Britain in the Biathlon and ski orienteering, and more recently had undertaken a series of astonishing expeditions across the high plateaux of the world. On one occasion, he skied with two Norwegians for more than 1,000 kilometres above the Indian Himalayas in winter. On another trip they traversed the Carpathian mountains in four weeks, surviving solely on what they carried upon their backs. Guy was invariably cheerful in adversity, his enthusiasm and strength always a tonic when endurance was sapped and the wind chilled – as it often does in our profession.

In these final days of April, however, he was preoccupied with co-ordinating the administrative arrangements, so that we should be ready to react when our orders came. Months later I was to discover that he and his family had returned from a day's skiing in the Pyrenees to find a note from the British Consul left at their holiday home. All that night they raced through France for the ferry, and Guy was back with us on the second day. It was just as well. By then both the jetlagged Operations Officer and myself were spending most of our time at one conference or another.

The Operations Officer was Ian McNeill, a bright and forthright captain. He had recently graduated from the Army Staff College at Camberley, arguably the finest preparation in the world for what we might have to do – control a unit in battle. I had selected him as 'Ops Officer' just a few weeks earlier, despite mutual reservations; he had only commanded his company for a few months, and this is a highly prized time in an infantry officer's career. Characteristically, he accepted disappointment without demur. It was now his business to provide me with the essential information and advice on which to make plans. Then he must transcribe them swiftly into concise and comprehensive orders which everyone, including me, could understand.

Another invaluable quality, from everyone's point of view, was Ian's resilience to the Vaux tantrum, which would dash itself to pieces against his meticulous politeness before subsiding harmlessly, or in embarrassment. He could make one feel utterly unreasonable merely by impassively responding 'Very good, Colonel', although this was transparently not the case from his point of view. Everyone in authority must yearn for compatible and discerning subordinates. Perhaps no one more than a commander in war, facing pressure and fatigue which test relationships to their limits. My own shortcomings include impatience and irascibility (tactfully designated 'a mercurial temperament' in various reports over the years). In Ian McNeill I found a soothing influence, as well as a loyal and capable subordinate. He was to be of inestimable help in the months to come.

The initial series of planning meetings was held at HQ Commando Forces in Plymouth. These were far from the structured, functional affairs we were used to. One of the great strengths of a small Corps like the Royal Marines lies in the total familiarity with which we are able to set about our tasks. Years of practice together are crucial because an amphibious operation is one of the most complex of military evolutions. It must be mounted in consecutive stages, each of them vitally dependent upon one another. From the outset it is imperative to know the task, the mission. Next, the location for a landing must be identified. After that, availability of shipping and stipulated timings will determine the plan for execution.

At this early stage Brigadier Julian Thompson and the staff of 3 Commando Brigade had been told none of these things. Indeed, in the event we set sail without a defined mission, loading as ships were made available. It was the beginning of a bold, unorthodox deployment, urgently driven with decisive political direction and sustained by constant adaptation to the changing circumstances. Later, we basked in almost unbelievable luck, when St Jude could justifiably have been claimed to be British. But during this preparatory confusion, it was the commitment, foresight and professional capability of the Services, supported by their civilian agencies, that got the Task Force to sea.

An early Orders Group ('O' Group) at Brigade included the Commanding Officer of the 3rd Battalion, the Parachute Regiment, Lieutenant-Colonel Hew Pike. At that point we realized that this was not to be just a 'Green Beret' (Royal Marine) affair, although we had no idea of the scale of the force that would eventually be deployed. Initially it had seemed that it would comprise the three Royal Marines Commando units, (40, 42 and 45 Commandos), our own artillery, engineer, and logistic support, and a Rapier missile anti-aircraft battery. But now, in addition to the Royal Marines forces, there would be 3 Para and two troops of light tanks.

For a while we wondered how even half of us could fit into the Royal Navy's few amphibious ships; then the astonishing news came through of SS *Canberra*'s requisition. Eventually, on Sunday 4 April, a more formal 'O' Group clarified, in impressive detail, who would go into which ship and with what. 42 Commando was to embark in the *Canberra*, already en route to Southampton from Gibraltar. As it happened, we had discreetly slipped one of our own subalterns on to the last connecting flight to Gibraltar, thus securing an invaluable foot in the camp – or rather deck space – before anyone else. Lieutenant Tony Hornby, the innocent-looking Assistant Training Officer, proved so plausible a manipulator of statistics that we reached Ascension Island before it was proved that 42 Commando held more desirable territory on board than it was entitled to. For the moment, however, the notion that we would sail to war in a luxury liner seemed most bizarre to me. The rest of the unit were in no doubt that it was an excellent idea.

Amid the frenzied preparations, I had been pondering a separate problem which, ironically as it turned out, concerned the Major-General commanding Commando Forces, Jeremy Moore. He was shortly to retire. I felt that his distinguished association with 42 Commando, during which he had twice been decorated with the Military Cross, should be recognized. Phil Wilson, the Adjutant, was not impressed with the idea of any ceremonial on top of our preparations to sail in a few days' time. But we decided that the situation could be turned to everyone's advantage with a farewell parade for the General before relatives and friends, in the traditional way. Some swift calls secured us the Band of Commando Forces, and the General agreed to review the parade and accept a presentation. Suddenly the idea seemed to catch on. Everyone began enthusiastically rehearsing for a major occasion which would obviously attract many spectators, including the media. I started to wonder if we hadn't overreached ourselves.

As it turned out, we had not. The mood was well caught by an old friend of the Royal Marines, Geoffrey Underwood, the Defence Correspondent of the *Western Morning News*:

COMMANDOS PARADE FOR FALKLANDS CRISIS

A bleak wind sliced across the parade ground at Bickleigh Barracks today as 42 Commando paraded before their departure for the South Atlantic and a possible battle for the Falkland Islands. The Dewerstone glowered in the background under dark clouds as Major-General Jeremy Moore, who commands Commando Forces, spoke to the hundreds of officers and men on parade in full fighting order ...

After the review, General Moore was presented by Lt-Col

Vaux with a pewter statue of a Marine in mountain and arctic warfare uniform kneeling in skis and firing a self-loading rifle. The parade moved off the square after Lt Col-Vaux had given the final order '42 Commando, to the South Atlantic – Quick March'.

An astonishing wave of publicity followed from that order to 'March to the South Atlantic'. Months afterwards, friends in America told me of seeing it on CBS News, while BBC TV and Radio featured it for several bulletins. But the order was nearly not given at all. After belatedly deciding to revive an old Royal Marine tradition of ordering a parade to march to its final military destination, it seemed prudent to inform our press organizations in case of some security 'hang-up'. Sure enough, a message came back declaring that the management in London did *not* approve of announcing a march on the Falklands. Ruefully, the idea was dropped. But, on the day of the parade, I mentioned it to General Jeremy. He pondered for a moment, before responding, with a perfectly straight face, that if marching to the Falklands sounded too jingoistic, he really could not see how mentioning the South Atlantic as our destination could offend anyone …

Before the General's parade, however, there were other problems to be sorted out. Early on the morning of the day our stores were to move to Southampton, I received an anxious call from Colonel Richard Preston, Chief of Staff, Commando Forces … 'I can't tell you more on the telephone, but we are on our way to task one of your sub-units elsewhere at minimal notice. How soon could they be ready to fly out with arctic-warfare equipment?' I responded tersely that this would depend upon whether we could stop the convoy even now rolling through the main gate. Some fifteen minutes later, after vigorous 'whipping-in' by Adjutant and RSM had restored the situation, the staff arrived. Richard briefed me that one company group from 42 Commando was to come to six hours' notice for an airmove to Ascension Island. This force would embark immediately to recapture South Georgia.

By this time I knew where South Georgia was and a lot about its dangerous terrain and vicious climate. We had been informed that it was held by at least a hundred Argentine troops with strong naval support. The plan to recapture the island included elements of both Army and RM Special Forces with several RN ships in support. Only a hundred arctic-warfare-trained troops could go and they were to take all their winter equipment, including skis. From the moment they were detailed, everyone in the company group was to be confined to camp and 'incommunicado'. The rest of the unit were not to know of the mission. As the briefing came to an end, Ian McNeill and I looked at each other wryly as we wondered which monumental problem to tackle first.

First I had to decide who should go. That must take into consideration the company commander and his subordinates, and also which sub-units could be most easily rearranged to do the job. We must also decide what specialist support should be added and identify the most accessible transport from which to offload equipment needed. I had a separate worry. One of my three rifle companies was to be despatched on an evidently hazardous mission, under someone else's control. I was not at all happy with the circumstances, and it was then that I first considered putting Guy Sheridan in overall command. This was not a decision to be taken lightly. I had been a second-in-command myself and knew full well how I would need him in the weeks to come. So would the company commanders, who looked to him for direction and co-ordination. On the other hand, his qualifications were unique, and instinct also told me that an experienced major like Guy Sheridan was more likely to resolve dissension within a force drawn from several units than a younger company commander. In any case, the latter should not be diverted from his own responsibilities. Later, when I sent for Guy, it struck me that real danger and grief could be close to all of us.

That decision taken, it was easier to choose the company commander for the South Georgia party, since I could afford to retain the two most experienced for whatever awaited us elsewhere. As it happened, I had not the slightest doubt that Captain Chris Nunn, who had just successfully completed his first winter in command of 'M' Company, was the right choice. A short, resolute, ebullient man, and an experienced light helicopter pilot, he had the charisma and adaptability for this unconventional task; I was also confident that he would work well with Guy Sheridan. Soon we had agreed upon a company group that included a precious section of the unit's Reconnaissance Troop, who were all tried and trained specialists in mountain and arctic warfare. We decided to include two of the six 81-mm mortars from Support Company but also asked for a naval gunfire support control team from the specialist Royal Artillery unit which is attached to Commando Forces.

We were now joined by an old friend, Captain Douglas Keelan, another international mountaineer of repute. He had been sent to advise on South Georgia itself, which he knew well. I decided that we need not tell 'Munch Company', as they were known in the ribald Royal Marine vernacular, of their destiny yet. That could wait until after the parade for General Jeremy. Instead they were warned they would sail on a different ship because there was no space on *Canberra*. That night my wife Zoya laid on a small supper party for Guy and Molly Sheridan, with Douggie Keelan there as well. We had all been close friends for many years, so it was a relaxed and happy occasion, but as I watched their laughing faces in the firelight I hoped privately that we would all do this again in the years to come.

Next morning, as soon as the General's parade was over, the RSM met me outside the unit gymnasium, where 'M' Company Group had been assembled. His extensive experience in mountain and arctic warfare made him especially conscious of how hazardous this enterprise would be, and his advice and suggestions about the men or equipment we should choose had already proved invaluable. Now he told me that the Company had already worked out that it was not just sailing without us; the presence of all those specialized support elements had put paid to that little deception. To begin with I told them what I thought should happen, then cautioned them to remain flexible because war never turns out the way one expects. Finally I tried to warn them not to underrate the enemy, before wishing them well. We were not to meet again for over four months. They were to experience danger, physical adversity, disappointment and loneliness. On the other hand, they were to become famous overnight, albeit somewhat undeservedly. Throughout it all, however, they maintained their morale and professional standards.

By now, increasing emphasis was being placed upon the professional commitment of individual marines. We were about to step abruptly out of the familiar, controlled environment in which a commando normally functions. Soon we would be on a large, luxurious ship run by civilians, shared with strange units from other services. The close-knit disciplined relationship of officers, NCOs and marines might be drastically diminished by factors outside our control, and it seemed particularly important to instil in everyone a real sense of personal responsibility. There was some ruthless pruning in those last few days, aimed at leaving behind the few who might give cause for concern. On two occasions I invoked a rarely used military custom, publishing on orders the names of disciplinary offenders who, in addition to more conventional penalties, were to be 'left out of battle'. Undoubtedly this had a profound effect. But we also had to leave behind many more men than were needed for the Rear Party, because of the supposed limits on accommodation in *Canberra*. Frustratingly, after we had sailed there turned out to be spare places on the ship.

One of our sadder tasks was having to turn away many volunteers who yearned to come. Most were those who had just left the unit, but who still remained on our books during their last leave. It had been decided that these ranks were to be retained in the UK and that no additional men could be 'recruited', with only two exceptions. Much to our delight our previous RN doctor, Surgeon-Lieutenant Ross Adley was retained so that the newly joined Surgeon-Lieutenant Nick Morgan could go to South Georgia, while Captain Matt Sturman, RM, who was on foreign service leave, volunteered to forgo that and joined as an extra 'Battle Adjutant' within Commando Headquarters. Both officers were to prove invaluable during the campaign.

Once the parade for General Moore was over, and with 'M' Company addressed, it was time for us all to make our own good-byes. In the past few days there had been little enough time for much attention to my wife and three children, but I was also conscious of other officers and SNCOs whose homes were not in or near Plymouth, some of whom had been unable to see their families at all since recall. I had married a 'Service daughter', and a Royal Marine one at that (we both try to excuse such lack of originality by pointing out that we met in Bermuda). Among many advantages, I found in Zoya a wife for whom unexpected separation at short notice is accepted as inevitable. Whether that makes it any easier only she could say. My two elder daughters were old enough to understand that this crisis could lead to fighting, but we all conspired to reassure my nine-year-old son that this was merely an exciting adventure for Daddy. I still have a photograph of them waving a banner as we marched by on the day of the parade: ' "FOUR-TWO" CDO IS MAGIC, ARGIES ARE TRAGIC'.

On 8 April Dennis, Ian, Phil and I set off for Southampton in the staff car, the three of them chuckling at the command '42

Commando, to the South Atlantic – Quick March' on radio news bulletins. As we drove across the West Country in the spring sunshine it seemed like a relaxed start to another exercise.

Our embarkation was swift and efficient. In no time we were settled into this spacious and elegant, if strange, environment, which was to represent security, comfort and friendship for so many of us in the weeks to come. Before we sailed the following evening I had a visit from an old friend, David Storrie, then commanding Royal Marines Poole. A natural warrior, with more than twenty-five years' military experience around the world's trouble spots, he was typical of scores of my contemporaries for whom the Falklands crisis proved desperately frustrating, because they were left behind. Much of David's command was already sailing with us. But he knew that, come what may, he had to remain to look after the rest of it. We joked cynically that this would just be a run to the sun and back, but I felt real sympathy, as well as relief at my own good fortune. In the end, about a third of the Corps was left out of the campaign. It is a measure of the camaraderie among Royal Marines that, afterwards, this divide was never, on either side, to be a problem.

Canberra sailed at twilight in an exhilarating blaze of military nostalgia that could have been a realistic scene from a feature film. In past centuries, expeditionary forces for the Crusades, Crécy, Agincourt, had sailed down Southampton Water. More recently loaded troopships had set out for wars around the Empire. Now the Royal Marines and the Parachute Regiment Bands vied with each other to stir the martial instinct. A crowd of relatives, sightseers, dockers and officials waved, or cheered, appropriately. We slipped away smoothly, the darkness of our passage illuminated intermittently by flashes of goodwill from friendly headlights. I sipped a gin-and-tonic on the wing of the bridge and reflected that going to war seemed to have its compensations. If indeed we really were going to fight.

2

A CRUISE ON *CANBERRA*

In my profession, the words 'requisition' and 'billeting' are familiar enough, if a little outdated. They have usually carried with them the stigma of reluctance, or resentment, on the part of the hosts, but nothing could have been further from that than our experience of *Canberra*. From Captain Dennis Scott-Masson and his officers, through Lauraine Mulberry and the girls to Geoffrey in the bar or Arthur in the engine-room, we were made hearteningly welcome on this graceful and spacious floating hotel. And what a readjustment they had had to make! At one moment the ship was on a Mediterranean cruise, with a sedentary clientele seeking relaxation in the sun. Within less than a week *Canberra* was carrying more than 3,000 Green and Red Berets, most of whose owners were less than twenty years old. Worse, her swimming pools were boarded over, her superstructure mangled. Elegant lounges were converted into canteens, sun decks became cluttered with ammunition boxes. The ship's broadcast resounded with inarticulate or conflicting directives; the circular promenade deck was thronged with joggers; water consumption quadrupled. The dish most in demand, predictably, was chips. Perhaps even more traumatically, a Royal Navy 'liaison' team, headed by a senior four-ring Captain, assumed authority to co-ordinate the transition from passenger liner to troopship. It was a measure of the tolerance and goodwill displayed by the entire ship's company that the new management seemed to aggravate us far more than it did them.

An essential ingredient in the lasting and harmonious bond between us all was the fact that *Canberra*'s crew were in the hospitality business; another was certainly that P&O is a

23

disciplined, motivated, and extremely professional company, with its own long-standing traditions and morale. Here was the common ground on which we forged the closest links possible between a military and civilian organization. These were to prove critical in the sudden flare of war, as well as so memorable afterwards, when we returned together. I shall never cease to think affectionately and with pride of the 'Great White Whale', in which 42 Commando was doubly fortunate to go down to war, and to come home afterwards; there is a host of others who would say the same.

There were, however, plentiful ingredients for dissension. Inter-unit rivalry is a way of life in the Services, even amongst Royal Marine Commandos. Now we had to contend with another major unit, whose members wore the red beret of our rivals in élite mystique, the paratroopers. Worse than this, however, our predominantly aggressive group was catapulted into close proximity with a ship's company operating under different rules, with a group of girls and some 'camp' equivalents thrown in. Finally, that nightmare of Whitehall bureaucrats and object of suspicion to most senior officers, the press, had at the last minute materialized in a motley group, ready to sail with us. Given all these elements, firm but discerning direction was called for – luckily it was on hand.

Resident landlord, and thus *de facto* 'seigneur', was *Canberra*'s Captain, Dennis Scott-Masson, an imposing and affable man whose somewhat reserved nature was belied by a deep, rumbling voice that seized our attention during the almost nightly broadcasts. Of all the individuals whose world had been turned topsy-turvy by this crisis, his transition must have been the most traumatic. Although he was a long-serving Royal Naval Reserve officer, I doubt if he seriously believed that his beloved ship might actually be sunk. Weeks later, as we stood helplessly on her bridge at the height of the initial Argentine air attacks, I caught a memorable glimpse of his face. It was a mask of horror and outrage, as if some madman was trying to destroy his family. For the moment, as we sailed south, he grappled uneasily with a host of unfamiliar problems, ranging from how to black out this floating skyscraper, to where he should allow the military to fly their plethora of flags.

Meanwhile, he and his officers steadfastly retained the ambience of a cruise liner, with generous drinks parties, formal dress in the evenings and invitations to dine at their tables. He was backed up by a highly professional team. The Deputy Captain, the relaxed 'Sammy' Bradford, had commanded his own ships across the world, and Martin Reed, the lean, saturnine Chief Officer with formidable social stamina, was almost equally experienced. Commanding Officers were permitted on *Canberra*'s bridge from the outset, so we had plenty of opportunities to watch the strict but paternal direction being exercised over the junior staff, with impressive and reassuring results.

Elsewhere in the ship, the technical and administrative departments functioned equally smoothly. We never lacked for facilities, comfort, or simple response, however difficult our requests might be. Maurice Rudderham, the Purser, suddenly found himself feeding more than 3,000 ravenous young men, with his foreign staff replaced by RN or RM cooks. To make things worse, even rationed beer evaporated at over 7,000 cans a day! Down in the Bureau, normally the rendezvous for passengers changing money or making sightseeing arrangements, the brisk and capable Miss Mulberry co-ordinated a joint organization that gradually overcame the difficulties of adjusting the ship's routines to our imposed presence. There were only some fifteen of the female staff who had volunteered to sail with us, so there was a natural concern that, amongst 3,000 or so of the 'rapacious and licentious', we – or they, at any rate – were bound to face problems. There were none of any consequence, however, either going down or on the way back, a testimonial to the character and commonsense of those girls, as well as to their multitude of male shipmates.

Naturally, all this co-operation did not simply just happen. It had begun with an advance party flown on board off Gibraltar and was consolidated at Southampton into what was starkly termed Naval Party 1710. Totalling around ten officers and more than fifty assorted ranks, it provided the link between the liner and her embarked force, with the task of guiding *Canberra* through her transition into a troopship within the Task Force. Luxury liners do not replenish at sea, zig-zag through convoys in the dark, disembark hundreds of troops into landing-craft, or close up for action against air attacks. Each evolution poses complex and demanding problems, and to bring about this transition the Royal Navy selected one of its more unconventional figures, Captain Christopher Oldbury Burne. A dynamic and idealistic officer, with every right to be called a 'real sea-dog', Chris did not have a lot of 'form' in the harmonious co-operation business, and initially seemed insensitive. Fortunately, I had known him well over the years, and knew this to be misleading.

'Beagle' Burne, as he had been nicknamed years before after managing the Royal Naval College hounds, was a tall, gaunt individual with a heart of gold. According to Phil Wilson, he had 'forgotten to switch off his afterburners', but this was simply because his boundless energy seemed so overwhelming. Once determined on a course of action, little would deter him from seeing it through. Stories of his impetuosity abounded, of which my own favourite illustrates that selfless determination which eventually was to win him almost universal devotion. On one occasion, while at sea as Captain of HMS *Coventry*, he confronted the life-buoy sentry on the ship's stern by inviting him to prove the system and jump overboard. When the sailor sensibly demurred, the 'Beagle' carefully took off his cap and leapt over the rail himself.

Such endearing sincerity was less obvious to begin with, for he ruffled clouds of feathers throughout the ship. The journalists, in particular, took exception to his outspokenly jaundiced view of their presence on board, and derisively dubbed him 'Captain Fawlty', after John Cleese's character in the TV comedy. (In fact, Chris Burne, who was extremely well read as well as endowed with a keen sense of humour, could probably have upstaged them by suggesting a more literary buffoon.) As it was he concentrated on whipping *Canberra* into shape in the shortest possible time.

On the military side, we had also been provided with an arbiter, partly to keep three strong-willed Commanding Officers under control (as Brigadier Julian Thompson later revealed), but mainly to provide an overall authority for the 3,000 or so embarked sailors, marines and soldiers. Colonel Tom Seccombe was also the Deputy Brigade Commander, separated deliberately from the actual Headquarters travelling in HMS *Fearless*. If any disaster should befall the HQ on passage south, or after the landings, he could instantly provide substitute leadership. A solid, urbane and reassuring figure, he had served in the Royal Marines Special Boat Squadron before commanding his own Commando in Northern Ireland, and had that deceptively easy knack of conversing equably with dukes or dustmen. His swift banter and outrageous anecdotes endeared him to the troops, but he was also a discerning and determined officer. He possessed an unerring knack for detecting the 'ungodly', as he benignly termed anyone who disrupted the delicate fabric of our seaborne coalition. A subtle rebuke usually followed, with an apt quotation from Evelyn Waugh or P.G. Wodehouse, whose works he could declaim at will to admiring journalists. 'Uncle Tom', as he was affectionately known, in fact provided exactly the cohesion that was needed. Our long-standing friendship did not deter him from reprimanding me firmly when 42 Commando's manipulation of *Canberra*'s living space was detected, nor did it prevent me from being genuinely contrite – for a while, anyway.

We lived opposite each other in palatial staterooms, each with its own bathroom, normally reserved for the super-rich on world cruises. Apart from having enough space to hold a full-sized Commando 'O' Group, mine contained a well stocked bar that was replenished daily by Christine, the maid. I wondered if other Royal Marines COs had ever gone to war like this, meanwhile reassuring Marine Green, my MOA – batman – that he had not been totally supplanted by the nubile counterpart provided by P&O.

All of us were extremely conscious that the comforts of *Canberra* could prove disastrous to our fitness unless firmly controlled at all levels. In the Officers' and Sergeants' Messes the word was merely passed, but in the men's canteens, where beer only was served, that was rationed to two cans per man per day. In fact, the limitation was based upon necessity rather than distrust; unlimited beer was simply not available. Since they regularly deploy in ships, the Royal Marines are anyway accustomed to such restrictions, but no one else seemed particularly perturbed.

That may well have been because of the intense physical training which had been instituted from the outset. Each day, starting at 0700 hours, every available upper deck space was allocated to a designated unit for some form of endurance or strengthening exercise. Throughout the ship the high-pitched cries of physical training instructors rose above the thumps and groans of sweating bodies pushed to the limits. Around the quarter-mile of Promenade Deck that encircled the ship, small groups, whole platoons, or even formed companies of around a hundred men, ran remorselessly. At first they wore only boots and PT gear. Later they carried full equipment. These were the fittest troops in the British Army, and we were determined that they should remain

so. They did; indeed, some marines and paratroopers stepped
ashore in the Falklands in better shape than when they embarked
in *Canberra*. This had proved possible for two main reasons. First,
because we were on a cruise liner with the space in which to train;
second, because we carried the specialist instructors to ensure that
this was done safely and progressively – without that expertise
much effort would have been counter-productive. (Happily, since I
was almost the oldest soldier aboard, I was in training for the 1982
London Marathon; a lifetime addiction to long-distance running
certainly helped me at this time.) All sorts of other training
activities filled the rest of each day: weapon handling and radio
procedure, field-craft, survival techniques, aircraft recognition; the
list was endless. Live-firing at floating targets and intelligence
briefings on the Islands themselves also took place. Two aspects of
our training, in particular, were later to prove crucial.

The first of these was that comprehensive first-aid instruction
was given a particular emphasis, with all marines and soldiers
being shown how to suppress bleeding, insert drips, administer
pain-killing drugs on themselves or their comrades. Much of the
impetus for this came from an old friend Surgeon-Commander
Rick Jolly, an experienced Commando medical officer who had
seen hard times with us in Northern Ireland, and who knew how
critical instant appropriate treatment can be. Later, in the
Falklands, he was to command the Field Hospital ashore at Ajax
Bay, where over a hundred serious casualties from both sides were
operated on without a single death. On *Canberra*, however, he
caused us some concern by proposing that everyone should attend
macabre presentations during which he illustrated different
wounds with a series of gory slides depicting ghastly mutilation
and death. Naively, I worried that this might create squeamish-
ness amongst the younger elements, but in the event the marines
found the slides hilariously funny. They teased each other
gleefully, employing their own special brand of black humour:
'Hey, Merv. What's a sucking chest wound?' 'Well, I can tell you
wot a f— ...' 'Bollocks! It's nature's way of showing you've been
in a fire fight ...'

The other subject on which, fortunately, we placed much
emphasis was supporting-fire control. Normally, practical training
in this is limited for anyone below the rank of sergeant, and even
NCOs are lucky to get much first-hand experience. There are
simply not enough artillery rounds or mortar bombs available,

and priority is given to the specialist Forward Observation Officers and Mortar Fire Controllers who operate as part of Commando Headquarters or with the rifle company commanders. It was already obvious, however, that in the Falklands unit manoeuvre would be less likely than fighting patrols; the ability of a marine in a rifle section to call down supporting fire accurately could therefore be decisive. We were lucky in having our Royal Artillery fire-control teams with us on the ship; lucky, too, because, in the case of 42 Commando, the whole battery had just been with us in Norway for three months. Not only did they teach us technique, but they also transmitted comprehension of what guns and mortars could achieve. The seeds of essential confidence in fire support were sown while we were outward bound in *Canberra*.

I had a personal preoccupation at this time, which concerned how we would carry our enormous burdens once ashore. More than twenty years earlier I had been incredulous when on the night before we flew into Port Said during the Suez Crisis, the marines had been issued with a mountain of ammunition to be stowed and carried. In 1982, we would have to carry even more. Every individual needed to test his own load, and how he should pack it, even if this meant breaking open sealed ammunition cartons (which is the reason why this exercise is never realistically practised in peacetime). Sure enough, in the first sections to make such tests marines actually fell down as they shouldered their overweight, unbalanced packs. We persisted, however, with troop subalterns and JNCOs conducting endless experiments. Eventually an assembly was devised, which was tabulated and photographed, and then circulated to the rest of the Commando. By the time of the landings, fighting-order and rucksacks had been adjusted to individual requirements. When those adjustments were complete, the stooped owner 'promenaded' with his burden until he was satisfied with the fit. This was to make a considerable difference during our interminable moves through the mountains.

Besides marines, soldiers and sailors, two other segments of *Canberra* society played notable parts throughout the voyage south. The more influential section, in the long term, was composed of the twenty press reporters who finally gained political reprieve and were allowed to sail, despite vehement protestations by 'the Beagle'. The more popular, on the other hand, was the Band of Commando Forces, Royal Marines.

Martial music has exhilarated the military for centuries, but the versatility to play a variety of music is perhaps the most important aspect. The Royal Marines musician spends several years being trained so that he has just that versatility. Amongst other roles, the band must be able to entertain Royalty, as well as the Royal Navy while embarked in ships. Captain John Ware, LRAM, RM, and his band predictably seemed more at home on *Canberra* than anyone else, and their music made an inestimable contribution to settling-in the embarked military force. They played us on board in Southampton, and again as we sailed the next day. On passage they unstintingly provided concerts, unit sing-songs, mess-deck 'smokers', Church orchestras, dance bands, groups, soloists; there was even Band Corporal Monahan, with his unique repertoire of traditional sea shanties. When *Canberra* was in company with other ships, the musicians continually volunteered to fly across to them to provide similar entertainment. Between their performances, the members of the band trained earnestly for their role as stretcher-bearers should *Canberra* take on casualties after the landings. Subsequently they were to entertain a second brigade's worth – this time of Guardsmen and Gurkhas – after *Canberra* collected these troops from South Georgia as reinforcements for us in the Falklands.

'The hacks', as Tom Seccombe typically dubbed them, were a predictably mixed assortment of Fleet Street representatives. Later they would endure adversity with us both impressively and uncomplainingly. However, this was not our perception to begin with. The Argentine invasion came so unexpectedly that most newspapers had been panicked into 'scrambling' the first available journalists, since a number of foreign correspondents were already out of the country. Although not all of these substitutes were in the war-reporter mould, this probably eliminated some pre-conceived notions on both sides, press and military. A high proportion of the press group were understandably doubtful that we would ever sail south of Ascension Island and to begin with this gave them a jaundiced view of the Task Force. But three weeks of living closely with us also offered them a unique chance to observe and assess the military's capability, as well as to get to know us.

There is little doubt that the understanding and mutual respect which resulted made a profound difference to the public's support for the war, although the wrangling over censorship or the timing

of bulletins (which was absolutely nothing to do with the South
Atlantic 'hacks') must have diminished that.

Max Hastings, the son of a famous Second World War
correspondent, used to contrast this old-style rapport we succeeded
in establishing on *Canberra* with his other experiences of war
reporting, particularly in Vietnam. There, correspondents flew into
the zone of operations, saw only a battle or major manoeuvre, and
were then wafted away from the fields of fire and their
anonymous, bitter, combatants. Antiseptic staff officers, who
lacked all feel for the troops, would then return the pressmen to the
fleshpots of Saigon.

On *Canberra*, harmony and mutual respect were given time to
develop. But they could not simply be created around the bar,
although that certainly helped. It was slightly disconcerting to
discover that each unit was destined to look after two, or perhaps
three, correspondents who would be affiliated to it. I was even
more put out when told that they would select us, not the other
way round! A yet more traumatic adjustment was to follow when,
hung-over one morning, I swept into my office for Commanding
Officer's Orderly Room – to be confronted by several journalists.
'CO's' is normally a formal, discreet procedure involving the
Adjutant, the RSM, and those officers responsible for the
individual who is to be promoted, drafted, counselled or rebuked. I
was not best pleased when Phil Wilson loomed over me and said
brightly: 'This is our press team, Colonel.' And, in a whisper, '*You
must welcome them – now!*'

It was my first conscious meeting with one individual in
particular. John Shirley, soon to become a friend, would share all
of our dangers, and would write about them sensitively and
perceptively both during and after the war. At this moment,
however, he epitomized the 'pinko press' to me, as he dubiously
surveyed us through his wire-rimmed glasses, dressed in faded
jeans and scruffy open-neck shirt. As I recall, my clientele that
morning included a marine receiving an official commendation for
assisting the police in making an arrest, with another who was
reprimanded for violently rejecting the homosexual advances of a
Canberra steward. Then came a sergeant in Support Company
whose father was dying. Sergeant Dave Mitchell was therefore
entitled to be flown back from Dakar but, in a moving explanation,
turned down this right, making the point that his expertise with
the Milan missiles might prove crucial. That later turned out to be

so, and this revelation of selfless commitment obviously impressed, if it also puzzled, our new observers.

Patrick Bishop of the *Observer*, who wrote one of the first, vivid impressions of this war, later described some unexpected perceptions, from his point of view as a journalist:

> We tended to make crude assumptions about what these men would be like. Few of them matched the stereotypes. There was something Victorian about many of them. Most of the battalion commanders had been educated at the better known public-schools and gone straight into the Army. The Para and Marine Commanding Officers tended to be practical, spartan men who shared all the discomforts their men had to put up with.

Max Hastings was a literal giant amongst these literary gentlemen. Untidy, polite and charming, his courtesy belied an incisive mind and an insatiable curiosity. He had several military books to his name already, as well as real experience in reporting wars over the last decade. This campaign experience was to ensure that he contrived to be where it mattered throughout the Falklands battles. He was eventually designated 'Journalist of the Year', though not without outraging most of his less ruthless or determined colleagues. He and I were to experience some dramatic events together, a number of which are graphically described in *The Battle for the Falklands*, the highly successful book which he wrote with Simon Jenkins in 1983.

In the first few weeks on *Canberra*, however, Max was feeling less than benevolent towards the management, which he found ponderous, inflexible, if not downright unsympathetic. These were tense days of apparently mindless censorship on articles about the embarked force which reporters like himself thought emasculated their stories. They were particularly aggravated because the censorship was exercised by MOD press officers, who seemed to operate on no clear directive. These 'Minders', as they were known, used 'the Beagle' or 'Uncle Tom', and eventually the Commanding Officers, as their shields against the combined wrath of the 'hacks', which created tension amongst us all. It became more personally frustrating when Max wrote a feature on Lieutenant-Colonel Nick Vaux, 'ex-steeplechase rider whose wife breeds Connemara ponies in the West Country', but was not allowed to reveal the unit I commanded in his despatch from

Canberra. In the same week, however, as we soon discovered, a national tabloid carried pictures correctly identified, of all the unit Commanding Officers.

Less than a week after sailing, I celebrated my forty-sixth birthday. It was an event which I had planned to keep as quiet as possible. As the Commanding Officer of 42 Commando was several years older than the other two on board, it seemed prudent not to alarm the constituents. 'Uncle Tom' and I therefore planned to drink a discreet bottle of bubbly together before dinner. So it seemed a little surprising when, at about 1800 hours, I was summoned urgently to the bridge. On arrival Tom and Phil Wilson engaged me in a boring conversation about ship's administration which seemed to go on for ever. At last the Adjutant and I returned to my stateroom to finalize details. As I reached to open the door I remember saying bleakly, 'Phil, I hope this won't take long, as I have some other things to do.' 'No, Colonel,' he replied, 'I don't suppose it will ...'

I opened the door to discover that I was the cunningly duped guest at a surprise party, which every officer of 42 Commando seemed to have conspired to attend. There was even a small ensemble from the Commando Forces Band playing the traditional song as I walked in. Champagne corks popped, greetings were hurled at me, and before long a magnificent cake was produced, decorated with a crest emblazoned in the unit colours. I was also given an original greeting card with a glorious 'Argie' cartoon on it, signed by all the officers and warrant officers.

It was a striking reminder that trust, loyalty, friendship, are crucial to anyone who has responsibility for the success, or survival, of a group of people. When those qualities are spontaneously and affectionately demonstrated in such a way, it is profoundly moving. For an hour or so we forgot what the future might hold, indulging in the relaxed, amusing badinage that is both timeless and peculiar to groups of military comrades. Perhaps the most special moment of all came later when Albert Hempenstall, our bearded, outspoken Padre, called me over to the window (*Canberra* staterooms have nothing less) as a flapping, ink-spattered banner loomed down, bearing the legend 'Happy Birthday Boss! From the Lads'. The ship was plunging through the seas at around 20 knots, while my window was several decks down and, to those above, appeared as just another light in the dark. Now I was even more inclined to agree that 42 Commando really might be 'magic'. The card from my family which mysteriously appeared on my desk said that they hoped I wouldn't be too lonely on my birthday ...

A few days later we arrived at Ascension Island, which considerably changed our perception of this rather carefree adventure, as it seemed to us then. To begin with, the international situation was now clearly deteriorating. General Alexander Haig, the US Secretary of State, shuttled fruitlessly back and forth across the Atlantic, while the Secretary-General of the United Nations, Señor Javier Pérez de Cuéllar, whose name was now being sonorously declaimed in almost every BBC World Service Bulletin, had commenced a series of increasingly gloomy predictions. Ominously, *Canberra* was now anchored with a flotilla of warships and an imposing array of supporting merchantmen, as the big jets rumbled interminably overhead into the island's airfield, Wideawake. Support helicopters bustled frenetically about the anchorage and, almost as soon as *Canberra*'s propellers settled, the Brigade staff appeared, to bombard us at once with queries or directives.

During their overcrowded passage on the Assault Ship HMS *Fearless*, in advance of us, the Brigade staff had experienced great difficulties in keeping in touch. The secure signals system (in other words, communications invulnerable to interception), was so overstretched that *Canberra* became effectively incommunicado, except for encrypted high-priority messages. Now that communications were restored, overdue and important liaison intensified, with returns, nominals, maps and intelligence data constantly being exchanged. Manpower or equipment statistics had to be constantly updated as planning intensified. Most important, we were all able to see 'The Commander' himself, something which had always been so important to troops before battle. Our Brigadier, Julian Thompson, a keen military historian, knew this better than most. He spent every moment he could spare on board *Canberra* or other ships carrying elements of his force, watching what went on and being seen to do so. He was, in this respect, particularly prominent in the imaginative and vigorous training programme which was now instigated ashore.

Before 42 Commando really became absorbed in that, however, our morale was galvanized by events several thousand miles away. Less than a week after we arrived at Ascension came the dramatic, fantastic, news that South Georgia had been retaken. There is no record of how we first learnt this news, but it was probably in a message from Brigade Headquarters. I had been informed under the strictest secrecy about forty-eight hours beforehand that a landing in South Georgia was imminent. But now official bulletins were rapidly engulfed by conflicting news flashes from all over the world. There were also 'inside stories' that various hacks passed on to me after ship-to-shore conversations with their editors. Eventually the anxiously awaited message from our own people came:

> FROM: HMS ANTRIM
> TO: SS CANBERRA
> FOR: LT COL VAUX CO 42 CDO RM FROM SHERIDAN THE 42 CDO FLAG FLIES HIGH OVER GRYTVIKEN. MUCH TO TELL YOU WHEN WE REJOIN WHICH WE NOW LOOK FORWARD TO.
> SEMPER. FI.

(Semper Fi. is a traditional way of signing off in the United States Marines, with whom I had just completed a two-year tour. *Semper fidelis*, 'ever faithful', is the USMC's motto.)

The Commando signalled back:

> Very many thanks for your welcome signal that we were so proud to receive. All ranks from here send congratulations on your outstanding success achieved in daunting circumstances. When we have sorted out the rest of the South Atlantic we look forward to a spectacular Four-Two reunion at Bickleigh. Did you have the right wax?

Guy Sheridan was probably one of Britain's greatest experts on waxing cross-country skis, so the joke seemed appropriate. We assumed that 'Munch' Company must have skied any approach to Grytviken, but in fact this was not the case at all – the Company did not get ashore until after the surrender. But at first all of us on *Canberra*, as well as the press at home, considered them victors and sung their praises accordingly. Here is a typical extract from a *Daily Mirror* account, which reached us very quickly now that we were in Ascension and at the end of an RAF pipeline:

MAJOR GUY LEADS THE BATTLE CHARGE

The men of the 42 Commandos leaped into action behind 'Boy's Own' hero Major Guy Sheridan.

The mountaineer and cross-country skiing expert is

second-in-command of the battalion.

He has seen active service in Aden, Malaysia and Oman, and spent several years on Arctic warfare exercises in Norway.

It is not known from which task force vessels the Royal Marine invasion force came.

But they were all from M Company of 42 Commando stationed at Bickleigh Camp, on the edge of Dartmoor, near Plymouth.

With blackened faces and carrying self-loading rifles, they were ferried in by helicopters.

They were backed up by mortar teams and squads with handheld anti-tank guns that can knock out reinforced concrete bunkers.

Two hours later after a running battle with Argentine troops the Union Jack was flying again over the islands.

Although there was little, if any, bloodshed the Marines emphasised that the successful retaking of South Georgia should not be underestimated.

It was obvious that this story was not only wildly romanticized, but also gave inadequate recognition to the motley force that, in the event, Guy had assembled in order to seize decisive advantage of an unexpected reversal in Argentine fortunes. There was, however, absolutely nothing we could do from *Canberra* about press coverage in the UK. I remained content to note the proud and happy faces around our unit notice-board as they avidly read each and every signal, news bulletin or press cutting. A tremendous fillip had been given to the self-confidence and commitment which a unit must have for war. As far as I was concerned, any inspiring illusions would be dispelled gradually and sensitively. Anything which would bond the team together and strengthen their morale was not to be missed.

The night after the news of South Georgia's recapture, we naturally celebrated at the bar. At some point, late that evening, I found myself joking amidst a noisy group that included an officer from another unit. He kept on trying to tell me something. Eventually he made himself heard: 'Well, Colonel. Great achievement by "Four-Two", but I fear it may be your swan song.' My consternation was obvious. 'You see, with only two rifle companies, now 'M' Company must garrison South Georgia, you certainly can't expect a major task. Reserve unit and holding the beach-head ...' He withdrew, as I caught Ian McNeill's inscrutable eye.

The next morning, we met with Phil Wilson in unspoken determination to try and avert this crisis. I remembered my father-in-law's stories of how the first Royal Marine Commando units were formed in the Second World War. To begin with, hand-picked individuals were despatched to find a further few 'as good as themselves' – perhaps we could do something similar? Indeed we could!

Phil instantly identified an officer, just arrived on board *Canberra*, who had all the motivation in the world to lead a company of his own against the Argentines. Captain Mike Norman had lately commanded the Royal Marines Garrison in the Falklands, where they had resisted, gallantly but unavailingly, that overwhelming Argentine invasion of just a few weeks ago. Now Mike Norman, a huge, craggy, taciturn man, was on board as a very reluctant press officer, having been repatriated to Britain from captivity. I asked him to come and see me, and we then had one of the briefest but most encouraging dialogues of my career. 'How long have I got, Colonel?' was his simple reaction.

Whatever my response, I certainly couldn't have restricted him to only forty-eight hours. Yet within that time-scale a radiant Phil informed me that Mike had recruited nearly a hundred individuals who possessed, more or less, the rank-structure and training for a rifle company. Many of them came from Mike's original garrison, most of whom were also on board; others were specialists – cooks, clerks, armourers and vehicle mechanics. All had been sent to *Canberra* in the final hours before she sailed, to be allocated by Brigade Headquarters wherever they might be needed. Fortunately, in the Royal Marines everyone is trained primarily to fight in a Commando unit, with his specialization as a secondary skill. By internal rearrangement within the rest of 'Four-Two', we were able to provide this band with any missing expertise. Somehow, by underhand means, the partnership of Dennis, our QM, and Mike, or 'Sparks and Norman', as they came to be indignantly cited by their counterparts, assembled a rifle company's worth of weapons and equipment. We never discovered how, although there was a shrewd suspicion that some of the automatic weapons might have come from the unit reserves of my friend at the bar!

That night, we signalled Brigade Headquarters that 42 Commando was now fully reconstituted, ready to carry out the same tasks as any other unit. After the war John Chester, the

Brigade Major, confirmed that this news came as a welcome surprise, for it enabled Brigade HQ to consider us for any option. For me, it was the beginning of another memorable association, this time with a new sub-unit within Four-Two. The men of 'J' Company, as it was designated (the other rifle companies being 'K', 'L' and 'M'), were to perform with distinction, in danger and adversity, before, appropriately, re-hoisting the British flag over Government House.

In the meantime, however, it was our detached 'M' Company that had moved into the limelight.

3

SOUTH GEORGIA REGAINED

At 2200 hours on Good Friday, 9 April 1982, two hours after *Canberra* slipped her moorings in Southampton, 'M' Company 42 Commando took off from Brize Norton in an RAF VC10, bound for Ascension Island. Some of them were able to watch our own departure on the BBC's nine o'clock news. I had spoken to Guy Sheridan back at Bickleigh earlier in the day, so I was aware that they were soon to be launched on 'Operation Paraquet'; already it seemed an age since we had marched off the parade-ground together, less than two days before.

For Chris Nunn, the 'M' Company Commander, it was a moment of excitement, but also one of reflection. His family's commitment to whatever was to come was heavy. He was on his way in secret, with his wife, Siobhan, and parents believing that 'M' Company was with the main body of 42 Commando in *Canberra*. His brother, Richard, had already flown a Scout helicopter onto a Landing Ship Logistic (LSL) in Portsmouth, to embark with the rest of the Brigade Air Squadron. Their last meeting had been some four days earlier, over one of the Sunday lunches they frequently attended at their parents' house in Cornwall. David Constance, his best friend, and a brother-in-law since 1972, had somehow got out of his training job at the Commando Training Centre, to join 2 Para at Aldershot as their Royal Marine liaison officer. Their involvement, as things unfolded, meant they were leaving behind a level of worry and concern in a family which was probably unique in this war.

Nearly twelve hours after take-off, 'M' Company landed at

Ascension, to be met by the familiar, reassuring presence of Major Jonathan Thomson, commanding the Royal Marines Special Boat Squadron (SBS). This highly specialized clandestine organization (our own smaller, maritime equivalent of the SAS) was to gain most unwelcome exposure as a result of the Falklands campaign; just as the SAS had unhappily lost their anonymity after the storming of the Iranian Embassy in 1981. A section from Jonathan's squadron was to be attached to Sheridan's group, which would give him the capability to insert trained reconnaissance patrols by canoe or inflatable boat onto the South Georgia coastline. If necessary, these SBS teams could make an underwater approach into enemy-held waters, where their training would enable them to pass back information for an amphibious landing, or possibly even sabotage enemy shipping.

With an equivalent SAS troop for land operations on its way, Guy felt that he had more than adequate means of gaining the intelligence required to plan the recapture of South Georgia. Specific knowledge of enemy strengths and locations prior to landing was, of course, essential. The weather and terrain were so hazardous that to land even a few miles from the objective could prove futile, and the details of estimated strengths of Argentine forces at specific places were very sketchy indeed. Guy had also asked for·a section of his own specialization, the Royal Marines Mountain and Arctic Warfare Cadre (M & AW Cadre). This equally exclusive organization had just been with us all winter in Norway, where they train intensively in protracted survival under extreme conditions, snow- and ice-climbing and long-distance ski marches. More important, though, the Cadre contained a number of officers and NCOs who, like Sheridan, had wide and varied mountaineering experience all over the world – some, indeed, had spent time in the Antarctic, including South Georgia. It was decided, however, that the space available precluded additional special forces; in any case, the SAS troop assigned to mountain operations was being sent out to join the group.

A welcome initiative on Jonathan Thomson's part had been his arranging for everyone to test-fire their weapons before sailing from Ascension. So, in the last real sunshine they were to enjoy – briefly – for many weeks, 'M' Company enthusiastically prepared their varied ordnance for battle. Meanwhile, Guy Sheridan was discovering just how complex his responsibilities were to be. The South Georgia Task Force Commander, Captain Brian Young, of the County Class destroyer HMS *Antrim*, had been allocated the Royal Fleet Auxiliary (RFA) *Tidespring*, in which it was sensibly decided to embark the whole of 'M' Company. The remainder of the military force was to be split between HMS *Antrim* and another escort, the frigate HMS *Plymouth*. Sheridan advised that his own HQ, with Chris Nunn and all the support elements, should be consolidated in HMS *Antrim*, which meant that the SBS and SAS troops still to join could be placed in HMS *Plymouth* and HMS *Endurance*, respectively, when they had made their rendezvous with the force. On Easter Monday, however, when the South Georgia Task Force rendezvoused at sea for a last replenishment with the RFA *Fort Austin*, a whole squadron of SAS, instead of just one troop, transferred. This disconcerted everyone, particularly the Navy, while the presence of a second major, Cedric Delves, immediately created uncertainty about command arrangements. These problems were not alleviated by the subsequent operational order from the Commander-in-Chief Fleet, Admiral Sir John Fieldhouse, in his HQ at Northwood, which, on 15 April, was dropped to the Task Force by parachute from an RAF Nimrod. Amongst much other detail, culminating bizarrely with the signature of a Lieutenant Nelson, the order stipulated quite specifically that only one troop of SAS was to be attached. Eventually the three troops were split between the various ships, with their HQ also on *Antrim*. Later, the position was clarified: Sheridan had overall command of the 250-strong Military Force, although Delves's special communications meant that he could speak independently to his own commanders. Joint planning for 'Operation Paraquet' – which everyone recognized as a most hazardous venture – could now begin. Officially codenamed 'Paraquet' (as in small, long-tailed parrot), the plan was at first opposed by Brigade HQ, which allegedly signalled Northwood 'Kill Paraquet before it kills us'. Shortly afterwards the spelling was unofficially amended to 'Paraquat' by Task Force members but the plan was endorsed.

The following day, 13 April, saw one of those unique naval occasions that combine tradition with emotion. At 1100 hours the Royal Navy's Ice Patrol Ship, HMS *Endurance*, rendezvoused with the three task force vessels. Late in March she had been at the end of her commission and about to return home, when she was ordered to remain on station around South Georgia, on which a number of Argentine scrap-metal men had landed. It was her

Royal Marines, under Lieutenant Keith Mills, who had conducted such a spirited and brave defence of the island when it was invaded on 3 April, before sensibly surrendering to a superior force. Now, as *Endurance* took station under a clear sky, it seemed fitting that the crews of the other ships should line their decks to give her a rousing three cheers in the Navy tradition. She steamed past before turning to head south once more – this time in company with a small task force of considerably greater fire-power than her own twin Oerlikon guns and two Wasp helicopters armed with outdated SS12 missiles.

On Saturday 17 April, Guy Sheridan prophetically noted in his personal diary that the South Georgia operation would be so unpredictable that only a swift and simple plan made sense. By this time the councils of war had exhaustively evaluated the possible approaches to the whaling stations of Grytviken and Leith, where the Argentines had to be. Guy consistently warned against one of the major hazards: 'In my directive to D Squadron SAS, I advised them, on my own experience, to avoid glaciers like the plague ...' Captain Nick Barker of *Endurance* took the same line, pointing out that there were landfalls on the eastern side of the island which involved far less risk, as well as much easier approaches, than a march over glaciers. When the SAS argued that secrecy was paramount, Barker allegedly retorted: 'It's not exactly as busy as Brighton Front round there, you know!' Nevertheless, the eventual SAS plan, endorsed by higher authority, was for an approach march across the Fortuna Glacier.

By 21 April the ships were within sight of the island and its adjacent icebergs. The weather was appalling, which boded ill for flying, as well as operating ashore. A series of plans had been drawn up by now, all dependent on obtaining prior information about the enemy, and with the emphasis on quick reaction to any perceived opportunity. Several rehearsals of 'cross-decking' – moving troops from ship to ship by helicopter – to consolidate the force had been conducted, in order that ship and helicopter crews could practise the unfamiliar business of loading the military into their anti-submarine helicopters. These aircraft had to be stripped of their radar for troop lift, however, and for as long as that was the case the task force was even more vulnerable to the submarine threat which had been ominously predicted.

After one abortive attempt, made in minimal visibility and with the wind gusting viciously between Force 8 and 12, the SAS

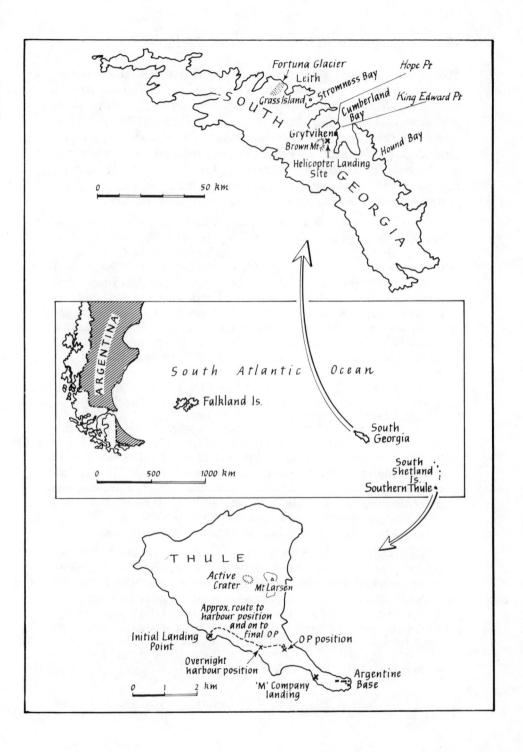

Mountain Troop was inserted onto the Fortuna Glacier in the early afternoon of 21 April. The barometer then dropped steeply and storm-force winds swept across the area. By 1800 hours *Endurance* was plunging about in a Force 11 gale. Later, at 0300 hours on the 22nd, she managed to put her SBS patrols into Hound Bay, where they were to attempt to cross to Cumberland Bay by boat for a look at the enemy in Grytviken. On the glacier, however, the situation became desperate overnight, as Max Hastings graphically described in *The Battle for the Falklands*:

> From the moment that they descended into the howling gale and snowclad misery of the glacier, the SAS found themselves confounded by the elements. 'Spindrift blocked the feed-trays of the machine-guns', wrote an NCO in his report. 'On the first afternoon, three corporals probing crevasses advanced 500 metres in four to five hours ...' Their efforts to drag their sledges laden with 200 pounds of equipment apiece were frustrated by white-outs that made all movement impossible. 'Luckily we were now close to an outcrop in the glacier and were able to get into a crevasse out of the main blast of the wind ...' They began to erect their tents. One was instantly torn from their hands by the wind and swept away into the snow. The poles of the others snapped within seconds, but the men struggled beneath the fabric and kept it upright by flattening themselves against the walls. Every forty-five minutes, they took turns to crawl out and dig the snow away from the entrance, to avoid becoming totally buried. They were now facing katabatic* winds of more than 100 mph. By 11 a.m. the next morning, the 22nd April, their physical condition was deteriorating rapidly. The SAS were obliged to report that their position was untenable, and ask to be withdrawn.

Guy's cryptic notes starkly take up the desperate saga:

> John Hamilton [the SAS troop second-in-command] forecast cold casualties imminent. They had to be extracted rapidly. So we embarked on a horrific series of events which Divine Providence somehow influenced because we got everyone back. Three Wessex helicopters led by Ian Stanley flew in, couldn't locate the patrol in the weather and returned to refuel. They went back in appalling weather, found the patrol, but on flying out, one Wessex 5 crashed! The passengers from this were picked up jointly by the remaining aircraft which then set off

---

* Very high gusting winds caused by air flowing downwards as, in this case, down a mountainside.

again. Then the second Wessex 5 crashed! The solitary Wessex 3 arrived safely on board *Antrim* and brought the story with it. Atrocious weather and white-out were to blame. But now we had 13 men ashore who needed rescue pretty quickly if they were to survive the dreadful conditions on the glacier. It was not possible to fly off until the afternoon came, when Ian and Chris Parry [his co-pilot] again took off. We all thought there was little chance of anyone coming out alive. About half an hour later Ian radioed to say he had found them and was picking them up. What we didn't realise was that Ian had assessed that this would be the only chance and that to take half the survivors would leave the rest out for the night and everything that meant. So he put the whole lot in on top of each other and flew back to *Antrim* 16 men up! Quite unbelievable, and what a daring and skilful pilot Ian Stanley is.

Daring and skilful indeed, for not only was this one of the bravest single acts of the war, it also averted disaster, and the failure of our first military operation at a politically crucial moment. Who can say what consequences might have followed futile casualties on this scale? But without any troop-lift helicopters left, the recapture of South Georgia was now hardly feasible. A few days before this rescue, Chris Nunn, an experienced helicopter pilot himself, had conducted trials on a 'Humphrey', as the Wessex 3 anti-submarine helicopter was affectionately known. After stripping out the radar equipment, he and Chris Parry had agreed that no more than five or six troops could be lifted, depending on the equipment carried. To have brought sixteen men out in one helicopter during a major storm was little short of miraculous. Later, Nunn described Ian Stanley's 'controlled crash' onto the heaving deck of *Antrim* as one of the greatest feats of flying he had ever witnessed. Lieutenant-Commander Ian Stanley was subsequently awarded the only DSO given to a pilot in that war, as well deserved a decoration for valour as any in the Falklands campaign. Sadly, Captain John Hamilton, who I was later to meet briefly on Mount Kent, was killed on West Falkland towards the end of hostilities while putting up a ferocious display of courage against overwhelming odds.

In London and aboard HMS *Fearless*, carrying Brigadier Thompson and the 3 Commando Brigade staff, news of this episode had been received first with anxiety, and then relief as the magnitude of the regain was appreciated. In the meantime, Sheridan and Delves concluded that their activities so far had been masked from the enemy by the weather. Further reconnaissance was therefore feasible. Guy proposed to Brian Young that this time they should launch the SAS Boat Troop. At just after midnight, on the night of 22/23 April, during a lull in the weather, *Antrim* slipped into Stromness harbour and dropped off five SAS inflatables, with their crews. Although the engines of only two of the flimsy boats appeared to start, the warship could not remain long in those hazardous and confined waters. A bearing for Grass Island, where they were to tie up, was passed to the last boat, and then *Antrim* stole away, with the wind beginning to gust once more. At about 0700 next morning the Boat Troop commander signalled that two of the Gemini craft were missing, although the crews of the other three were established ashore and observing the enemy. Once again, the idefatigable Ian Stanley took off in deteriorating weather. He returned at around 1030 hours, bearing the three very fortunate occupants of one of the boats, which was being steadily blown out into the South Atlantic. Of the second there was no sign for the moment, and soon the weather precluded further searches. There was a further setback when one of the SBS sections, which had been launched into Cumberland Bay, signalled that pack-ice had punctured their Geminis, which would now have to be replaced if they were to continue with their mission.

'We were getting behind with intelligence, so with pressure coming from Northwood I began to think of direct military action against Leith ...' But as Guy was making plans for an impromptu operation, there came the bombshell that radically changed the conduct of the operation. At 1830 hours on 24 April, Northwood informed Captain Young that an Argentine submarine was believed to be in South Georgia waters, reportedly a 1940s-vintage American-built Guppy Class vessel. Elderly she might be, but she was armed with torpedoes, had a British-trained captain, and was undoubtedly looking for the Royal Navy. Within half an hour of receiving this news, the decision was taken to send *Tidespring* and *Endurance* clear of danger, where they could hide amongst the icebergs. The odds in favour of the attackers had been eroded drastically.

On board *Antrim* there were sixty assorted Royal Marines and SAS. *Plymouth* and *Endurance* carried two troops of SAS and one

SBS section between them, but none of the remaining helicopters could land on their decks. As a result, Guy could not count on the sort of numerical superiority classically recommended for an initial assault. But next day, as this operation against Leith was being organized, the equation dramatically altered. Early on the morning of 25 April, Ian Stanley, enjoying a memorable war, sighted and then successfully depth-charged an Argentine submarine sailing sedately on the surface five miles out of Grytviken. Follow-up attacks with helicopters from the recently arrived HMS *Brilliant*, and *Plymouth* and *Endurance*, forced the submarine, the *Santa Fe*, to limp past King Edward Point, on the surface and, in an obviously damaged state. Here was a classic military opportunity. The enemy was momentarily unbalanced. The advantage must be taken as fast and as vigorously as possible, something which Guy Sheridan quickly sensed:

> We had to take action as soon as possible to maintain our momentum and ensure the eighty sailors in that submarine did not reinforce the garrison. So I told Chris Nunn to get the organization for the Leith landing stood by at 30 minutes to move.

Frustratingly, Guy had to wait several hours before his chance came, while naval debriefs and discussions concerning the attack on the submarine were completed. Finally, approval was given for landings to go in at 1445:

> I gave hasty orders at 1345 and then went round the marines in the main passageway of the ship to talk to them. They were all keen to go, faces blackened and ammunition bristling from every pocket. I had about seventy-five men – about half the opposition we expected; so it was a gamble! Three troops of about twenty men were commanded by Major Cedric Delves SAS, Captain Chris Nunn RM and Lieutenant Clive Grant RM, with Surgeon-Lieutenant Crispin Swinhoe RN in my tactical headquarters. I had two 81-mm tubes and each man carried two high-explosive bombs ...

All that contingency planning and cross-decking practice was about to pay off.

The key to this plan was Naval Gunfire Support. Directed by Captain Chris Brown, RA, from *Endurance*'s Wasp helicopter, *Antrim* put down a spectacular creeping barrage towards the old whaling station at Grytviken. Brown placed shells all round King

Edward Point without damaging the settlement, and finished with a flourish, dropping a salvo onto a small outcrop called Hobart Rocks, some 300 yards offshore. This so demoralized the enemy that, even before the British force – landing from helicopters while the bombardment was in progress – could close within small-arms' range, the Argentines had hung out several white sheets. As Guy Sheridan reached the top of the ridge that had screened the fly-in, he saw that the battle was effectively over. While Cedric and his men 'legged it' down the other side of the ridge, towards the settlement, the wily Sheridan summoned a helicopter to fly him forward for the surrender, urgently calling for the ships now to show themselves in Cumberland Bay. This combined appearance of land and sea forces eliminated any second thoughts the enemy might have had. At 1715 Cedric's sergeant-major was running a Union Jack up the whaling station's flagpole, while Sheridan accepted the surrender. South Georgia had been recaptured.

With hindsight, it seems likely that the captain of the damaged Argentine submarine had tipped the scales after he and his crew had swarmed ashore with an alarming account of attacks by three different types of helicopter. Even without his two years of training with the Royal Navy, the captain would have known that the helicopters' presence meant that several large warships were off the coast. Once the bombardment had started, and with the sound of helicopters landing on the other side of Brown Mountain clearly audible, he probably persuaded the garrison that discretion was certainly preferable to valour. Later that day, and in similar vein, Guy made an Argentine officer radio the Leith defenders some miles away, telling them that unless they capitulated on the following day 'they must suffer the consequences'. In response to a certain amount of Argentine obduracy, he explained to the interpreter this meant 'annihilation or surrender'.

The day concluded as amazingly as it had begun. *Antrim* asked Sheridan to invite the submarine captain and the garrison commander, Major Astiz, to dine on board. The motive was, however, more cunning than magnanimous, the Navy being suddenly nervous of underwater sabotage. When both enemy officers accepted with alacrity, enjoying the hospitality extended in a thoroughly relaxed manner, it was assumed that the alarm had been false. Eventually Guy got back ashore, to collapse into bed: 'What a satisfying day, but I cannot believe that we are in

Grytviken without a single casualty – seventy of us to one hundred and thirty-seven of them! A *nice* day!'

Leith surrendered as ordered on the following day. Against significant odds, and despite diabolical weather conditions, the Royal Navy ships and aircraft had conducted a series of desperately dangerous manoeuvres without detection and without losing a single man. Although the military force had suffered serious reverses to begin with, these had not been allowed to diminish the resolve to land and recapture the whaling stations, and thus the island. Eventually there was a reversal of fortunes, and on this the small task force capitalized swiftly and unremittingly. The re-taking of South Georgia was, in so many respects, a minor prelude to the main events in the Falklands. That little victory must also have come as a tremendous relief to the anxious leadership back in the UK. To complete the success, the last missing SAS Gemini crew were picked up a day or so later.

Next day, 26 April, an effective working relationship between friend and enemy was soon established by 'M' Company escorts, as both prisoners and the new RM garrison willingly set about cleaning up Grytviken. Unfortunately, this understanding was almost immediately shattered when an 'M' Company guard shot dead Chief Petty Officer Felix Artuso, whom he judged to be sabotaging the captured submarine. At the time, the *Santa Fe* was being moved around the cove under the Navy's supervision, with RM guards providing security. The Argentine rating *appeared* to open valves which might have flooded the submarine. This was not what the lance-corporal had been briefed to expect, and he reacted accordingly. In the misunderstanding an innocent POW lost his life, while a young, alert Royal Marine had to face protracted inquiries and endure his own misgivings far away from home. At one point, Chris Nunn was instructed to deliver him up to confinement in cells in a ship, but he successfully protested against that. The junior NCO was eventually completedly exonerated, but it was, as Guy commented, a melancholy incident which soured the landing operation. After the shooting, the Argentine captain and those of his crew who had been present at the time had to be separated from the remaining prisoners, and the initial rapport between POWs and their captors was never re-established. The purpose of moving the *Santa Fe* was never made clear to those ashore. But whatever the reason, the co-ordination of the operation clearly left a lot to be desired.

Early on the morning of 30 April, in blustery and brooding weather, Artuso was buried at Grytviken with full naval ceremony. HMS *Antrim*'s chaplain officiated, and many of her officers and a contingent from her ship's company attended the service. The crew of the *Santa Fe*, led by their Captain, were also there, having been shipped in from RFA *Tidespring*. It was a sad and moving occasion, made more so when the young Marine bugler immaculately played the Last Post and the Reveille. The notes whipped away by the wind, echoing around the mountains and mingling with the sound of the volleys fired by the guard of honour. Although obviously moved, the Argentines remained impassive in their grief. This was probably just as well. Lying hidden in the broken ground around the burial place were Sergeant John Napier and five other snipers, in case emotion should turn to violence.

On the day before the funeral, Thursday 29 April, as soon as he had unpacked to settle in for what he imagined might be a prolonged stay, Guy Sheridan received the traditional 'pierhead jump'. Within two hours he was aboard HMS *Brilliant*, a Type 22 frigate, and en route for the main Carrier Task Force – arrangements were being made for him to rejoin the body of 42 Commando. Guy felt some misgivings about leaving South Georgia. The island's garrison was still being organized, while the rest of 'Four-Two' remained, at Ascension on *Canberra*. But he assumed that the main landings on the Falklands must be imminent. By lunchtime on the 30th, he had been flown on board the carrier HMS *Hermes*. There, he imagined, a great deal of interest would be shown in the recapture of South Georgia, and his immediate future might be clarified. But he was wrong on both counts. With the exception of Colonel Richard Preston, who listened to his story and explained that the main landings were still some time away, no one paid any attention to the man who had commanded the military force in 'Operation Paraquat'. Later that afternoon Preston arranged for him to fly on board *Plymouth*, which was returning to South Georgia. Within a few days, Guy had rejoined Chris Nunn and 'Munch' Company. Their sojourn had only just begun when the spotlight shifted from South Georgia towards the Falkland Islands. It was only after the war that we learned of their lonely vigil, and of the difficulties they had to face.

4

POISED IN ASCENSION

While 'M' Company had been dominating the headlines, the Amphibious Task Force had taken full advantage of the convenient pause in Ascension Island to reorganize, restow and rehearse. Each function would critically improve our ability to conduct the essential amphibious operation; essential because, until we were established in the Falkland Islands, we could not engage the enemy ashore. With most of the force now assembled at Ascension, each unit could be grouped with its supporting arms and services. In 'Four-Two', we now knew the artillery battery, engineer troop, anti-aircraft section (nicknamed 'Blowpipe', after the hand-held missile they operated), Forward Air Controller, Naval Gunfire Support Officer, and so on, who would be attached to us for specific operations. Whenever possible, these elements cross-decked, so that they could then train and live with the parent unit. When lack of space prevented this, the representatives of the supporting arms joined unit HQs, in order that planning and orders involved them directly. My 'O' Groups almost doubled in size as a result, although most of the faces remained familiar since we had all worked together before.

On the logistics side, Brigade HQ gained at Ascension the invaluable chance to rearrange cargoes which, before sailing, had been loaded hastily into the first available hold without regard to ownership or function. Weapons and ammunition were restowed so that they could be moved ashore, by either helicopter or landing-craft, according to a logical priority. The vast stocks of supplies had to be broken down into accessible and functional loads; they also had to be dispersed in case of loss. Similarly, the mountains of supplementary items which were now being flown out from UK had to be incorporated in this ceaseless and complex activity. This involved helicopters, landing-craft, lighters and sectional rafts (called Mexeflotes) criss-crossing the anchorage with every conceivable configuration of stores for war. To make matters more difficult, Ascension Island has no harbour, jetties, or beach capable of providing facilities for the stacking and initial sorting-out of material. The only available space was at Wideawake airfield itself. That, however, was crammed with Phantom fighters, Nimrod reconnaissance aircraft, a squadron of bombers, another of tankers, and an ever-changing miscellany of helicopters, apart from the constant stream of VC10s and Hercules which provided the air bridge from home. The incoming freight created a vast stores park that threatened to swamp the airfield's existing facilities. We waited impatiently and often unavailingly for designated cargo. (We never did receive the cases of beer despatched by Vaux Breweries in Newcastle to 'Four-Two'. Probably they never got past the reception encampment!) We did, however, get one important load, a small but invaluable consignment of weapons and equipment for our new 'J' Company, rushed out to us from Poole by the resourceful David Storrie when it became clear that even Dennis, the QM, couldn't acquire those locally.

On the training side of things, there were so many aspects of such importance that it was difficult for Brigade HQ to decide on the priorities. Ideally, we should first have practised the amphibious drills, and then rehearsed the landings. In practice, however, the coastal topography of Ascension ruled out such a programme, with the result that we had to do the next best thing, and practise disembarkation from each ship separately. Modern assault ships like HMSS *Fearless* and *Intrepid*, the two LPDs with the Task Force, have a sea dock as well as a flight deck. The option to use helicopters or landing-craft therefore involves comparatively simple procedures for marines trained in their use. The vast majority of the landing force was not in assault ships, however. Most men were aboard the passenger liners or the logistic landing-ships (LSLs), which, for the purposes of getting men ashore, are best beached or moored alongside existing piers or jetties. Furthermore, the two airborne units – we were to be joined by the 2nd Battalion, the Parachute Regiment (2 Para), now on their way to Ascension in the North Sea ferry MV *Norland* – had no training in amphibious techniques. Yet even this inexperience

palled beside the dilemma for all four units embarked in
commercial shipping. On these vessels, every procedure, starting
with the establishment in the ships of assembly areas and routes
along which heavily laden troops should move to the
disembarkation point, had to be worked out, proved, and then
practised. Next, we exercised getting off the ship. This posed more
special problems. Disembarkation either had to be by helicopter
from the *ad hoc* platforms, swiftly constructed in the UK and
lacking convenient access, or alternatively by landing-craft that
could only come alongside cargo ports many decks below. Control
was, of course the crucial aspect. Without it disembarkation would
degenerate into a spasmodic, disorganized struggle to get ashore,
when it was imperative that we should land a balanced force ready
for action from the outset. Ocean liners are not designed for such
activities. Nor do they possess the military communications to
co-ordinate them. Innovation and compromise were called for on
all sides.

The actual landing would almost certainly take place at night.
So disembarkation in darkness also had to be practised, especially
as the ships might well be under way rather than hove-to. Even
after several daylight runs, I watched with concern as hundreds of
our men, festooned with weapons and equipment, leapt across the
ever-changing gap 'twixt ship and landing-craft, the swell surging
and seething beneath them. A slip meant almost certain death.
Even if a man came up, he would most likely be crushed, although
two lucky marines did survive just such a mishap. To everyone's
secret relief, the availability of both landing-craft and helicopters
for such practices was severely curtailed by the need to use them
for re-stowing the vast quantities of stores.

We were also desperate to get ashore to fire our weapons. The
modern rifle and machine-gun require regular zero-ing of the
sights if accuracy is to be maintained. Almost more important,
though, was the need to familiarize troops with the specialized
weapons that, because of safety restrictions and financial
limitations, are comparatively rarely fired, or even seen, after basic
training. Within a rifle company, these include the 66-mm and
84-mm hand-held anti-tank projectiles. It was also essential to
create confidence in the larger and more sophisticated support
weapons – artillery, mortars, and the Milan anti-tank and
Blowpipe anti-aircraft missiles. It proved impracticable to
demonstrate all of these, because the island simply wasn't large

enough for an artillery range to be constructed there, and the RAF, understandably, drew the line at our firing guided missiles in their already overcrowded airspace. We did, however, manage impressive mixed 81-mm mortar-shoots, putting down smoke, illumination and phosphorus very close to the troops, as much to reassure them of the weapons' control as their efficacy. It was the demonstration of Milan's range and accuracy, however, that gained universal approbation. Milan is a long-range wire-guided anti-tank missile. The operator aims through an eyepiece and, after firing, the flare of the rocket merely has to be aligned constantly upon the target for a guaranteed hit. As each missile costs more than £4,000, they are not expended lightly; most training is carried out with dummy missiles, using elaborate electronic scenarios within the simulator that complements the system. Outside the Milan teams, riflemen rarely, if ever, see it fired, so we were determined to prove the weapon's lethality to the rifle companies. They might desperately need to rely on it, for the Argentines were known to have Panhard armoured cars on the islands. Before the assembled cohorts of both 40 and 42 Commandos, one of 'Four-Two's' marines unerringly struck the distant target, over a mile away and barely discernible, with his first missile. His section commander endorsed this accuracy with a second strike. No one was left in any doubt that Milan was a deadly weapons system.

3 Commando Brigade had also been provided with some light armoured reconnaissance in the form of two troops of Scorpion and Scimitar light tanks from the Blues and Royals. Although few of us had actually worked with armour before, its role and capability were well known to most officers and SNCOs. Ashore on Ascension, the features and characteristics of these compact, tracked vehicles, with their varied array of machine-guns and long-range rapid-firing cannon, were carefully explained by the two armoured troop officers. In the tradition of British cavalry, both had clearly spent some time on the playing fields of Eton, and favoured a more elegant style of uniform than their infantry counterparts. Nevertheless, their professionalism, and their absolute conviction that their tanks could operate across the boggy terrain of the Falklands, came over compellingly. Less than two years before I had been on the fringes of a lobby attempting, unsuccessfully, to persuade the US Marine Corps that tracks were more versatile than wheels for this type of armoured recce vehicle.

The war in the Falklands would soon provide an irrefutable endorsement of this very point. In the event, those eight light tanks were to skim across the steep, glutinous surface of the waterlogged terrain and provide devastating fire support for 2 Para in their final attack outside Stanley.

There was one vital organization which needed to use every possible moment ashore to set up its equipment and iron out electronic bugs. This was the Rapier anti-aircraft missile battery. Manned by specialists from the Royal Artillery, this delicate and complex system had been rushed aboard an LSL, onto which a further batch of vehicles was subsequently loaded. As a result, it proved impossible to carry out the essential testing and maintenance of the system's telemetry during the voyage out. On arrival at Ascension, the command and control system had to be stripped down, reassembled, and then tested with live firings against simulated aircraft. No sooner had all the equipment been extricated from the LSL and established ashore, however, than the whole Task Force was put at short notice to sail by a signal from the controlling HQ at Northwood. Unproven, Rapier was hastily flown back on board, the first of several reminders that the fog of war thickens in proportion to the distance between strategist and tactician ...

From the outset of 'Operation Corporate', as the recapture of the Falkland Islands was to be codenamed, it was clear that British air superiority would be a crucial factor. After the first 'O' Group in Plymouth, a number of officers, including myself, had probed warily about whether this could be guaranteed. We were assured that the naval assessment available up to then was unequivocal. Even if I had not seen for myself, at Suez, the ravages of close air support, everyone appreciates the total vulnerability of a flotilla of stationary ships disgorging troops and equipment ashore. It is a fundamental precept of amphibious warfare that the attacker must establish air superiority over the beach-head. Brigadier Julian had constantly stressed this requirement. But from now on, it became increasingly and disconcertingly clear that we must anticipate air attack during the landings.

Later, an ominous reappraisal was forced upon the maritime planners when the devastating potential of air-launched missiles against surface ships was demonstrated by the Argentines. This threat compelled the carrier group of HMSS *Invincible* and *Hermes*, with their escorts, to stay further out in the Total Exclusion Zone, so that the endurance of their Harrier aircraft over the islands was therefore reduced. It would also take longer for the Harriers to react to incoming threats. Belatedly, it began to be acknowledged that the Argentine air force might be a great deal more versatile and dangerous than had originally been supposed. It is also clear now that few assessors had anticipated that the Argentine pilots would prove as resolute and tenacious as they turned out to be. Fortunately, the enemy's potentially overwhelming advantage was mitigated, unexpectedly, by the failure of many of their bombs to explode.

Luckily, perhaps, little of this was then apparent to us. Nor, of course, could we foresee the unbelievably courageous and quite devastating interceptions the Fleet Air Arm and RAF pilots would achieve until the threat was overcome. Even so, attack from the air was the closest-run aspect of the campaign, a risk which we were exceedingly lucky to get away with. As a recent instructor at the US Marine Corps Amphibious Warfare School, where the art is comprehensively taught and is constantly reviewed, I felt decidedly uneasy.

Amidst all this practical activity and tactical contemplation, I found the odd moment in which to ponder upon Ascension Island, this amazing carbuncle on the restless surface of the South Atlantic. I was intrigued to read that we had been preceded on Ascension by other Royal Marines, more than a century earlier; in fact there was a garrison fort atop the island which there might be time to visit. My first impressions of Ascension, however, were of its precipitous, volcanic slopes, covered in ash and clinker, which seemed reminiscent of a moon landscape as we perspired across them in the glaring heat. The coastline was almost universally barren and inaccessible, because of the unending ocean rollers that dashed themselves malevolently onto the rocks. But there was a single beach on which a craft could land, making possible a rare afternoon or two of 'banyans' – swimming and drinking beer – for the boys. From there, one could look up the sheer pile of the volcano to the distant summit where, astoundingly, there was a sort of skull cap of greenery in which, we were told, tropical birds sang and orchids flourished. Snaking enticingly up the mountain was a modern tarmac road, for which, at some time, the British taxpayer had been liable. The only flat part of the island was the airfield at Wideawake with, nearby, its associated housing estates whose inhabitants made it plain that they preferred us to keep our distance.

Eventually 'Uncle Tom' and I decided that we could afford a

break. Since he carried more clout, I left the provision of transport up to him. It was simply arranged, for Hew Pike kindly lent us his CO's Land-Rover and driver on a day when 3 Para were ashore training. A carefree group made up of myself, Phil Wilson, the RSM, Marine Green and a 42 Commando signaller in case we were recalled, joined *Canberra*'s Military Force Commander and his Provost Marshal (otherwise known as 'The Sheriff') Warrant Officer Bob Brown of the Royal Marines Police. Sure enough, after an impressive, switchback drive we eventually reached the edge of a lush green forest, which seemed aflame with the brilliant colours of orchids, hibiscus and bougainvillaea. Even more astonishing to me were the numbers of minas in their handsome black outfits with gold facings, flitting amongst other noisy, tropical birds. We had just such a bird, with the rather dull name 'Fred', back at home in Devon. His name belied his character, however, for Fred possessed a repertoire of expletives and remarks that often embarrassed strangers. His *pièce de résistance* was to whistle for the dogs, and then laugh derisively when they eagerly came. It was amusing to meet his kith and kin on top of an extinct volcano 4,000 miles from home, although I would have preferred to have encountered my eager spaniels or companionable labrador.

At the very top of this leafy grove we came upon the ancient farm where fresh vegetables for Ascension's inhabitants have been grown since 1823. There we left the vehicle, going on to ascend a few hundred feet to the original Royal Marine fort, cunningly constructed alongside the only freshwater spring on the island. This relic of wars gone by, in which our predecessors had faced different but no doubt equally daunting forebodings, provided the excuse for the reflection that we were probably better off than they had been – at least we did not have to remain here for four years! The old fort's garrison had, however, enjoyed one of the world's most panoramic ocean views, as they scanned the horizon for French ships that might appear to release Napoleon from nearby St Helena.

On the way down Tom, ever the gallant cavalier, came up with the idea of gathering flowers for two of the women officers on *Canberra*. Both warrant officers in our party exchanged tolerant smiles as their carefree seniors scampered through the trees, collecting handfuls of exotic blooms. But Mr Brown's grin became somewhat lopsided when Tom decided that he, personally, ought not to appear with a bunch of flowers in a crowded landing-craft alongside the ship. I took one look at the RSM and decided that it simply wasn't worth mentioning! Later, we swung on board with an aggressive-looking 'Sheriff' gingerly clutching his posy; mine was furtively shoved down the front of my shirt ...

During this period the COs and their operational staffs were made increasingly aware of how hydrography, geography, and intelligence about the enemy were gradually determining the selection of a landing-site. By now we knew that our landing force would be outnumbered by at least two to one. We had also been told that the enemy had concentrated the bulk of his force around the approaches to Port Stanley. Obviously, a direct assault landing near that town would be hazardous. But the number of potentially suitable beaches elsewhere was limited. The further we landed from Stanley, the further we must march to engage the enemy. The Falklands consist of two main islands, both of which were now garrisoned by Argentine forces. This was an additional complication, and the idea of making an initial landing in West Falkland was seriously considered for a time. It was eventually abandoned, however, both because of the subsequent problems of crossing the sound to East Falkland, and because the western island was closer to the mainland Argentine air force. The only advantage we seemed to have was that the Argentines would have infinitely greater problems in reinforcing from one island to another, because of their very limited and vulnerable amphibious lift.

The selection of any beach-head for a major amphibious landing is a complicated process for it requires specific information on tides, gradients, underwater obstacles, and the shore line. Most fortunately for the Task Force, such expert knowledge was available through the first-hand experience and research of Major Ewen Southby-Tailyour, Royal Marines. Ewen had recently prepared a book on inshore navigation around the Falklands. This was to prove almost as invaluable as his personal judgement and expert advice, until SAS and SBS reconnaissance teams were able to provide first-hand intelligence. It is an extraordinary tribute to both organizations that, from early May, patrols from the Special Air Service and RM Special Boat Squadron were operating all over the islands without detection. Throughout April, however, Brigade Headquarters, which prudently included Ewen Tailyour, was without up-to-date intelligence. There were not even any recent aerial photographs, since the islands' distance from the nearest RAF base precluded them.

On 30 April Brigadier Julian and Major John Chester, the Brigade Major, came on board *Canberra* to brief the COs, in strictest secrecy, on the options identified so far. Because any plan was subject to approval from Northwood, or to new intelligence from the Special Forces, these options were fairly wide-ranging. At that stage, the favoured idea was for a landing at Cow Bay, less than 20 miles north of Stanley. We were told that Cow Bay had a restricted beach, exposed to the South Atlantic weather, where we would have to execute a complex assault with a mix of helicopters and landing-craft crucially co-ordinated. To me this seemed ominously complicated. Cow Bay was also well within range of the enemy's medium artillery in and around Stanley, and only a few minutes' flying time from their infantry reserves. We would have our own powerful naval gunfire and air support, but I remained apprehensive, and I could see that Malcolm Hunt, my 40 Commando counterpart, felt the same. Included among the alternatives was a place called San Carlos, which lay on the other, western side, of East Falkland, in sheltered waters and having several beaches that seemed tailor-made for an amphibious landing. It did not seem to rate very highly in the plans, however ...

All these plans were merely options then and we considered them chiefly in terms of our own tactical problems. However, all manner of other factors – air, naval, logistic, even political – bore heavily on the staff. In truth, our parochial misgivings were selfish as well as worrying. But they were soon to be exacerbated, for we speedily discovered that these critically sensitive plans became common knowledge in the Crow's Nest Bar (officers and 'hacks'), as well as among many of the SNCOs.

This was the beginning of yet another pressure imposed upon us by our peculiar circumstances. A passenger liner is not unlike a club, where an indiscretion or unguarded confidences are transmitted like a series of ripples across a pool. Furthermore, within our circle there was a professionally inquisitive element – the journalists – who could interpret an expression, expletive, or silence with experienced discernment. Although the press men on *Canberra* never prematurely revealed confidential information to their newspapers, their presence was a catalyst for gossip and speculation. COs were under pressure either to deny knowledge of plans which they knew must eventually be confirmed, or to tell their staffs what they *did* know, although this had been expressly forbidden. Regrettably, we never did seem to achieve a consensus within the three units.

Journalistic controversy was not all linked to Fleet Street. Our two RN Education Officers launched a 'local rag' called the *Canberra Buzz*. In the naval tradition, nobody was sacrosanct, however senior or important. As circulation swelled amongst the majority, so indignant complaints from outraged individuals increased. The most popular section of the paper was 'The Buzz', a column intended to satisfy the huge demand for shipboard rumour and gossip. 'Prince Andrew ordered home' and '42 Commando to lead the assault' were typically stimulating by-lines, but others proved more controversial: '*Invincible* reduced to one propeller' was another figment of their fertile imaginations. Somehow that was smoothed over, but the next provocation proved terminal. Our postal address had been published as BFPO 666. 'Some say these numerals may be a sign of the Anti-Christ,'* the next edition of the *Canberra Buzz* revealed. This was too much, as a deputation of Padres represented to 'Uncle Tom'. Censorship was decreed, but with commendable independence Lieutenant-Commanders Miklinski and Brown preferred to close down the paper.

By now, we were also becoming increasingly exposed to the premise that a conscripted, untrained, ill equipped and disillusioned Argentine garrison was deteriorating from hunger and exposure, and would be a push-over once we had landed. This view had largely come about because of the enemy's pitiful resistance on South Georgia, and was compounded by the increasingly jingoistic line taken by some newspapers at home. It worried us on two counts. First, complacency amongst the troops could, in adversity, prove disastrous. Second, we might be put to unrealistic risks should ministers and their advisers come to share such overconfidence. Bleak and aggressive briefings prevented the rot from setting in among the troops, but in some quarters in the UK a dangerously simplistic view was formed of how swiftly we could advance almost as soon as the force was ashore.

We had a succession of visitors while we were at Ascension, including the occasional familiar face from UK, since planning teams flew out and back in the space of a few days. On one

---

* 'Let him that hath understanding count the number of the beast: for it is the number of a man; and his number is Six hundred threescore and six.' The Revelation of St John the Divine, 13:18.

occasion Lieutenant-Colonel Paul Stevenson, RM, a friend and neighbour of mine, who had been co-opted into the expanding headquarters staff at Northwood suddenly appeared. Although it was fascinating to listen to his explanations of how matters were being dealt with both there and in Downing Street, I found it difficult to grasp that he would visit my family that very weekend. It seemed that we were still close to home, a feeling enhanced by topical newspapers, recorded video news and the incessant radio bulletins. But a glance across the sun-burnished anchorage, or a check in the atlas, reminded me that we were actually 4,000 miles from the cool scent of Devon moors, and the soft snuffle or familiar stamp of a horse in the stables.

Others who came aboard *Canberra* for a night of well deserved luxury and relaxation away from the spartan circumstances in which they were billeted elsewhere, included Andrew Whitehead, the CO of 45 Commando, Jonathan Thomson of the SBS, and Ewen Southby-Tailyour, our Falklands 'sage'. Andrew was aboard the Royal Fleet Auxiliary *Stromness*, with his unit split amongst several ships; indeed, we had one of his companies on *Canberra*. Despite the difficulties this dispersal posed for him, he showed no hint of resentment or envy towards my own luxurious quarters and convenient situation. After teasing me about being suborned by the plush life, we spent the rest of our time together speculating on the future. We agreed that hostilities were inevitable if the Task Force sailed south, that the Argentine air threat was exceedingly disturbing, and that the terrain was probably impassable for extended marches by heavily laden troops. Instead, we would have to move by helicopter, probably at night. Eventually 'Four-Five's' marines were to shoulder their burdens across more than forty miles of tussock and slush, marching all the way from San Carlos to Stanley.

Jonathan Thomson and Ewen both came over from HMS *Fearless*, where their living conditions could only have been described as primitive (Ewen slept in a bath each night because there was no room anywhere else). Both of them made joyful use of my shower and stateroom sofa, as well as the bar in Ewen's case. The abstemious and super-fit Jonathan ran for miles around the promenade deck, but consumed only gallons of soft drinks.

From the LPD, Jonathan could speak directly and securely through satellite communications (SATCOM) to ships of the task groups in the Total Exclusion Zone, or, as he had been doing, directly to Guy in South Georgia. Unlike the SAS, however, his SBS sub-units did not actually carry such sets with them. An SAS patrol commander could speak directly back to the UK or to Brigade HQ, while at a higher level SATCOM meant that the Brigade Commander, or the Commodore who would command our amphibious group for the landings, were now personally accessible to the planners at Northwood. Gone for ever were the days of blind eyes to telescopes, or circuitously routed despatches ...

Ewen Tailyour was an old and favourite friend. I had known him since he was a boy, because his father had been my first Commanding Officer. An elegant, witty, swashbuckling figure, once accurately described as the reincarnation of an Elizabethan sea dog, he epitomized the tradition of apparently feckless officers who nevertheless remain true professionals. Behind the relaxed banter lay unique experience in amphibious techniques, gained from nearly twenty years of operating RM landing-craft all over the world. In addition, Ewen is an offshore sailor of international renown, having successfully completed several Round-Britain races and travelled thousands of miles in other challenging voyages. His speciality, however, is inshore navigation, at which he is an acknowledged expert. His pilotage book on the Falklands was compiled while he was commanding the garrison there some years before. Apart from local fishermen, no one in the world then knew as much about this coastline as Ewen. A suave, gregarious bon viveur, he instantly adapted to *Canberra*'s social scene, and contrived to spend as much time with us as possible. He could always find plausible reasons, for his amusing and fascinating lectures on the islands were in constant demand. But Captain Christopher Burne, RN, began to cast an increasingly jaundiced eye in Ewen's direction. He was not an accredited resident of *Canberra*, whose comforts irresistibly lured would-be 'gate-crashers', although these were unceremoniously ejected by 'the Beagle' as soon as he discovered their presence.

The legend of the 'Great White Whale's' Senior Naval Officer was already becoming established. Lieutenant-Colonel Mike Rose, SAS, a sophisticated and intellectual Guards officer, but with little experience of the Navy, flew on to *Canberra* one evening. As he paused to gain his bearings, a voice from the darkness rasped: 'Who the hell are you, and why are you skulking around my ship?' A bemused Rose arrived in the Crow's Nest Bar, declaring: 'I have just been attacked on deck by a lunatic in the uniform of a Captain, Royal Navy ...' Another story, no doubt embellished with poetic licence, involved the Leading Seaman Communicator, a perpetually harassed individual who rushed incessantly between 'the Beagle' and the communications centre. Chris became concerned that the rating in question might be cracking up, so decided that it might be prudent to arrange an unknowing interview between the Signalman and a psychiatrist in the embarked medical squadron. This was duly fixed on the pretext of sending the sailor to deliver a signal to the Surgeon-Commander in his cabin, where a casual chat could be used to disguise a more serious purpose. Later, Chris Burne was sombrely informed by 'The Shrink' that his chap was indeed deranged, and must if possible be repatriated. Concerned at how to break the news to his faithful subordinate, 'the Beagle' muttered diffidently: 'Er, Watkins, do you remember that officer you delivered the signal to this morning ...?'

'Well, actually, Sir, it wasn't me, because I was too busy. Atkinson went along instead ...'

Elsewhere on *Canberra*, the fitness programme continued unabated from dawn till dusk, even though the promenade deck was now beginning to resemble a crumbling motorway, with potholes and cracks marring the composite surface. The companies or platoons, laden with weapons and equipment, tramped and doubled in the same direction for mile after mile. When I wasn't punishing my own ageing frame, I would stand on the sidelines with the RSM and watch the snake of sweating marines and paras, flanked by their officers and NCOs, stamping endlessly by, as if in some bizarre ceremonial. Even below decks, one was just as conscious of this activity. Bulkheads shivered as the rumble of the men's passage increased to a crescendo overhead. This made concentration or relaxation impossible, so that we had to limit all such training to certain times of day, for otherwise no one could have slept. Not surprisingly, the five weeks of undiluted training had produced a lean, mean-looking band of warriors with feet like leather. Equipment now seemed moulded to the body, and men carried their weapons as extensions of themselves. Like athletes preparing for an Olympiad, we were approaching the peak of readiness, but thereafter would come the danger of gradually getting stale if a landing did not follow. It was also obvious that once the Task Force sailed south towards the Antarctic winter, deteriorating weather would prevent training on the upper decks. It was vital – and would become more so – that we should not be inactive too long.

It was now apparent that international diplomacy could not avert conflict. Before leaving Ascension on 6 May each unit chose to have a 'smoker', as they called it, where officers and NCOs joined their troops in the men's canteen for a last 'get-together'. John Ware and his band were at 'Four-Two's', helping to create the boisterous camaraderie which will always be one of my best memories of this time. We were completely at ease with each other, and full of confidence in ourselves. Every now and again the cheerful chatter would die down for a 'Four-Two Special', which might be a solitary comedian unerringly ridiculing the officer establishment, some sort of song, or a musical group. Marine Maurice Toombs was a particular favourite. He had adapted the old Cliff Richard hit 'Summer Holiday' to altogether more sinister verses, predicting a fate that would shortly overtake 'The Spics' on the Malvinas. The song was in the most appalling taste from an outsider's point of view, and unashamedly vicious, too. But aggression had now to be encouraged, and morale fostered, in every way possible. I asked for an encore. Once again, we all roared out those ghastly threats with gusto.

The evening ended when, quite spontaneously, the band launched into a patriotic theme. Suddenly, unexpectedly, certainly out of character for the predominant generation present, we were all on our feet, singing lustily and emotionally. But the songs were those that, nowadays, only have an annual, implausible airing at the last night of The Proms. We might have been a battalion on a troopship to South Africa, the Dardanelles, or India. As I watched those bronzed young faces, raised in martial chorus, it was clear that each and every one had accepted the coming challenge. They knew that, in success or disaster, they were committed together, and felt that this was how it should be. I knew then that, given the chance to close with the enemy, we could unleash a fearful ferocity.

In an article about 42 Commando, John Shirley had quoted me as saying: 'You have to have a violent and uncompromising attitude to this job. It's what you get paid for. War is about generating violence and we have to generate more of it more quickly than the other side ...' Looking about me at the 'smoker', with the whole Commando in full voice, I recognized that this was precisely what we could do.

On this memorable evening, most of us finally accepted that killing the enemy, or the fear of being killed, were ordeals that had to be faced. The time had come to stimulate, rather than suppress, the potential for violence that simmers within élite forces. We were going to war.

5

SOUTH ACROSS THE ATLANTIC

At twilight on Thursday 6 May, we weighed anchor and set sail in convoy, like countless task forces before us, towards a strange coastline and an unknown enemy.

3 Commando Brigade's staff were still evaluating reconnaissance reports received from SBS and SAS patrols operating across the islands. By now, the landing-site options had been dramatically reduced, as new hazards eliminated so many of those considered, including Cow Bay. San Carlos was increasingly preferred, providing the Special Forces could confirm that the Argentines had not established a significant presence there. San Carlos Bay offered a sheltered anchorage, with three beaches suitable for unit landings, as well as the space for troops to move out rapidly and deploy tactically. Almost more important, the bay was overlooked by a semi-circle of hills high enough to inhibit hostile aircraft attacks. If we occupied the reverse slopes to the enemy direction, then these hills would also make a formidable obstacle to any advance from the interior. After the sinking of HMS *Sheffield* on 4 May, no one was in the slightest doubt about the lethality of Exocet. But the hills of San Carlos should effectively mask ships in the anchorage from such attacks, even the 'Great White Whale' – or so we hoped.

I was warned that, whatever the outcome, 42 Commando would after all provide the reserve for the landings. This was a bitter pill to swallow. Illogically, we all still thought in terms of fighting for the beaches, even though Brigadier Thompson and his staff were striving to ensure that our arrival should be as far away from the enemy as possible. Because the reserve should not be required to fight for the beaches, 42 Commando was, more encouragingly, tasked with planning swift follow-up raids against enemy garrisons at Goose Green and Port Howard. Current intelligence indicated that Goose Green was held by about a battalion of the enemy. Port Howard seemed a far more formidable objective, containing an Argentine Brigade HQ and an artillery battery, as well as the equivalent of a battalion of infantry. We therefore concentrated on a military appreciation of the enemy's advantages and intentions at Goose Green, which seemed to suggest that their primary purpose was to hold the local airstrip. This provided a base for their close air support, notably the Pucara aircraft which, although propeller-driven, was heavily armed and specifically configured to attack troops on the ground. The most vulnerable aspect of the Argentine garrison appeared to be the main supply route between the airstrip and Stanley. If this track could be cut and held, with artillery or mortars denying aircraft the use of the strip, then we would seriously interfere with the enemy's operations at Goose Green, and would perhaps force him to leave his positions to attack us. We would be extremely vulnerable to fighter ground attack from the mainland, but, even at that stage, we naively supposed this to be unlikely. The whole concept of our plan was, of course, based upon the availability of helicopters, and upon our having an artillery battery in support.

Meticulously, Ian McNeill preserved one of the map traces we sent to Brigade HQ. It shows our outline plan for the objective that was later to become a household word overnight after 2 Para had carried out, in different circumstances, a more daunting operation at Goose Green. After the war I visited that bleak, open heathland, and found it littered with the stark relics of a vicious infantry battle, in which aggression and personal courage had finally prevailed. My professional admiration for the achievement of 'H' Jones and 2 Para was tempered with relief that we had not had to 'blood' ourselves against such odds.

As the ships sailed on, the pace and pressure of preparation gained in intensity. All too frequently, COs had to fly to other ships to attend briefings, trips which entailed noisy, buffeted flights over rough seas in crowded helicopters. During these excursions, we would hover again and again over the smaller ships as other planners were winched up or down. As a veteran passenger, I knew that all the skill and experience of the RN pilots could be

neutralized in seconds by mechanical failure, or a drastic change
of wind conditions. Each flight between ships of the Task Force
made me more conscious of the odds on collapse into the icy
waters, or a fiery death on some vessel's superstructure. Just such
a fatal calamity overtook a Sea King helicopter, crowded with men
of the SAS, cross-decking from HMS *Hermes* to an assault ship
after an outstandingly successful raid on the enemy aircraft based
at Pebble Island. There were only two survivors out of the
twenty-two invaluable Special Forces experts.

One trip which I made very willingly, however, was to HMS
Fearless on 13 May for the formal, 3 Commando Brigade 'O'
Group. There each commanding officer was to be given the
detailed instructions for his mission during the landings. In his
book *No Picnic*, Brigadier Julian Thompson vividly described why
this military ritual is such an important preliminary to battle.
Meticulous preparation, co-ordination and stage management is
required by the staff, as well as a compelling performance from the
commander himself. For it is then that a leader briefs his
subordinate commanders on how he expects them to risk their
own lives, and those of their men, while carrying out his particular
plan for battle. Not only must everyone understand the orders –
they must also have confidence in them as well. Subsequently, of
course, the whole orders procedure needs to be successfully
repeated all the way down the line, from commanding officer to
corporal.

It was lucky for all of us that the commander and staff of 3
Commando Brigade RM together made up such an experienced,
professional, harmonious team. They had worked unstintingly to
ensure the 'O' Group's success. Twenty-four hours beforehand,
each unit had received a detailed operation order clarifying the
role of every component of the military force which was to
establish itself ashore. With this clarification were pages of
statistics listing map references, codenames, radio frequencies,
supporting-fire tasks, logistic priorities and timings – altogether,
the document was nearly fifty pages long. We needed all
twenty-four hours of that lead-time to absorb, discuss and place in
perspective this tapestry of the landing.

At the 'O' Group, the Brigadier was able to illustrate his
intentions for each unit against the detailed background of the
operation order. His own orders were delivered formally and
precisely, but with that personal touch for each CO which has

always characterized British briefings of this kind – individual reassurance is never more important than at such moments. 'Nick. I want you to remain on board *Canberra* in reserve until called forward ...'

I sat there in the front of the throng of officers who had crowded into the wardroom of HMS *Fearless*. There were two other Royal Marine Commando COs, our Parachute Regiment counterparts, and the commanding officers of an artillery regiment, two helicopter squadrons, a logistic regiment, a squadron of engineers. Ranged behind us were row upon row of representatives from all over the Task Force. This included the naval, air and gunnery support, special forces, landing-craft, air defence, the medical organization, communicators, logisticians, air controllers. This was to be Britain's largest amphibious operation since Suez, involving nearly 5,000 men – there must be no chance of doubt or ambiguity about the plan. The soundness and clarity of those instructions were confirmed when, after the briefing, not one of us raised a query.

Throughout his crisp and confident orders, Julian Thompson was seeking to put over his own conviction that the landings in San Carlos were merely a means to an end. It was vital, he emphasized time and again, for every man to recognize that establishing the beach-head would merely provide a secure logistic base from which to push forward towards the enemy. If we were besieged there, our reaction must be a swift breakout towards Stanley and the main Argentinian positions. The Brigadier also explained that reinforcements were expected before the final battles.

The San Carlos plan was for the four fighting units (2 and 3 Para, 40 and 45 Commandos) to establish a perimeter around the high ground under cover of darkness. This meant using landing-craft, since comparatively few ships' decks could be used by helicopters at night. After first light, one battery of guns with the necessary ammunition would be flown in to release those ships restricted to naval gunfire support for the troops ashore. The most urgent priority was for the Rapier battery to be lifted on to selected heights, where the firing-posts could provide an umbrella of missile defence in co-ordination with the anti-air systems of RN ships around San Carlos. Thereafter, all helicopters and landing-craft would concentrate on completing a carefully programmed move of men, equipment and stores to various beaches or positions. The tight, forty-eight-hour time-scale for all these operations was based on two critical assumptions: that local air superiority would be maintained, and that logistic shipping could unload continuously.

'Four-Two' was to remain on *Canberra*, at instant notice for a summons forward, although this would inevitably entail the diversion of vital helicopters and landing-craft from their designated landing tasks. I was keenly interested in the command and control system that would prevail if our move became necessary. Another principle of amphibious warfare is that control of all amphibious forces is retained by the senior naval commander – Commodore Clapp in this case – until the military are effectively established ashore. This control includes direction and co-ordination of the 'movement assets'; in other words, the landing-craft or helicopters we required would be under naval control, even though 3 Commando Brigade HQ might call for 'Four-Two' as reinforcements while they were setting up ashore.

In the event, this did not prove as much of a problem as we had expected, for Brigade HQ was still trapped on board HMS *Fearless* by air attacks when it was decided to land us. It was, however, subsequently decreed that control of both helicopters and landing-craft would remain afloat even after Brigade HQ was established ashore. No doubt there were compelling reasons for that decision, but this was the second violation of the principles of amphibious warfare. I believe that it had unfortunate consequences for the best use of movement assets during those critical first days in the beach-head.

The Brigade 'O' Group was our cue to arrange a collective briefing for the officers of 42 Commando. Just as the staff of 3 Commando Brigade had tabulated a mass of essential data, so Ian McNeill and his team now transposed that mass for us. Being in reserve, we had the simplest of missions – 'don't call us, we'll call you!' – but it was vital that junior leaders at every level should understand the landing plan. Eventually they might find themselves intervening during the various phases within any part of the beach-head. In some ways it was more difficult to prepare for all these eventualities than for a specific task. Much of the essential support and co-ordination remained uncertain. Which battery would be supporting us for what contingency? Where and how would we be landed? When could companies expect re-supply if timings were unpredictable?

It was, however, a familiar, almost reassuring, routine after the winter training in Norway. I knew the personalities and experience of all the company commanders except Mike Norman, and the new Battle Adjutant, Matt Sturman, who had replaced Phil Wilson. This was not as a result of Phil's duplicity over birthday parties, but because of his unrivalled experience with the Commando's support weapons, the 81-mm mortar and Milan anti-tank missile. I was convinced that these would play a critical role in the actions to come, and it made sense to place the best-qualified officer in charge of such assets. Matt, on the other hand, was a proven commando adjutant. I knew that he would run our main HQ, with all its complex of communications and specialists, efficiently and independently. That was going to be particularly important, since it was obvious from the terrain that the alternative tactical headquarters would be on foot and well forward most of the time. Tac HQ includes the CO, his Operations Officer (Ops Offr) and Battery Commander (BC), together with their essential communication and protection parties; other advisers would come along according to requirement.

42 Commando's Battery Commander was David Brown, a major in the Royal Artillery, who also brought with him two Forward Observation Officers and a strong communications team. A special light regiment of artillery forms part of Commando Forces Royal Marines, the volunteer Royal Artillery gunners qualifying for the same green beret. The BC advises a unit's CO on how best to use his available artillery support, and then co-ordinates its provision. The observation officers are attached to the rifle companies and have a similar role, although their main function is actually controlling the gunfire by direct observation of where shells land. David Brown, a neat, tactful and most professional officer, possessed the self-confidence and relaxed sense of humour that ensured our personal relationship was always easy. Although we did not then know one another well, his obvious pride in the battery, and his commitment to our interests, were reassuring. The observation officers, Captains Chris Romberg and Nick D'Apice, were both strong characters who could ski as fast and drink as hard as any of my own officers, with whom they maintained a competitive but easy-going relationship. This team spirit also extended amongst the marines and their gunner counterparts.

One way in which the Commando might acquire intelligence, once ashore, would be through the Reconnaissance Troop, which

was led by a tough young lieutenant, Chris Mawhood. Royal
Marine Commando units have been unique for some years in
maintaining these specialized teams, sometimes described as the
CO's 'eyes and ears'. The sixteen or so members will invariably be
hand-picked, experienced men, and are usually parachute- and
mountain-warfare-trained. I was more than satisfied with our
recce team, which included several highly trained snipers. RSM
Dave Chisnall, who came from a distinguished background in this
field, rated them as well above average. We were, however, short
of one section and the troop second-in-command, Sergeant John
Napier – they had been sent to South Georgia with Guy Sheridan.

Communications in modern warfare are not only crucial, they
are also increasingly complex, so that COs have to rely heavily
upon the knowledge and technical advice of their comparatively
junior Signals Officers. In 42 Commando this expertise was
provided by Charlie Eggar, a fresh-faced, conscientious lieutenant
who also stoically endured my impatience and frustration at the
occasional failures of his expensive technology. But most of the
time it did work, thanks to the unflagging skill of his fifty or so
signallers and technicians who manned and maintained the radio
nets we could use constantly in the field. Charlie once cryptically
remarked to me that my own Signals Corporal, John Adams, had
been hand-picked for his endurance. Where I went so did Corporal
Adams, constantly monitoring the nets, briefing me on
developments while I concentrated on other events, fetching
officers to their own sets so that I wasted as little time as possible.
Whenever we halted, he would instantly set up aerials and adjust
frequencies. Before we set off again, he would have anticipated the
preparations for moving. For more than a year we drove, marched,
skied in unison, often sharing food and shelter, instinctively
co-operating to dominate the medium of communication through
which control of a fighting unit is maintained. He was an
essential, utterly reliable element within the personal group on
which I depended so much.

Another member of Tac HQ was Marine Green, who was
charged with looking after my domestic requirements on
operations. In the field, there is too little time for officers,
particularly those with command or planning responsibilities, to
cope with the incessant distractions of cooking food or setting up
shelter. But if these practical problems are not taken care of, the
quality and endurance of leadership is inevitably and increasingly

eroded. The marines themselves sardonically referred to Green as my 'flunkey', although they were quick enough to help him whenever that became necessary: 'You're not expecting him to eat that crap, are you? Look, slip in some of this "go-faster dust" [curry powder]. We want the little bugger on the ball, you know ...' Green, sadly, was a lousy cook, although a reliable campaigner in other respects. This made life frustrating at times, as well as tedious, because I took some pride in my field cooking. It was one of the activities I most enjoyed, as a relaxation from responsibility. Arctic rations are dehydrated, and so must be reconstituted with gentle boiling and careful blending in order to retain flavour and consistency. In North Norway, time spent over a cooker also provides essential warmth inside tents or snowholes while inmates get ready to snuggle down into sleeping-bags. In the Falklands, however, we had no shelter for most of the time, and my rations reflected those bleak circumstances.

The rest of Tac HQ was made up of a mixture of signallers, drivers, and the Provost for protection, meticulously directed by the indefatigable RSM. David Chisnall was one of the youngest ever selected in the Royal Marines, and one of the most wary and accomplished field soldiers I have known. For nearly fifteen years he had alternated between unit Reconnaissance Troops across the world, and the Mountain and Arctic Cadre. He had also completed over ten winters in North Norway, climbed to 'severe' standard in the Alps, qualified as a ski teacher in a Norwegian school, and completed a bewildering variety of special operations training. Immensely strong and lithe, he moved like a wild animal through cover or at night, with an instinctive awareness of danger that was to save my life at least once. Despite this primeval nature, however, he was invariably well turned-out; indeed, I once wrote in a report that he could be found 'as immaculate and unruffled on top of some mountain in a gale, as he was when directing unit ceremonial on the parade ground'. WO1 Chisnall was younger than me, and we had not served together before, but we liked each other from the outset, a particular advantage in such a crucial relationship within the unit hierarchy.

The RSM is the senior non-commissioned rank, and it is he who safeguards the men's individual interests, using, if necessary, his exclusive access to the CO. This paternalism must be matched by unremitting enforcement of professional standards, especially amongst the SNCOs, to whom he is the equivalent of a Mafia

'Godfather'. David Chisnall was perhaps less imposing than my first RSM in the 1950s, a fearsome figure who would crash to attention with a daunting salute before declaring in stentorian tones: 'Mr Vaux, Sir! It's time you had your hair cut again, and have you written to your mother this week?' But Chisnall was just what was needed for 42 Commando in the 1980s. His only drawback, as far as I was concerned, was that he was teetotal – hangovers were never shared experiences on early morning ski trips or at Orderly Room.

Until now, there has been only oblique reference to the two men who would lead 'K' and 'L' Companies. Once again, the relationship between a CO and his rifle company commanders is one which must be adapted to the personality and experience of individuals. A frustrated company commander is of little use in battle, when mutual confidence and freedom of action count for all. In peacetime, of course, authority and direction are less flexible, and the two company commanders and I had had our ups and downs in Norway the previous winter. Gradually we all adapted to my particular way of running the Commando on exercise or in barracks.

Captain David Wheen, who commanded 'L' Company, had been a wild young subaltern and Navy skier in the same unit where I first had to accept the restrictions of desk and telephone. I envied him then, and wondered now how he apparently still managed to seem a military 'free spirit'. This was largely due to his boundless enthusiasm for doing what he enjoyed, as well as to a lively and friendly personality. All of which made him a popular and relaxed company commander, if not always a conscientious administrator. In adversity he was robust and determined, especially in the Arctic, where he was as much at home on a pair of skis as any local. A typical memory of David is of him outfacing a Norwegian major as they hurtled ever faster down an icy, ever-steepening slope. Eventually the Scandinavian prudently turned up his ski tips to slow down and acknowledge defeat, while Wheen swooped on down the slope with a triumphant whoop. The major bone of contention between David and myself, the subject of some amusement to signallers and officers on the unit command net, was that OC 'L' Company seldom responded on the radio as quickly as the CO thought he should. In Norway, the plausible excuse for this was that the signallers could not ski as fast as their commander. At one stage, this led me to order officers on the command net to carry their own sets. Although unpopular, this order speeded up communication dramatically, particularly David Wheen's!

OC 'K' Company was a very different personality. Captain Peter Babbington was another expert in support weapons, as well as an experienced Arctic operator. His dour, single-minded attitude to the parochial interests of his company could be either reassuring or aggravating, depending upon whether these coincided with the Commando's more general intentions. His charges, of course, reciprocated with a fierce loyalty and keen response to all Peter asked of them; nevertheless, his strong convictions and vigorous personality made him a firm disciplinarian. He was a thoroughly practical soldier – imperturbable, resourceful, absolutely determined once embarked on a course of action. Even though there was some truth in the topical joke that 'Four-Two' did this, while 'K Commando' did that, I knew that Peter and his men could be relied upon when it mattered.

The original Brigade plan had stipulated that the first two units ashore at San Carlos would be 40 and 45 Commandos. This had not been decided by any regimental prejudice against the Paras, but because the Staff had reasoned that Royal Marine experience would be an advantage during the disembarkation in the dark from unfamiliar commercial ships. If there were to be delays, then Brigadier Thompson did not want them during the first crucial wave. This could only comprise two units in the landing-craft available. Such misgivings turned out to be well founded – on the day, 2 Para, in a changed order of disembarkation, took over an hour longer than the stipulated time to disembark from the labyrinth of the lofty MV *Norland*. They had not had the time to practise at Ascension, having left the UK after the other units.

This change to the orchestration of the landings was an interesting example of just how flexible such plans must remain, right up to the last minute. Special Forces intelligence had begun to indicate the movement of what appeared to be an Argentine intervention force into the Goose Green area. This was disconcerting, since it meant that such a reserve could be swiftly moved by helicopter to anywhere along the western coastline, including the San Carlos area. The Brigadier reasoned that such a force might seize the heights of Sussex Mountain as soon as our landings were detected. This would be potentially disastrous, as the feature dominated much of the beach-head. 2 Para, who were to occupy Sussex Mountain, were therefore moved up into the first wave in place of 45 Commando. This meant that the Red and the Green Berets would now hit the beaches simultaneously. All of us agreed that was a thoroughly appropriate beginning to this joint enterprise.

But, just forty-eight hours before D-Day, there were far more drastic rearrangements to come. While the Task Force wallowed through steadily increasing seas, CINCFLEET's staff in Northwood suddenly signalled that 40 Commando and 3 Para must transfer from *Canberra* into the two amphibious ships, *Fearless* and *Intrepid*. Keeping all three units together in a single ship, it was now belatedly judged, was unacceptably dangerous. Although no one disputed our vulnerability, the order caused consternation among the embarked staffs. They had evaluated the options during planning at Ascension, and had concluded that the risk of landing most of the brigade from *Canberra* had to be taken. An LPD has the 'overload' capacity to carry up to 700 troops for very limited periods. Each unit now comprised almost that number of men, but both *Fearless* and *Intrepid* were overloaded already. Had they been in the LPDs, the commandos and paratroopers would have been forced to endure serious privation and lack of rest during the rough, two-week passage from Ascension. That would have diminished unacceptably their capability in a major, perhaps protracted, battle on landing. In any case, the loss of an overcrowded LPD, one of the two largest and most important ships in the amphibious task group, would have been just as disastrous as the destruction of *Canberra*. The lines of communication smouldered in the heat of last-minute argument ...

There was to be no compromise. So, in the finest tradition of Royal Navy resourcefulness, frantic arrangements were made to cross-deck from a luxury liner far out in the Atlantic, more than 1,200 heavily equipped men – all in one day. Two major limitations instantly became apparent. The first was that helicopters could not be used because the extra flying hours required for cross-decking would cripple them for forthcoming operations. The second was that only unexpectedly favourable weather could allow the LPDs to 'dock down' and float off their landing-craft for use in a sea transfer. A daunting third option would be to shuttle men individually slung on jackstays, while the three ships steamed close together with lines strung between them.

No one knew how long this might take, or whether the elements would also prevent this operation. Over any form of transfer loomed the ever-increasing threat of Argentine interference, particularly from submarines.

That night, there occurred the first of several almost miraculous events which could plausibly have been included in Grimms' fairy-tales. On Wednesday 19 May, against all weather patterns and predictions, the seas calmed sufficiently throughout the day for both units, with all their gear, to transfer to the LPDs without serious mishap (although one marine from 40 Commando fell in between *Canberra* and a landing-craft, and survived). The day ended with both units miraculously packed into the assault ships, despite daunting hazards in a sea state 4. Without that practice at Ascension, and the superb seamanship of the RM boat crews, the transfer would not have been possible, but we had also been unbelievably fortunate with that lull in the weather.

By now, we were poised on the edge of the Total Exclusion Zone. Argentine planes could and would attack us, as they had done just a few days earlier when HMS *Sheffield* had been sunk. The trauma, as well as the tragedy, of that event had reverberated throughout the Fleet. On *Canberra*, Chris Burne briefed us to prepare for air attacks against the ship, despite her pack of escorts. He decreed that all available machine-guns must be sited around the upper decks, in order to put up a curtain of lead against low-level aircraft. I am ashamed to admit to an almost total scepticism at the time that this could do any good against the supersonic menace we were facing. And once the other units had landed I was even more reluctant to conform, since I wanted our weaponry and ammunition reserved for an instant move ashore. How wrong I was, and how effectively that foresight prepared *Canberra* for her ordeal at San Carlos.

But an even greater danger faced us during the last twenty-four hours, as we came into range of the enemy's air-launched Exocet missiles. It was obvious that the Argentines must go for the amphibious task group and that the troop-carriers, particularly *Canberra*, the largest of them all, would be considered prime targets. Could our far-flung escort ships detect the Super Etendards in time? Would they be able to intercept the deadly missiles as they streaked above the wave-tops from over the horizon? If a modern destroyer could not survive their impact, what chance had a vulnerable luxury liner?

But elfin providence came to our rescue once again. 20 May –
D-day minus 1 – dawned foul and filthy for aviators, with minimal
visibility and confusing clutter appearing on radar screens. All day
it remained so, while the Argentine air force vainly sought for us,
until the skies lightened the gloom into a starlit evening. For a
second time the elements had enveloped us with their benevolent
protection at a critical moment.

That evening, the Military Force Commander, Colonel Tom
Seccombe, made a short broadcast, which concluded:

> Finally, I would like to congratulate all the members of the
> Embarked Military Force for the exemplary way in which they
> have behaved over the last six weeks. A great many people who
> are not connected with either the ship or the Military Force
> were quite needlessly apprehensive about a situation which place
> 2,500 marines and paratroopers in a comparatively confined
> space for an extended period of time. Those fears, as most of us
> supposed they would, have proved quite groundless, due in no
> small part to the way in which the ship's company of the *Canberra*
> have looked after us. In return we will do all we can to look after
> them. I cease to be Military Force Commander tomorrow and
> move to the Landing Force HQ, always providing it is possible
> to get me to *Fearless*. Thank you all for the support you have
> given to me and to my small staff over the last few weeks – Have
> an Interesting Week!

The time had also come for me to speak to 'Four-Two' before we
went to war. A spacious passenger lounge is no doubt easier for the
purpose than an olive grove in Tuscany, a plain in Russia, or a
creek run in Virginia. But across the centuries it can never have
been easy for commanders to look down upon young, resolute,
faces that soon may be frozen in death, or contorted with agony.
The British are an undemonstrative race, and nowhere more so
than in Her Majesty's Forces, where affection and trust are often
concealed behind regimental loyalty and military discipline. It
would have been embarrassing to have said how incredibly
fortunate I considered myself. Probably disquieting to dwell upon
the courage that I knew would be shown, or upon the sufferings to
be endured. Certainly banal to suggest that every man who fell
must be a personal loss. Instead, I sought refuge along those well
worn paths of understatement and banter, mixed with general
encouragement to everyone to take what might come in their
stride. There were reminders, too, of our morale, comradeship,

professionalism – even a reference to the justice of our cause: the rest of it mostly concerned tactics, or the enemy. I wondered afterwards whether my words had achieved much. By the end of the war I had forgotten almost everything that was said.

Nearly three years later, Kim Sabido, the IRN reporter who accompanied us, unearthed his tape-recording of that address. He wrote to tell me so, but then lost it again before I could check whether this is an accurate description ...

The call to arms is suspended above every professional serviceman. Many, of course, hope that trumpet will blow, to provide the exhilaration of conflict, or the satisfaction for years of training and commitment. But, as time goes by and routine dulls, others increasingly hope that it will not. On board *Canberra* were individuals for whom retirement loomed increasingly close. Suddenly, often for the first time, they faced the belated dangers of war. Among those that I knew, however, there seemed to be no misgivings.

For myself, I desperately wanted to prove that this unit could fight and win. Like a racehorse trainer, I sensed that our peak of potential was imminent. Inevitably, however, the test of battle must mean death and mutilation. Would that turn victory into revulsion?

It was the conviction that the Task Force was at last committed to war that brought on my solitary reflections. Eventually I stifled such doubts. We must accept the risks of the profession we had chosen, for the country paid and maintained us to do so. Firm and confident leadership was now essential. I could only hope that it need not prevent the sparing of casualties.

6

SAN CARLOS LANDINGS

In the remaining hours of D-day's eve I packed away the things I would not be needing – shirt-sleeve order, a lightweight suit, my swimming trunks. I paid the mess bill anonymously pushed under my door with the tactful heading 'Before disembarking from your cruise on *Canberra*'. Wrote those letters to loved ones that one reads about in other soldiers' memoirs.

A few nights earlier there had been a commanders' 'last supper', kindly arranged by Dennis Scott-Masson. As I had looked around the immaculate table at those familiar, pleasant faces – Uncle Tom, the Beagle, Malcolm Hunt, Hew Pike and 'H' Jones of 2 Para – it seemed impossible that, within a week, some of us might have been killed or maimed. I accepted this and worried about my family accordingly, although, egotistically, I believed such things would not happen to me. Instead, my fears were of some catastrophic personal misjudgement, of being left out of the battles, of causing unnecessary casualties, of failing to last the pace. The last reservation had a disconcerting relevance, because a youthful passion for racing horses over jumps had left my back with less than its original flexibility. Although I could still parachute, ski, run, swim, even dance after a fashion, a wrenching slip or a careless heave occasionally immobilized me for days. If prayers could be quantified, that fear probably rated the most piety as I fell into a fitful sleep in my king-size bed …

At about 0200 hours I had moved up onto the bridge to watch the unwieldy amphibious task group steal into Falkland Sound. Many RM officers have as little desire to serve at sea as sailors yearn to soldier in the field, but throughout my career the seamanship of the Royal Navy has invariably impressed and reassured me. That was so now, as calm, confident voices passed executive radio orders that were instantly implemented into simultaneous manoeuvres by thousands of units of inexorable horsepower. One miscalculation, misunderstanding, or hesitation could lead to a disastrous series of collisions. Instead, the mass of ships, 'painting' so closely together on our radar screen, slipped undetected between the black headlands, the whole operation flawlessly orchestrated from on board *Fearless* by Commodore Mike Clapp and his staff.

Almost at once, the calm of the night was shattered as a frigate began to bombard some target on Fanning Head, which loomed over the entrance to San Carlos Bay where the landing-craft must pass. In the distance we could also hear sounds of a more serious engagement, as a squadron of SAS put in a diversionary attack on the Goose Green garrison to the south. Despite these disturbances, however, the dark shoreline remained silent and inscrutable as the first laden landing-craft began to circle impatiently around the two assault ships and *Norland*. The offload was running late, and those now embarked were already pleading over the control net to be allowed to run into the beaches on their own. These requests were prudently – and firmly – turned down. Eventually, the complete flotillas formed into organized patterns and, as I watched, slowly dissolved away into the loom of the shoreline. By now there was complete silence again, except for the muffled throb of the escorts, prowling ceaselessly around us. Over the air I began to hear the clipped voice of Ewen Southby-Tailyour, passing cheerful sitreps back to a tense Brigade HQ as he conned the waves of landing-craft into their various beaches. This is one of the most dangerous moments in any amphibious operation, when a storm of fire from onshore can decimate troops packed tightly into vulnerable landing-craft, all surprise, momentum, numerical advantage being irretrievably lost. Despite the known presence of SBS patrols already in the vicinity, it was a huge relief to hear the codewords for successful landings being declared by the units as empty landing-craft hastened back for the second wave. Once these had taken on more men and headed inshore again, some of the amphibious ships and STUFT (ships taken up from trade) steered into San Carlos Water behind them, while RN frigates and destroyers took station around us in anticipation of what was to come. Dawn was already pinking the sky. We knew that air attacks must follow swiftly on the sunrise.

Nevertheless, *Canberra*'s routine continued regardless. There was a cooked breakfast provided for everyone, served as efficiently and cheerfully as if we had been octogenarians cruising in the Mediterranean. Afterwards I walked around to visit the companies which had been dispersed into the additional lounges once used by 40 Commando and 3 Para. No one was under any illusion that this was for their comfort, and I felt particularly unhappy that most men were completely shut off from the outside world, and would remain so until our disembarkation. The best we could do for them was to provide a running commentary over the ship's broadcast. Each man was kitted out to fight for forty-eight hours without replenishment, while our rucksacks were stacked and labelled on an upper deck, ready for immediate fly-off. Various problems worried me, one being that all our 'B' Echelon – follow-up stores and spares – was also in *Canberra*, and it would be difficult to get it ashore quickly. Another was that Ian McNeill was already having difficulty in contacting Brigade HQ through the voluble maze of radio nets – and the war hadn't really started yet. The marines themselves were tense, but as jokey as ever: 'Is it true there's a unit ski race this weekend, Sir?' 'You mean I'll miss the Farnborough Air Show AGAIN?' ... On my way back from visiting the companies, I stopped in to say goodbye to the girls, who seemed, sensibly, to have concentrated in Lauraine Mulberry's domain. They were cheerful, if a little apprehensive, and I was cheekily rebuked for not wearing my life-belt correctly. We had made so many friends in that ship. Now it almost seemed as if we were abandoning her.

I went up to the bridge, to find that day had dawned brilliant, cloudless, exhilarating. The sun sparkled across calm waters, and I could see soft moorland sloping gently down to the shoreline, while skeins of wildfowl flew tamely around the anchored ships. The STUFT ships now appeared very prominent in their mercantile livery; on one, the name *Elk* stood out in bold white letters against a russet background (I hoped that this one would not attract too much attention, since she carried enough high-explosive to blow us all out of the water with her!). *Norland* lay some distance away, also seeming to flaunt her presence, while the various other Ro-Ro ferries seemed poised for just another Channel crossing. *Canberra*, however, was infinitely more imposing than any of them, with her beguiling contrast of rust-streaked cream hull and prominent yellow funnels.

By now, the logistic landing ships (LSLs) were craning cargo onto their collapsible rafts, called Mexeflotes, which are slung over the ship's side on passage. Above the water, a miscellany of helicopters clattered about the anchorage. The scene was comfortingly familiar, like just another NATO exercise off Greece or Gibraltar, Denmark or Norway. Only Chris Burne seemed restive: wily, experienced 'salt-horse' that he was, he sensed only too well that this was no rehearsal. On the wings of *Canberra*'s huge bridge and around the upper decks, our GPMG teams fiddled nervously with the belted bullets as the ship's broadcast began to relay warnings from the carrier task group far out at sea. 'Air raid warning YELLOW. Bandits at fifteen miles. Turning away. Air raid warning ...'

When they came, I don't recall being alerted beforehand. Suddenly, around Fanning Head, appeared the distant, graceful silhouettes of swept-wing fighters. The aircraft looped leisurely over HMS *Plymouth* in Falkland Sound, before swooping malevolently down to cloud her in a haze of smoke, spray and orange flashes. As I watched, mesmerized, I became aware of Chris Burne shouting: 'Open fire! Open fire now! Take cover!' Approaching us at low level, from nowhere, as it seemed, was what I recognized as a Pucara. The aircraft was twisting and turning through a screen of explosions and tracer that rose up to meet it, with flashes of gunfire from its wing-tips and nose. I just had time to realize that our 'Great White Whale' was the target before the aircraft turned away towards the hills. By now I had become enraged at this marauder, but equally furious with the Blowpipe team on the deck below us, who appeared to be incompetent in the operation of their equipment. Rather as a horse reacts to uncertainty in its rider, so the missile seemed to reflect the team's confusion. The wretched device hiccupped half-heartedly upwards before fizzing pathetically back into the sea.

The next attack was altogether more serious. We had plenty of warning from the air defence radio net, but still the wave of howling, streaking shapes arrived like thunderbolts from the blue. The noise in those fleeting, fearful seconds was overwhelming. Explosions boomed around us, the air was filled with flashes and streaks of light, machine-guns crackled, lookouts shouted, the ship lurched and reverberated to detonations in the water. Just as suddenly as they had appeared, the enemy were gone, jinking and weaving over the crestline, so low that one hoped they would fail to clear it. For a breathless moment or two the spray around two LSLs across the bay seemed to hang as a cloud in the air. More reassuringly, an oily smudge in the sky beyond indicated that something had hit someone. Predictably, almost everyone claimed to have downed an aircraft, although this was transparently not the case. Indeed, our air defence seemed alarmingly ineffectual until one listened to reports of 'splashes' out at sea, as Harriers downed both incoming raiders and fugitives fleeing home. The Argentine pilots were evidently hampered in their attacks by the ring of hills, which masked them from the ships until they were over the bay, with only a few seconds in which to line up on a target. It appeared possible that flashes near aircraft might be causing the pilots to take evasive action against missiles. I passed the word to our GPMG teams that they should fire hand-held flares towards the incoming aircraft in addition to the tracer we were already using. Like me, however, they must have already concluded that our eventual destruction was merely a matter of time.

I remember, rather to my surprise, that while all this was happening I was pacing up and down the bridge wing alongside Chris Burne, who obviously considered such activity to be appropriately Nelsonian. From now on, he was to establish himself as the director of *Canberra*'s tactics throughout the war, but at this moment he expressed another concern: 'Nick, you have got to get your boys ashore where they can fight – while you still can.' I suspect that he already knew the ship would have to get away if she could, but he shared my unspoken conviction that absolute priority must be given to landing our vital component of the military force. I dashed away to the military operations room. There, however, it proved impossible to make radio contact with Brigade HQ. An exasperating hour or two later Ian sent me a message that Brigade had acknowledged our predicament, and had placed us on stand-by to move at short notice. We were more than ready when, around 1400 hours, – and several air attacks later – four landing-craft hove in our direction.

I returned to the bridge to say farewell to an ebullient Burne and a slightly less sanguine Captain Scott-Masson, whose beloved ship rested in such obvious danger. Then I went below to catch the last landing-craft. As Tac HQ passed along the passageways, many of the crew came forward to wish us luck, despite their own preoccupations. I recall particularly seeing Geoffrey, a gentle, middle-aged waiter from our bar, who had spent all his peaceful career on cruise liners where neither violence, nor the military, normally intrude. He was obviously, and understandably, nervous of the air raids. I shook his hand and assured him that he would see his beloved mother again, for he had once told me that she was his only relative. I was rewarded with a tight smile, and the promise that he would include me in his prayers.

When Tac HQ swung on board the packed LCU, I saw to my surprise that Tom Seccombe was standing imperiously on the stern above the well-deck. I clambered over to join him. As our craft throbbed urgently towards the shore, he related some hair-raising experiences during the landings, when several enemy aircraft had flashed over the flotilla. We were luckier, and reached land without mishap. I decided not to remonstrate about the recklessness of the Deputy Brigade Commander; in any event it was probably just as dangerous on *Canberra*. Lest 300 years of amphibious tradition should be compromised, the landing-craft put us ashore where it was too rocky to beach. So we began as we were to continue – with wet feet.

Behind us we left Main HQ, most of our stores, and everyone's rucksacks. No doubt some sage declared this to be an undesirable logistic situation when Ptolemy waged his campaigns, and I was certainly unhappy about it myself. But Lieutenant Frank Allen, the resourceful assistant to the Quartermaster, who was in charge of 'B' Echelon knew how rapidly we might need our packs and resupply from his stores. I was confident that he would get our material ashore at the first opportunity. Our misgivings persisted, however, as we heard the waves of attacking aircraft thunder in against the ships while we proceeded inshore. Frank himself wrote in his diary:

> 1455: Repeated air raids since lunch. I've lost count of the number of times I've lain in stairways and corridors whilst aircraft have attacked the shipping. So far *Canberra* has escaped damage although a bomb just missed us during the last raid before lunch.
>
> The warships in the Falkland Sound have drawn the fire of the attackers in almost every case. *Glasgow* has been holed, *Antrim* has an unexploded bomb aboard, *Ardent* has been badly damaged and looks as though she may sink.

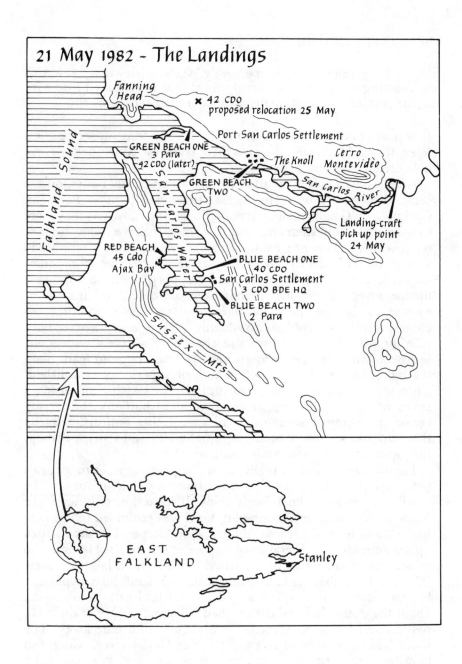

21 May 1982 - The Landings

Fanning Head

× 42 CDO
proposed relocation 25 May

Port San Carlos Settlement

GREEN BEACH ONE
3 Para
42 CDO (later)

The Knoll

Cerro
Montevideo

GREEN BEACH
TWO

San Carlos River

Falkland Sound

San Carlos Water

Landing-craft
pick up point
24 May

RED BEACH
45 Cdo
Ajax Bay

BLUE BEACH ONE
40 CDO
San Carlos Settlement
3 CDO BDE HQ

BLUE BEACH TWO
2 Para

Sussex Mts

EAST
FALKLAND

Stanley

I keep remembering the lovely peaceful dawn we saw this morning – the water was still, the clouds were tinged rose with the coming sun, and skeins of geese trailed across the sky ...

It was at about this time that Captain Scott-Masson sent back a telex to P&O Head Office, which stylishly concluded: 'Have delivered passengers as requested.'

After we had landed at Blue Beach, around 1600 hours, orders came through for us to move east beyond 3 Para at Port San Carlos. Two Gazelle helicopters had been shot down as they were moving into the settlement, and it seemed that we might be sent on to exact vengeance from a fleeing enemy. The Commando swung off confidently in a tactical advance, the companies leap-frogging forwards in mutual support, with the mortars manoeuvring in sections so that they could respond instantaneously to hostile fire. Corporal Adams reported that all communications were 'Go'. Suddenly I felt a huge sense of both relief and confidence. We were safely ashore, where we knew our business, with the finest troops anyone could hope to lead. Soon the landings would be complete and air superiority established. Then would follow a swift breakout from the beach-head, using a series of heliborne manoeuvres at night to outflank the largely conscript enemy. I seem to recall speculating optimistically on these lines as we moved along to John Shirley and Patrick Bishop, the journalists who had landed with us.

I was brought back to reality as we began to move into 3 Para's positions around the wooden farm buildings that made up the small settlement of Port San Carlos. It looked exactly as Ewen Tailyour had so often described it, but I was reminded that others had associations with these islands when Corporal Adams struck up an animated conversation with one of the locals. He had also served there; indeed he was married to a Falkland Islander. Hew Pike of 3 Para, looking brisk and warlike, was still busy deploying his men onto the crestline above us. He had little information about the enemy beyond the crashed helicopters. One of these lay twisted and burnt on a small slope about half a mile away. The other had sunk without trace in the San Carlos river, which ran parallel and to the right of our line of advance. We moved on purposefully, reluctantly declining the steaming cups of soup being offered by excited children from the settlement. I was struck by the 'Englishness' of it all, including the mud, and several hairy ponies which already seemed to accept the light helicopters flying low over their paddocks, and the distant clamour of air raids. As we advanced east across heather slopes that closely resembled Lowland pastures, a Gazelle landed alongside us. Brigadier Julian Thompson was on board. It was good to see him, and to hear his confirmation that the beach-head was established and his HQ safely ashore, but he was clearly concerned about delays in the logistic build-up caused by the air threat. He warned me that *Canberra*, with some other vulnerable shipping, must sail that night. I expressed alarm about our men and stores still on board, and he agreed that these must, if possible, be offloaded. My immediate orders, however, were for 'Four-Two' to follow the enemy along the river line, but to take up a defensive position before last light. The Brigadier exchanged some swift banter with my provost escorts, then the Gazelle lifted away in a swirl of dried grass. Peter Cameron, his pilot, also commanded the Air Squadron, and was obviously stunned at the loss of two aircraft so early on. We were old friends, and I could see that he was deeply affected by the casualties, one of whom was the youngest pilot in the 3 Commando Brigade Air Squadron.

We continued our advance until suddenly, long before I expected it, we were into a 'contact'. In a delayed and uninformative report, David Wheen told me that his right-hand troop was engaging some enemy on a knoll protruding into the inlet about a kilometre away. Sure enough, through my binoculars I could see his sections skirmishing forward, with covering fire being brought down on to what looked like a cave. But although this went on for some time, we could discern no fire being returned. Then, as abruptly as it had begun, the attack abruptly stopped. I had begun to suspect the truth, even before we received confirmation on the Gunners' net. It was all a false alarm: '... enemy section now identified as jumble of rocks. I say again, enemy ...'

I was furious. An hour earlier we had been radiating purposefulness and professionalism. Now we were shooting at boulders. Wasn't this exactly the sort of impetuous, trigger-happy behaviour that company commanders had been warned against? Why hadn't the troop subaltern personally gone forward to confirm a positive sighting? Surely no one had seriously expected isolated Argentine soldiers to commit suicide by holding a position with their backs to the water? David Wheen tactfully agreed with all of this, but sensibly pointed out that the troops were excited, as well as angered by the sight of the helicopter wreckage. Several officers and SNCOs had observed the target, which really did look like a machine-gun team in cover, and the point section commander had decided to shoot first, even though he knew he might be wrong ... as we moved off again I realized that it wasn't only individuals at the 'sharp end' who were in a state of tension. I must curb my impulses more than anyone, or confidence in the leadership could suffer. When I explained to Brigade HQ that the incident had been a false alarm, I was even more mortified by their understanding attitude.

By now it was late afternoon, high time that we began to decide our dispositions for the night. Ian McNeill had already tactfully mentioned this a couple of times, but I still smarted from the incident, stubbornly determined that we were going to catch up with the fleeing enemy. At last it became obvious that they had eluded us, by which time we were all tired from forcing the pace over demanding terrain. The options now open to us lay between climbing several hundred feet to the crest of Cerro Montevideo – where there would be shelter and cover amongst the crags – or descending to the rough ground below. The Brigadier had indicated that he would like us on the heights if possible. Unrealistically, I now attempted to achieve that. Darkness caught us halfway up a bare, exposed slope, and vulnerable from all directions. The ground underfoot was boggy and there were precious few landmarks for reference, or depressions to give cover. I had made a poor tactical decision, about which I agonized for the whole night. Although an aggressive move from the Argentines seemed unlikely, I was convinced that it would be extremely dangerous to allow movement outside our ill defined perimeter.

Several times before on operations I had observed how tactical carelessness or misunderstanding can lead to self-inflicted casualties. 'Own goals' is how we derisively refer to them when the opposition is involved, 'Blue on Blue' is the cosmetic evasion for declaring that comrade has fallen victim to comrade. Usually it is at night. Most often it occurs amongst inexperienced infantry. All the ingredients for such an occurrence were ominously with us. Already that afternoon we had listened to messages about a similar incident in 3 Para. If it could happen to them in daylight, the probability of a similar clash in the darkness of this unknown terrain was desperately high. I was determined that it should not occur. The tragic futility of such casualties at the outset of operations would be deeply demoralizing. The suspicion that they might have arisen because we were unprepared would make matters worse. All movement outside the perimeter was strictly forbidden, except for one fighting patrol. This was sent several miles up river to check on some buildings where the fleeing enemy could be sheltering. They were told not to return until after first light. At least we would know that any movement around us was not 'Four-Two'.

As dawn broke the next morning, we ascended swiftly to the crestline, acutely conscious of our vulnerability to air attack. There I set out what is called a 'linear defence', which is adopted when there is no real alternative to a straight line! From the top, we enjoyed a bird's-eye view for miles to the north and east, with the San Carlos river looping below and behind us. About a kilometre down the ridge was one of 3 Para's companies, so that together we formed a strong perimeter around the north-eastern segment of the beach-head. At least we now had an invaluable chance to settle down to field routine and tactical awareness, since there were no known enemy concentrations anywhere in the vicinity. That evening, the large packs were flown out from *Canberra* to everyone except the CO. 'Sunray's'* rucksack, said a plaintive message from Frank somewhere over the horizon, had been left on the ship. It would be sent on at the first opportunity. I was given a spare rucksack belonging to an NCO who had been injured in the landings. For the moment its contents sufficed, although the socks didn't fit and I missed my own sleeping-bag. My war didn't seem to be starting too well.

At this time I was taking a special interest in 'J' Company, because they were still such an unknown quantity. Mike Norman was obviously a hard and experienced campaigner, and I became increasingly reassured by the capability and confidence of the junior leadership. One of the troop officers had been 2/IC of the Falklands garrison under Norman. It was useful to have so much local knowledge within the unit, although by no means all of this new company had been imported from outside 'Four-Two'. Both the Chief Clerk's young brother, Marine Malcolm Cook, and the Orderly Room Clerk, Marine David Devenny, had swopped type-writers for 7.62 SLRs and a place in a rifle section. The

---

* Sunray – radio codeword for a commanding officer.

Commando was also augmented now with a Blowpipe section from the Brigade Air Defence Troop, which flew up to join us so that it could fire at passing raiders fleeing home down the valley below our positions. My doubts about this cumbersome weapon were not diminished after several misses, which we considered could only bring down undesirable fighter ground-attacks upon us. We did, however, enjoy a more reassuring sight one morning, while the Brigadier was visiting us, when Rapier missiles scored a lurid 'left and right' on two Argentine aircraft. The cheer that echoed round the hills would have done credit to any First Division match.

We stayed on our high ridge for two days, almost the most comfortable of the war despite the wind and rain which predominated, just as everyone had said they would. It had become clear by now that helicopters were at a premium, and we began to worry how we should get off this feature, carrying our large packs and all the extra equipment. I judged that we might get down into the valley overnight, but on foot we could never reach the air defences around Port San Carlos before dawn. The thought of 400 or so heavily laden troops moving across exposed ground in daylight nagged at me continually. On 23 May, we received orders to move back to an area between Port San Carlos and Fanning Head. There we were to establish a position to block any enemy thrust behind 3 Para. I was, however, as dubious about the selected terrain as the validity of the threat. McNeill, Wilson and I flew forward to reconnoitre the ground, which proved to be a featureless, boggy, windswept slope that ran down to rocky beaches inaccessible to landing-craft. It was absolutely unsuitable in every respect, and guaranteed to erode the Commando's morale and survivability – the classic example, it seemed, of a superficial map appreciation by hard-pressed staff. We flew over to Hew Pike's HQ and I explained my dilemma. I realized that we would have to put forward an alternative location to get out of the one selected for us, but we would need his help to do so. Our proposal was that 3 Para should 'move up in the bed' and let us take over the eastern end of San Carlos settlement, with 42 Commando rifle companies digging into the re-entrants beyond. Not only could we then contract the perimeter, but we could also concentrate all the logistics and administration for two units into one area. Hew, with characteristic consideration and flexibility, agreed to adjust his positions, although that would involve obvious inconvenience for his battalion.

Our next move was to proposition Brigade HQ, something to be undertaken with diffidence, since it was clear that they were under enormous pressure. Air raids had seriously disrupted the offload, and naval losses were becoming increasingly alarming. The logistic plan had had to be fundamentally revised, from resupply directly off the ships to stockpiling thirty days' worth of war stores ashore. With limited movement resources and an uncertain programme of ship movement into San Carlos each night, this was a logistician's nightmare. And, at the same time, we had heard rumours that the Brigade Commander was being pressed from the UK to close with the enemy even though he advised that this was premature. As tactfully as possible, I spoke to John Chester, the Brigade Major. He was clearly not pleased that plans should be changed simply because 42 Commando wished to go somewhere else, but he was attracted to the advantages of co-location. 3 Para's willingness to co-operate clinched the matter, although John confirmed that we would have to make the move under our own steam.

Having achieved my purpose, I made a quick recce of the settlement, and bumped into Ewen Tailyour down at the jetty, where much of the ship-to-shore resupply was taking place. As we enjoyed a swift update on our experiences, he suddenly suggested that 'Four-Two' should be recovered by landing-craft. The San Carlos river ran directly below Cerro Montevideo, so instead of making that hazardous trek back we could be ferried under cover of darkness. It was a brilliant suggestion, and one that only Ewen, with his great local knowledge and experience, could have conceived. As it was, when he turned to one of the locals for confirmation that there was sufficient depth of water for the landing-craft, the islander emphasized that it would be marginal. This was good enough for both of us, and I radioed orders ahead to the unit; by the time we flew back to the position preparations to move were well under way.

Ewen only had two of the larger landing-craft available, but we calculated that with some crowding the whole Commando could be extracted in two lifts. The time-scale for the move, from embarkation after dark to completing both sorties up and down several kilometres of winding river, was just about right. We did not anticipate any enemy interference en route, but it took little imagination to visualize what the carnage might be on a crowded landing-craft aground in daylight and at the mercy of hostile aircraft. I was also concerned about stragglers getting lost in the dark as groups of laden men stumbled down long, rough slopes to the rendezvous. This was on a tiny inlet along a meandering river, which had to be reached at a precise time. The danger of stragglers was emphasized at a hasty 'O' group, with detailed instructions for careful and regular checks by all junior leaders. In the circumstances it seemed only fair to provide Ewen with moral support, so I decided to sail with him on both sorties.

We set off after last light on a dark but reasonably fine night. From the enclosed bridge at the LCU's stern visibility was very restricted, because of the huge bow ramp. Below the raised platform on which the coxswain stood there was a cubby-hole housing the simple radar, while behind us throbbed the twin engines. Surprisingly for such a large craft – capable of carrying a complete company or two main battle tanks – the crew consisted only of a colour sergeant, four RM crewmen and a Navy artificer. Such teams operate together over long periods, either based in assault ships or as part of independent landing-craft squadrons. This group had by now been working intensively in great danger for several days, although there was no hint of that as everyone laughed and joked, passing around delicious cups of strong cocoa. Ewen darted about like quicksilver, constantly taking sights, consulting the charts, checking the radar. At the same time he regaled me with an effortless stream of anecdotes, teased Colour-Sergeant Johnston at the helm, smoked cigars and poured us strong drink from a flask. He was truly in his element, and I felt confident that we were in the best of hands.

As the river banks closed in, I could see that the channel became very narrow in places, where the dark water swirled and foamed around hidden rocks. When the river widened there were obviously shoals, and on two nerve-racking occasions we ran aground, despite having instantly gone astern at the first hint of trouble. The second LCU pulled us off, however, and all these hazards were meticulously marked on a chart to prevent the same thing happening to heavily laden craft on the way back. Ewen guessed that ours were the largest boats ever to have navigated this far up river, which made our silent passage up the lonely, glimmering waterway even more memorable and exciting. Rounding a tight left-hand bend, we found ourselves running towards a pale strand of gravel. Beyond it there winked a red pinpoint of light to indicate the Commando's rendezvous.

The companies streamed silently aboard, except for muttered acknowledgements as the JNCOs whispered those timeless nicknames British troops have always adopted amongst themselves: 'Smudge ... Taff ... Chalky ... Sticks ...' As we hauled back into the stream on our kedge anchors, I walked down one of the catwalks to explain briefly what was happening, ending with the ever-popular permission to smoke under cover of the well-deck. The return passage turned out to be pleasant and restful for everyone in both lifts, although embarking and disembarking had meant wet feet. I was particularly pleased by the quiet efficiency with which the move was achieved, and by the favourable comments from Ewen and his crews. Tragically, we were never again to see Colour-Sergeant Johnston and LCU Foxtrot 4. She was lost with all hands in an air attack a few days later, while providing similar dedicated support to another element of the landing force.

Early the next morning, the RSM came to find me. I was forcing down one of Marine Green's tepid concoctions at the time, and reflecting smugly on the night's move and our new and favourable situation. From his expression I could tell that the news was not good. A marine from 'K' Company was missing, presumed left behind on the beach. I was outraged. Already we were into the air-raid time-scale, so any attempt to reach him overland or by river would be very dangerous. In any event, there was no knowing what he would be doing, or where he might be. A helicopter was the obvious solution, but I refused even to ask for one, in the circumstances. All concerned were roundly castigated that the checking process had so miserably failed, especially the Troop Officer. Just as total gloom had descended, and while Corporal Adams was attempting to get through to Brigade HQ with the news, Mr Chisnall informed me that one of the raiding craft cox'ns had, bravely but recklessly, set off up river with the Troop Officer and Sergeant. These boats are highly manouevrable and extremely fast, but they are still vulnerable to ambush or air attack. Within an hour, however, the rigid raider was back bearing a sheepish truant, who had been found still asleep beside the beach. It was not his day. A few hours later he was wounded during an air attack and swiftly evacuated to a hospital ship. Before the end of the month he was being visited in a Plymouth hospital by my wife.

On 25 May a helicopter fetched me for a Brigade 'O' Group in the HQ overlooking San Carlos Water. It was a clear, sparkling morning, although it was difficult to appreciate the scenery as we skimmed the contours. Everyone on board was too preoccupied with looking out for enemy aircraft. There had been two raids already that morning, in which one of the logistic ships had taken yet another unexploded bomb. I was particularly horrified by the sight of the smoking hulk of HMS *Antelope*, lying broken in the bay. She had escorted *Canberra* most of the way south, and her sinuous power and rakish lines had epitomized all that is both graceful and awesome about a warship at sea. Now only the bows and stern protruded above her final resting place – one of all too many RN ships that had paid the price for getting us ashore.

The Brigadier and his staff were in sombre mood. The problem of unloading stores was about as difficult as it could be. Modern merchant ships are designed to discharge containerized cargo in port, using cranes or brows. In San Carlos Water, however, their varied loads had to be adapted to load into landing-craft, or be winched off by helicopter. In many cases the respective heights of ships and landing-craft were incompatible for direct transfer of stores and the bulk-ferrying Mexeflote rafts, in particular, could not co-ordinate with the bow or stern ramps of some Ro-Ro vessels. Most ships had only one landing platform, to which all helicopter cargo had to be shifted prior to offloading. A severe limitation, as well as a significant comparison, was that purpose-built naval ships achieved an offload rate of 90 tons per load, while most merchantmen could barely manage 20 tons. Short-term cuts to amphibious capability in the past were now having long-term consequences.

The air movement assets available were not much better. Altogether there were eleven Sea King helicopters available for logistic movement, augmented by five smaller Wessex. But just to lift the initial gun battery ashore with adequate ammunition required eighty-five sorties, which meant that eight Wessex helicopters would each have to fly more than ten sorties of around fifteen minutes. The original plan had included a reinforcement of twelve more Wessex, as well as four giant Chinook helicopters, for the breakout, but these had been embarked in the ill-fated *Atlantic Conveyor*, which was to be sunk by Exocet before she could reach San Carlos. Luckily one Chinook was airborne at the time, and so survived to give invaluable support in later operations.

Because of these immense logistic and movement problems, the brilliantly successful landings were followed by frustrating delays. Air parity, let alone superiority, was not achieved for several days. During that hazardous period Argentine aircraft took an increasing toll of vulnerable shipping and forced a dramatic reappraisal of the logistic plan. As a result, it was decided to attempt to land as many stocks as possible, before the logistic ships had to be withdrawn from their hazardous anchorage. As these stores were landed – although not all the essential ones could be offloaded in time – they were hastily stockpiled in the only suitable area at Ajax Bay. From there, they still had to be moved forward to units, with the result that there were insufficient helicopters for tactical as well as this logistic movement. Like so many commanders before him, Julian Thompson's concept of operations was compromised by unforeseen obstacles which seriously hampered the deployment of his force. In the traditions of British military history, his problems were also less than fully appreciated at home, for initial success had understandably increased the pressure for a swift conclusion to the campaign.

None of the unit COs at the 'O' Group had much to contribute other than our futile pleas for missing stores, or vain speculation as to when we could move on. All of us acknowledged the impossibility of a breakout before we could sustain ourselves, but at the same time we feared stagnation, within the beach-head. No one doubted the troops' endurance or resolve, but they also required urgent purpose, and that was becoming hard to put over. 'H' Jones was especially frustrated, because a projected raid by 2 Para on Goose Green had been cancelled the night before through lack of helicopter support.

After the 'O' Group had ended, Mike Rose drew me aside and invited me up to his SAS command post. This proved to be a brigand's cave of specialist weapons and technological devices, where menacing individuals muttered quietly into unfamiliar radio sets, or pored over strange maps and diagrams. With devastating candour, he informed me that his patrols believed Mount Kent to be only lightly held, and thus vulnerable to a *coup de main* operation by helicopter. Would I like 42 Commando to take on the task? We gazed silently at the map together for a moment or two. There seemed little point in remarking that Mount Kent was more than 50 kilometres into enemy territory, nor did the significance of the proposal being put privately escape me either. I knew that Mike Rose held a more aggressive view than some of the

Brigade staff, which was entirely in keeping with his particular background. No action would be taken until the Brigadier was ready, but Rose could probably press his case more strongly with a Commando CO in support. The selection of which unit might eventually go could depend upon something as intangible as that. I took a deep breath, and said yes. 'Tremendous,' he said, with an enigmatic smile, 'I shall fly in with you when you go.'

I told the 'team' of our possible destiny that evening, in our new and very comfortable HQ in two crofters' huts at Port San Carlos. I now had a room to myself, although my conscience revolted against the double bed, which stood forlornly empty. Instead I slept on the ground like everyone else; albeit in the dry. Many others had to remain out in the open, but my floor at least provided a firm base for my suspect back, which had already begun to stiffen up.

Our first thoughts about an operation against Mount Kent concerned the tactics we could adopt within the available helicopter lift. It was obvious that the fly-in could only take place in darkness, and we assumed that a battery of guns with ammunition would also have to accompany us. While Phil and Ian were debating how many Chinooks were aboard *Atlantic Conveyor* and discussing the helicopters' payload, the duty officer appeared with the desperate news that the ship had just been sunk. Apart from the obviously appalling consequences of this for the Brigade's logistics, I couldn't stifle my own selfish disappointment at the realization that 42 Commando might now have lost a great opportunity. The helicopters on *Atlantic Conveyor* were to have provided troop lift, while those ashore were earmarked for logistic movement.

The next few days brought drama, tragedy and triumph. On the morning of 26 May, Northwood ordered Julian Thompson by SATCOM to start moving 3 Commando Brigade out of the beach-head forthwith. 2 Para was now retasked to raid Goose Green the following night, with 'L' Company to relieve them on Sussex Mountain, and the rest of 'Four-Two' as the stand-by reinforcement. 3 Para and 45 Commando were to march over 30 kilometres to Douglas Settlement and Teal Inlet, carrying all their equipment. 40 Commando was to assume responsibility for defending the perimeter of the beach-head. Brigadier Thompson's book *No Picnic* reflects the staff reaction at the time: 'It had become quite clear to 3 Commando Brigade that, apart from the whole-hearted support from the Royal Navy, the Brigade was on its own.'

The following morning we watched, almost numbly, as so many close friends in 'Four-Five' marched stoically up from the jetty, humping their enormous burdens. Everything, including support weapons, was being manpacked. Together with essential ammunition every load weighed at least 100 pounds, or in many cases, much more. Even the stalwart Andrew Whitehead seemed dwarfed by his rucksack, although if he anticipated hard times ahead, he showed no sign of it. His RSM, Pat Chapman, had served with me often in Norway, where he would swoop like a bird down the slopes regardless of weapons or equipment. Here, without skis, his wings were also clipped by weight and mud, but not his sardonic wit; 'Good morning, Colonel. Sorry to see 42 Commando has to be left behind again ...'

I felt truly fearful for them as they plodded away up the side of Cerro Montevideo, ponderous and exposed, and soon beyond the range of artillery support. They seemed so desperately vulnerable. Shortly afterwards, we were saying similar farewells to 3 Para as Hew Pike led them away briskly along the San Carlos valley. This was the start of the great 'Yomp', so much publicized in the press, which was to confound our adversaries because they could not comprehend such fitness or endurance.

That evening, there was an air raid on the Brigade maintenance area and makeshift hospital at Ajax Bay. Half a dozen men were killed, and nearly thirty were wounded. Surgeon-Commander Rick Jolly, RN and the Field Dressing Station had hoped to operate from *Canberra*, where surgery could have been conducted in so much better conditions. Now their difficulties were even greater, as they worked on alongside several unexploded bombs.

On the next day, 28 May, the unit stood to from first light at 30 minutes' notice to be flown forward to Goose Green. Over our Brigade radio links we could monitor snatches of that increasingly desperate battle; I was not surprised, therefore, to be summoned forward to Brigade HQ early in the afternoon. There I was told that 'H' Jones had been killed, and that 42 Commando would almost certainly be committed as soon as the situation became clearer. In the event, 2 Para took their formidable objectives unassisted, but our own 'J' Company was flown down at last light to support operations the next morning. By then, the will of the defenders to fight any longer had been broken.

Later the same day, 'L' Company on Sussex Mountain was relieved by 40 Commando. Then we heard that 45 Commando and 3 Para had already completed the first leg of their trek across the wilderness of rock and heather. As soon as they had been resupplied, helicopters would become available for troop lift. The Mount Kent operation was now 'on' again – and ''Four-Two' was still tasked to do it!

7

CHILL WINDS ON MOUNT KENT

On the evening of 28 May, we were formally tasked by signal to seize Mount Kent on the following night. Anticipated enemy strength was no more than a platoon of around thirty men who had been left to hold the feature. An SAS team in the area would secure a landing-site for us. The available airlift consisted of four Sea King helicopters with the surviving Chinook, and these would be on hand for limited sorties over several nights. A section of light guns with designated ammunition must be included in the lift forward, as well as some SAS reinforcement. Given this information, we could now calculate the size and shape of force needed for the mission and prepare orders accordingly.

It was obvious that this reduced airlift would preclude the use of more than one company group for the initial seizure of the position. But the hours of darkness should allow a second company lift before dawn. 'K' and 'L' Companies were immediately warned, so that preparations could start as early as possible. A detailed 'O' Group was set for the following morning, followed by rehearsals and co-ordination of helicopter arrangements in the afternoon. Commando HQ then set about the detailed planning of tactics, organization, co-ordination and logistics, which lasted through most of the night.

I was absolutely clear that Tac HQ must accompany the force. This was an unpredictable operation, in which plans might have to be changed decisively at an early stage. Direct communication between San Carlos and Mount Kent could not be guaranteed, either during the assault, or throughout the crucial following day prior to reinforcement the next night. We concluded that air defence was also essential, and so a Blowpipe section must be fitted in. Finally, we decided that a section of our own 81-mm mortars should complement the guns. Their trajectory and rate of fire would increase our ability to break up the enemy counter-attacks that seemed inevitable. Once this force had been broken down to fit into the available helicopter sorties, 'K' Company had to reduce by around thirty ranks. The BC, David Brown, also advised me that it would be best to fly in his guns and ammunition as close together as possible, so we allocated most of the initial Chinook lift to our artillery support. Because it took so long to load and secure the guns, however, this meant that the huge aircraft could not be available for the first troop wave. These capers are never easy ...

Next morning, the place hummed with activity and the sound of eager voices. Today's young serviceman is both astute and interested in what goes on within his sphere of activity. The unit had deduced already that either 42 or 40 Commando would have to be left behind to protect the beach-head. There was no doubt of the marines' positive reaction to the outcome, as the RSM and I wandered about the positions. On the landing-site I stopped to chat with Wilson, my driver, normally one of the CO's most constant companions. In his case he not only drove me thousands of miles in a staff car each year, but we had just spent days and nights together in the mountains of Norway, where his skill in manoeuvring the tracked, articulated Volvo 'Bandwagon' over treacherous terrain was second to none. Now he waited anxiously for our invaluable mobile command post to be offloaded from a logistic ship. Meanwhile he and his fellow drivers provided control and handling parties for the helicopters. I asked him if he would like to fly forward that night. He grinned in response, to declare with 'old soldier's' wisdom that he never volunteered for anything now. In any case, we both knew that his experience would be put to better use there at the stores landing-site in Port San Carlos.

I invited our 'hacks' to the Mount Kent 'O' Group later that morning, although space prevented their inclusion in the operation for the moment. By now we regarded them with confidence, as well as affection, and their comprehension of military tactics or logistic restrictions was almost instinctive. I felt that their despatches would be all the better for having shared in the planning of the operation, and trusted them not to release information prematurely. That day they were particularly upset

about the irresponsible BBC revelation of the attack on Goose
Green, although it was well known that this indiscretion had
originated in UK. David Wheen had told us of his consternation
when, shortly after relieving 2 Para on Sussex Mountain, he had
heard Goose Green declared as the British objective on the World
Service. Everyone liked and trusted the BBC field force reporter,
Robert Fox, who had had nothing to do with this appalling
indiscretion. Indeed, he was personally put at risk, since he
accompanied 2 Para throughout the battle.

The orders confirmed that 'K' Company would move straight
off for the top of Mount Kent once they were complete on the
landing-zone, several hundred feet below the summit. By then the
guns and mortars, with their ammunition, should be in place,
although Commando HQ and Blowpipe would still be flying in.
We should, however, be on the ground long before Babbington's
marines came into contact with the enemy. In any case, that was
Peter's show, not mine. He would have his own Forward
Observations Officer, Captain Chris Romberg, RA, directing the
guns, with a Mortar Fire Controller. As it happened he was an
experienced fire support specialist himself. At first light the next
morning we would attempt to get Blowpipe missiles up to him,
since it was clear from the map that the men carrying them would
never make it with those loads in the dark. The SAS already in
place on Mount Kent would provide guides as far as the summit.

Towards the end of the morning I began to fret that we had
received no word of any helicopter presence for the afternoon. An
operation of this complexity simply cannot be mounted without
detailed preliminary co-ordination, though we could probably
have dispensed with rehearsals. Even now, control of helicopters
was still retained by the Commodore on board *Fearless*, so the
hard-pressed Brigade Staff could provide only partial reassurance
to our anxious enquiries. A further distraction was that we had
remained at one hour's notice to move since first light, in case
surrender negotiations at Goose Green went wrong. Eventually
Matt Sturman managed to talk a passing Wessex down, and we
lobbied the pilot to impress on his own HQ that time was running
out. It was especially disconcerting to find that the Wessex pilot
seemed to have heard nothing about the operation, although he
could not have taken part, as he was not trained to fly with Passive
Night Goggles himself. Our anxiety over the airlift deepened as 'K'
Company started to assemble their stores on the landing-site. At

last, to our relief, we received an 'inbound' consisting not only of a
Sea King, but also the vital Chinook. As they settled amidst
clouds of debris, it seemed that our plans might prevail after all.

The Navy pilot of the Sea King, however, immediately
confirmed my worst fears. He declared that he and his crews had
only been tasked for the operation that morning, and so could
provide just two sorties that night, instead of the three we needed.
Worse was to come, however, from the RAF squadron leader with
the Chinook. He and his crew had been operating non-stop for
nearly forty-eight hours; it was essential that they should now
rest. One glance at his haggard, unshaven face and red-rimmed
eyes was enough to confirm his total exhaustion. He did offer,
with gallant self-sacrifice, to lift in the guns if the Navy could take
the rest of us. But the Sea Kings were committed elsewhere – to
reschedule them needed more time than we had left. The
infuriating, inescapable fact was that we were only going to get to
Mount Kent that night if the plan was drastically modified. It was
the bitterest moment of the war thus far.

There followed an arid and acrimonious conversation between
John Chester, the Brigade Major, and myself. I was furious that
we appeared to have been let down by the Staff, he was adamant
that they had done all they could. Both of us knew only too well
that circumstances might change at any moment, perhaps
irrevocably diverting resources elsewhere. Selfishly, I was more
concerned with getting my unit into battle than with recognizing
the pressures and strains prevailing in that HQ over the past few
days. While, as Brigade Major, John Chester might have been too
preoccupied with his own problems to realize that I might have to
tell 'Four-Two', for the second time, that they were not going to
fight after all. Eventually we reached an uneasy compromise; 'K'
Company, Tac HQ and the four 81-mm mortars would fly in that
night. The remainder would have to wait until the following
evening. Both of us knew that reinforcements would by then be
crucial. The risks had now intensified.

After a confirmatory 'O' Group, with most of us 'blacked-out'
and rigged for action, the laden files of the first wave began to
assemble in the twilight. I had a few quiet words with Peter,
before watching the Sea Kings grumble raucously off into an
ominous sky of scurrying black clouds. There would still be time
to return to the Command Post to monitor progress, before our
lift. My own 'stick', consisting of the RSM, MOA, radio operators

and Provost protection, was already assembling our associated load of equipment.

But we were to be thwarted once again. Halfway through the mountains, the four Sea Kings were enveloped in 'white-out'. This is an exceptionally dangerous condition, in which a swirling blanket of snow blots out all the pilot's reference points. Only an instant landing on instruments can prevent disaster. The helicopters were compelled to do so again and again before they could extricate themselves and return to base. Listening to the terse, fraught exchanges between pilots and their control provided tension enough. But when, on their return, I saw the drawn, silent faces of invariably cheerful 'K' Company marines, the extent of their ordeal was underlined. Strapped claustrophobically together in the dark, unable to hear one another properly, confused and anxious, they were confined apprehensively for nearly two hours. Spasmodically the engines bellowed and shuddered as the helicopters had lurched sickeningly while the pilots fought against the blizzard.

Dennis Sparks issued the lads with some rum which he had hoarded from somewhere, and I broached the first of my medicinal reserves from the CO's box for a tight-lipped Peter Babbington. Peter was normally so imperturbable that it was all too clear what he and his men had endured.

Uncertainty and tension persisted on the following morning. Reassuringly, early in the afternoon an RN movement control team at last appeared. Their expertise and special communications facilities, linked into Commando HQ, would infinitely improve control and flexibility once this complex move had commenced. The planning payload, determined by factors such as radius of action and flying conditions, had to be transformed into lists of men or equipment, and these in turn were governed by tactical considerations at the other end. There was no point in landing in tactical order, but without the right communications or ammunition, for instance. The Operations Officer, Ian McNeill, would be coming with me, which left Matt Sturman with responsibility for co-ordinating support for the operation from Commando HQ, and the logistic build-up in the days to come. I was reminded again of how fortunate we were to have acquired an additional officer of his capability and experience. Even so, this was one of those occasions when we desperately needed a second-in-command.

'This time lucky, sir!' said Mr Chisnall that evening, with the impassive conviction which RSMs seem to acquire. I sincerely hoped he was right. A swift trip to Brigade HQ and a sympathetic chat with John Chester, had revealed that too many other commitments were building up for the Mount Kent project to be kept alive much longer. But at least we now had the huge Chinook back, so that the guns and ammunition could fly in with us.

Mercifully, I had no idea then that the operation was almost cancelled yet again. A message was received at Brigade HQ which stated that the RN helicopter squadron could undertake no further flying for the moment because of over-commitment. In the end, only John Chester's vigorous personal intervention ensured that we would get a second attempt. So, as it turned out, previous misgivings about the Staff commitment to this operation proved to be premature and unjustified.

While I was at Brigade I bumped into Paul Stevenson. He had just landed with General Jeremy Moore's Divisional HQ in advance of 5 Infantry Brigade, after both had transferred from *QE2* to *Canberra*. Suddenly the mood of frustration and worry seemed to be lifting. Goose Green had been a fine victory. Two units – 'Four-Five' and 3 Para – were by now well forward towards the enemy. The air attacks were appreciably diminishing. Now we were to be reinforced. To cap it all, I got back to find that there was mail, bringing news of loved ones far removed from the discomfort and tension of present circumstance. Morale shot up accordingly. By the evening meal, which was being centrally prepared in a shearing shed, the conviction that we would get to Mount Kent this time seemed unanimous.

I chatted to several of 'K' Company's veterans of the previous night, to get a feel for their attitude towards a second attempt. No one was much looking forward to the flying, which seemed to have taken their minds off what might happen at the other end. Everyone knew that the next twenty-four hours would be the most dangerous, but the majority believed that once Mount Kent had been seized, we could hold it until reinforcement. It was quite clear that they were absolutely determined to get there. I had no doubts that they would succeed, once given the chance.

I realized that this might be the last time more than one company of 'Four-Two' would be together for the foreseeable future. Privately I memorized the young, keen faces in the lantern light. Already, so many of them had developed a maturity and hardness not apparent before. Their self-confidence was infectious.

Not everyone shared this euphoria, however, and some were to reveal subsequently their grave misgivings about the outcome. Frank Allen wrote in his diary:

'K' Company and Tac HQ are flying out at this moment to attack a position on Mount Kent tonight. They will be many miles inside enemy territory, isolated from help of any kind and against what is thought to be a platoon in defence. If they succeed – and their chances cannot be rated highly if the defensive positions are good – they face a day of hardship tomorrow. The Argentines will bring down fighters and heavy artillery on them once they realize their position has been overrun. I feel very strongly that this move is ill-conceived and unless the enemy have moved away we could lose many men. I'm thinking particularly of Kay Babbington, Robyn Whiteley and everyone at the Leys* now ...

On this occasion, weather problems had not been predicted, although it seemed unusually dark as the embarkation into the helicopters got under way. In certain sports, there comes a climax which fuses individual preparation with collective effort, heightening the senses and focusing concentration. For some, it may be the parade in the paddock before a race; for others, perhaps, the final brief in the dressing-room. For a journalist I suppose it is the rumble of the presses, for a newscaster the count-down to broadcast. For me, after so many commando heliborne operations or exercises, it is always the roar of the engines coughing out the hot, acrid fumes of burnt Avcat, the shimmering vibration of rotor blades thrashing at the air. Muffled shouts, raised thumbs, running figures heaving packs up to anonymous hands, before they disappear into the helicopter's black maw. Ever since Suez in 1956, this has always seemed a marvellously exhilarating entry into battle. I felt that excitement stirring in me now as 'K' Company lifted off towards the hills once more, and we settled down to monitor their progress for the thirty-minute flight.

This time, the problem seemed to be communications. We kept losing contact as the helicopters flew on towards the objective, although our SAS liaison could still talk to their own patrols. Soon after the time planned for touch-down, however, I got the good

* My home in Devon.

news that 'K' Company was safely on the ground. Now the Chinook would be starting its fly-in with the guns. That doughty RAF pilot would have personally supervised the loading and lashing down of the guns with their pallets of HE ammunition. Their mass and weight would have to be safely unloaded at maximum speed on arrival at the objective. We moved back out to the landing-site to meet the returning wave of Sea Kings. After the previous 'rehearsal', Matt Sturman had attached an additional radio operator with Tac HQ, so that I could remain in touch with the main Commando HQ until the very last minute. They in turn could speak to the helicopters.

On the LS, activity was building up to a crescendo as sticks assembled, loads were netted, guides appointed. The marshallers with their luminous batons took post. In the distance behind us we could hear the approaching roar of the returning aircraft. Then Matt came urgently on the air with the news that the flight leader was not prepared to go back again. Apparently, 'K' Company's landing-site had come under attack during disembarkation. The reports were confused about how serious this had been but, ominously, the SAS now lost communications as well. I still had no means of talking to the pilots until they had landed. The dilemma was excruciating, because Peter could certainly not attack without the next wave. But this was the time to cut our losses if we were ever going to do so.

The black silhouettes lumbered out of the sky and lurched to a cumbersome halt. As the rotors disengaged, I doubled forward to the lead aircraft and jumped into the back, where a helmeted crewman thrust me a headset. The flight leader sounded ominously grim. Shortly after touchdown, small-arms fire had broken out on the Mount Kent side of the landing-site. By the time the aircraft were unloaded, the action had been augmented by illuminants and mortar fire. This engagement now threatened the approach route, for unless the SAS reported a more favourable situation, further flying would have to be cancelled. Both the flight leader and I appreciated the premium on helicopters only too well, especially since these four Sea Kings were the only ones with crews trained in night-vision techniques. Any further hazardous night operations, and the constant insertion and extraction of special forces, also depended upon their survival.

Just a few weeks (or was it centuries?) ago, I had taken part in a very similar dialogue. At the time we had been deep among the snow-covered mountains above Bardufoss in North Norway, with the weather closing in as we should have flown forward for the moonlight interception of a ski-borne Norwegian battalion. Safety had predominated then, as it seemed that expediency must now. But at least I knew that these pilots would still get us in if there was the slightest justification. We agreed that the flight would continue 'burning and turning' until the Chinook got back. A few minutes later, Matt reported her inbound. But the RAF pilot had radioed that he was in serious difficulties, and could not lift in the crucial artillery ammunition. In numbed misery I realized that we had failed again ...

This time I listened in as the pilots talked to each other on the radio. As he had manoeuvred his airborne leviathan back through the mountains, Squadron Leader Dick Langworthy had flown into a snowstorm. This had temporarily masked his vision through the specialized goggles, causing him to lose height. While he struggled to regain control of the descending aircraft, it had smashed into the mirror-like invisibility of a lake, distorting the undercarriage before bouncing off. Although he had now successfully crash-landed back at San Carlos, he could not take off again without substantial repairs to the Chinook. 'How about enemy action on the landing-site beforehand?' 'Oh, *that*. No problem! The SAS have it well under control. You can fly back there without a care ...' If there had been time, I would have run over to embrace him.

But our problems were not over. The delay had eroded the Sea King's fuel margins. Now the loss of the larger aircraft meant that they would have to lift the essential artillery ammunition in the follow-up, instead of 'L' Company. Some critical decisions had to be made, then and there. In an urgent three-cornered dialogue between myself in the helicopter, the flight leader, and Matt Sturman, in Commando HQ, with the QM and Ops Officer shouting comment from the back of the Sea King, we revised our priorities. We could only afford one further troop lift; thereafter the Sea Kings would have to complete their availability with sorties of 105-mm artillery ammunition pallets.

We loaded up accordingly. Weight and safety restrictions were ignored as the troops piled in atop mounds of missiles, bombs, grenades and ammunition. Spare batteries ousted rations, surveillance devices replaced fuel. Passengers no longer had safety belts, or even seats. Aircraft loads ceased to have a tactical significance. In the middle of this frenzied reorganization the RSM tapped me on the shoulder, 'I think you ought to know, Sir', he snarled with evident resentment, '*that* reporter, Max Hastings, is trying to infiltrate one of the helicopters!' 'Send for him!' I howled distractedly, as yet another call came through from Commando HQ. Shortly afterwards the unmistakable bulk of Max loomed over me. 'Hello, Nick,' he said warmly, as if we were meeting unexpectedly while out shooting, 'how's it going?' I struggled to maintain my equilibrium. 'Max, I don't know what you're doing here, because you're not even one of my journalists, but in any event there are no spare places for correspondents, we haven't even enough for ourselves.' 'My dear Nick, there's no question of taking any of your places! I'm with Mike Rose. The Brigadier personally allocated me a place with the SAS reinforcements ...' I returned to more pressing problems, leaving a smouldering Chisnall to squeeze the Hastings frame into a helicopter.

At last it was done, so Dennis assured me, as he and I stood at the edge of the LS. We looked at each other for a moment, without speaking. He represented the best of every QM I had ever known, a loyal, dependable, almost mysterious figure whose pronouncements even COs queried at their peril. He was also a friend. We were the old men of this outfit, experienced, wary, conscious that soon we must bow out from the challenge and companionship that we loved. He straightened to attention and saluted me in the darkness. 'Good luck, Colonel,' he muttered, and turned to move away. 'My God, you old fool!' I declared. 'You think you may be saying a final goodbye, don't you?' He denied it fiercely but, as I clambered aboard the labouring helicopter, it was quite clear to me that he did.

Adrenalin sometimes obliterates normal misgivings. Although I am occasionally nervous in helicopters, there were no fears now. I was reminded of a point-to-point at Larkhill years before, when the new horse I was riding set off in the lead of a big division of the Open. At the first ditch his hooves resounded on the take-off bar like a tomb. It was obvious that we would not get far, which we did not. But the thunder and momentum of that mass of straining horse-flesh was overwhelming, as one abandoned self-preservation for the thrill of the race. It was the same now, and I sensed that this was so for everyone. Beside me Chisnall's challenging gaze scanned the faces for irresolution, while across the dimness I could

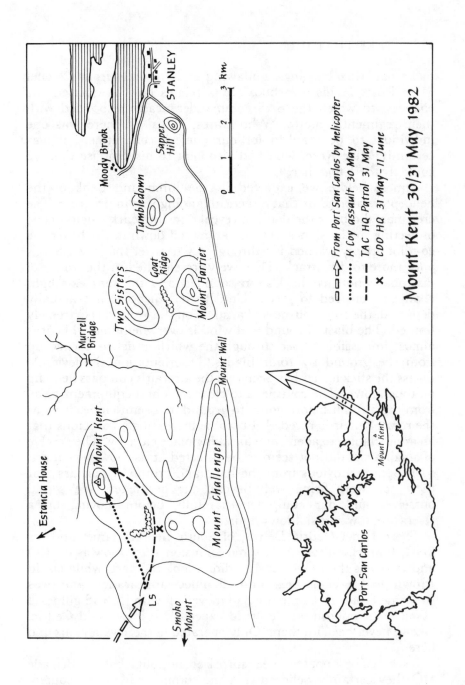

Estancia House

Smoko
Mount

LS

Murrell
Bridge

Mount Kent

Two Sisters

Goat
Ridge

Mount Harriet

Moody Brook

Tumbledown

Sapper
Hill

STANLEY

Mount Challenger

Mount Wall

Mount Kent

Port San Carlos

0   1   2   3 km

□→ From Port San Carlos by helicopter
········· K Coy assault 30 May
——— TAC HQ Patrol 31 May
–·–·– CDO HQ 31 May – 11 June
✗

Mount Kent 30/31 May 1982

make out Max Hastings, guffawing at some sally from Colonel Mike Rose. In his own book, Max relates how he queried our chances, to which the SAS commander neatly responded with their regimental motto, 'Who Dares, Wins'. If there was one individual to be thanked for our current commitment it was certainly Mike Rose, who had also kept to his promise that we could fly there together.

Almost before we expected it, the lurch and bank of the helicopters alerted us that a tactical landing was in progress. The crewman slid back the door, to reveal a reeling dark kaleidoscope of fleeting, rocky slopes. As we hammered down in the hover the co-pilot crisply warned me through my headset that the LS was once more under attack. Then we were engulfed in the frenzy of disembarkation as the klaxon sounded and the dim exit light changed from red to green. Until their helicopter has actually departed, the consciousness of a 'stick' on the ground is extremely limited. The blast of sound and wind is overwhelming, while it is almost impossible to see through the whirling debris sucked up from the ground by rotor blades. Disorientation is inevitable unless the stick leader has been told the aircraft's compass heading on touchdown. The routine is to clear men and equipment away from the aircraft before going to ground in a semi-circle. Now as the roar of engines receded, I became increasingly conscious that an appreciable engagement was taking place close by. The crackle of small arms did not seem to be directed at us, however, and it soon became obvious from the bang and crump of mortars that these too were firing well beyond the perimeter. We sorted ourselves and our equipment carefully before moving up a re-entrant towards shadowy figures.

There I met Cedric Delves, of South Georgia fame, and his 2/IC, John Hamilton. After some confusion as to who was the CO and who was the BC – clearly I didn't look the part, while David Brown had ever a neat and dignified appearance – it was confirmed that 'K' Company had moved off with its SAS guides. I asked what opposition we could expect. 'No idea,' said Cedric. 'We've never been up there. Only operated in these valleys around here ...'

It seemed best not to appear surprised, although back in Brigade HQ they certainly believed that the summit had been scouted. Deep-penetration forces like the SAS must adopt a low profile if they are to survive, and the necessary discretion is best judged on the spot. Observing, listening, and skirting around the Argentine positions was one thing. Probing onto a major position was quite another, since that might have provoked an overwhelming reaction. Anyway, we would find out what was on the summit soon enough when 'K' Company got there. I consoled myself with the thought that this could become the second 'Four-Two' success of the campaign.

Soon afterwards, the firing died down. The SAS had eliminated yet another luckless enemy patrol, and the fly-in of artillery ammunition was completed without further incident. About two hours later a laconic but elated Babbington confirmed that he and his men were on the summit of Mount Kent. The problem, he warned me, would be survival rather than the enemy, for the windchill factor at that height was well below freezing. I worried about them as we huddled under rocks in the rain. None of us had tentage or sleeping bags. But at least we were more sheltered from the wind in our valley.

8

ON THE WINGS OF
THE STORM

I awoke at dawn from a damp doze to the surprising sound of Mike
Rose apparently engaged in casual telephone conversation. He was
on the other side of some rocks speaking normally into a small
radio set, which I realized must be their SATCOM. It seemed
incredible that from our isolated, hazardous position, 8,000 miles
away, he could calmly converse with a colleague in the UK. It
underlined to me the pressures, as well as the advantages, of
space-age communications. These will inevitably become an
irresistible lure for 'chairborne tactics'; as we were already
discovering. But independent reports or individual opinions
by-passing Divisional Headquarters seemed equally likely to
create misunderstanding at one end of the command chain or
another.

It was time to set out with the Blowpipe missiles for 'K'
Company. The RSM began to concentrate our unwieldy group. I
had decided to leave Ian McNeill behind with David Brown; if
anything happened to me, they would maintain liaison and
direction between 'K' Company and Main HQ in Port San
Carlos. Apart from the six cumbersome missiles, and their dozen
or so handlers, we needed a strong escort team. Mike Rose and
Max Hastings also decided to 'come along for the ride'. At some
time the previous evening I had discovered that the latter had
bamboozled everyone, because the SAS had never given him a
place at all, nor had he permission from the Brigade Commander.
Indignation would have been futile, however; Max was a
professional journalist who sought news however he could get it.

As things turned out, he had not actually displaced anyone, and now was on hand to record one of the significant moves in the war. Anyway, I appreciated his initiative and had always admired his writing. My prejudice in his favour was suppressed by detailing him to carry a Blowpipe missile.

There were two particular dangers which I had discussed at length with the RSM, whose experience in this kind of situation was unrivalled. Our route covered several kilometres, and would take a number of hours. At any time we could bump into enemy patrols, or run into an ambush. Furthermore, Cedric also had SAS outposts of observation in place and we would have to ensure that we did not stumble into any of them without warning. Chisnall felt that the enemy, being less experienced, would tend to stay down in the valleys, so we planned a route around crestlines wherever possible. This also dovetailed with our other concern, which was not to get caught on exposed slopes by hostile aircraft or artillery fire. We were now within range of the Argentine heavy 155-mm guns, and their observation posts on Two Sisters or Mount Challenger would be able to direct devastating punishment if we were spotted. Before we set out, I saw Chisnall double-check in the SAS Squadron HQ that our route was known and that their OPs had been alerted.

We left well before first light. It was a jarring, slippery trudge in the dark with all that weight, and progress was slow. The hard-pressed missile men had not travelled out on *Canberra*, and the disparity in their fitness was worryingly apparent. Although their burdens must be shared, the fire-fighting capability of the escorts could not be compromised. In charge of this group was Sergeant Josh Shiel, the unit Provost Sergeant, for whom I had a special regard. A trained weapons instructor and sniper, his forthright and energetic approach did not endear him to everybody. But in circumstances like these he was at his best. The drizzle and sleet were unpleasant, but the wind and swirling mist concealed our movement and I prayed that both would persist after daylight. The RSM and I moved slightly ahead of the rest, in order to indicate the route more easily.

Thus it was that the RSM and I expended one of however many chances providence grants to each of us, as is told in the Prologue. At some reunion after the war, I met Colour-Sergeant 'Dinger' Bell of the SAS. He had held me in his sights as we loomed dimly out of the mist, heading up the slope towards his two-man OP.

Sharing a joke with a fighting patrol from 'L' Company on Mount Challenger

Corporal Mick Eccles (later awarded the Military Medal), 'K' Company, leads off a fighting patrol to Mount Harriet

The CO's 'O' Group. From left, front row: Sheridan, Babbington, Wheen, Norman, Sturman. In the second row, David Brown is behind Wheen and Norman; RSM Chisnall is in the second row from back, far left. 'The 'O' Group was a cold, factual affair, with the realisation that people were going to be killed tonight . . .'

Commando Headquarters 'saddle up' and move on

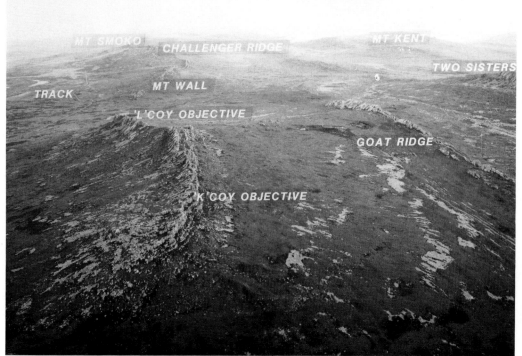

The battle ground

'Some chose not to surrender...'

'Others were only too eager to do so'

Sergeant Josh Shiel gleefully harasses the fleeing enemy with their own
machine-guns

'L' Company rest where cluster bombs have struck on the outskirts of Stanley

'Argies are tragic!'

The RSM (right) and 2/IC with Sergeant
Harradine ('L' Company) at Stanley Airport

Lance-Corporal Cuthell checks the credentials
of General Menendez

Sergeant John Napier looks down from the glacier to the Argentine base on
Southern Thule

'The ragged cliff-top dwellers'—Tony Hornby with Corporal Sharpe and the
troop from Mount Wall in Stanley

'Is Daddy really back?' Chris Nunn's children at RAF St Mawgan, July 1982

Presenting Mike Norman with his Mention in Despatches

Old friends meet again—with Colour-Sergeant Ray Rosedale at the first Mount Harriet Day Parade, 1983

RSM David Chisnall reads the lesson on
Harriet Day, 1983

Police Constable John Adams back in Stanley
with his family

Laying a wreath on Lieutenant Richard Nunn's grave, San Carlos, 1985

They had no inkling of our presence in the vicinity, so were certain we were Argentines. By coincidence, Bell was an ex-Marine who actually knew RSM Chisnall. His consternation at what might have happened almost matched my own! Fortunately, it was inopportune to hold a 'post-mortem' on the incident, so I left Mike Rose speaking vehemently to Cedric on the OP radio set, while we slogged on. In a curious way the episode seemed reassuring, because we had been spared. I muttered to Chisnall that I owed him a drink. Uncharacteristically, he agreed that this might be so.

Once it had become light, movement was increasingly dangerous. We were now amongst the crags on a feature opposite Mount Kent, which we could see rearing up into the cloud. In between us and our objective was a low valley, without much cover, and which I knew must be overlooked by Argentine positions just a few kilometres away. There was nothing for it but to plunge on down, and hope that visibility would not improve. We nearly made it. Then that perverse, unpredictable Falklands mist we came to know so well dissolved into bright sunshine. Suddenly we could see for miles. Above us was Mount Kent, much higher and steeper than I had imagined. On our right a series of jagged hills stepped away into the solid hump of the Challenger feature. Across our right front ran a rocky plateau, above which rose the majestic and unmistakable slopes of the Two Sisters mountain. Not only did we know that the Argentines had a major position there, but we could see them through binoculars, as they undoubtedly must have seen us. For a while we continued to descend, feeling conspicuously exposed, until another rain shower blanketed us in benevolent obscurity. This happened on several occasions, alternately exposing or hiding us for brief periods, but no shells burst around us. The cover on this slope was so sparse that it would have been senseless not to have kept moving. We pressed on nervously, expecting retribution at any moment.

At the bottom of the valley was a stone run, which at last would provide some cover, although it was a formidable obstacle to cross. These geological cascades were a feature that seemed peculiar to this bleak landscape, and made it all the worse to traverse. It was as if the mountains had vomited rivers of massive rocks, which meandered inconveniently in wide swathes across the valleys and re-entrants, making movement on foot incredibly arduous. For a heavily loaded man at night they were almost insurmountable. For vehicles they were impassable in any circumstances. Next to the cruel and capricious climate, I believe that most veterans of that war in the mountains will always recall stone runs as the greatest obstacle to progress.

As we reached this one, however, our feelings of relief were suddenly and dramatically changed as a new and fearsome threat manifested itself. For some time we had been hearing around us the intermittent sound of distant aircraft. That was to be expected, since Stanley was less than 20 kilometres away, and the Argentines used helicopters extensively for troop movement and resupply. It was certain that none of our own aircraft would be this far forward in daylight, unless they were Harriers, but they sounded completely different. The ever-present danger now was the dreaded Pucara. Intelligence had indicated that a number of these ground-attack aircraft were operating from Stanley Airfield. It was only to be expected that they would investigate last night's activities. Everything I had learned of their performance, at Goose Green and elsewhere, indicated that we must avoid being caught by them in the open, although Blowpipe could deter them, once launched. As the leading elements of our group clambered into the boulders, the clouds parted above a valley running down to our left. There, about a kilometre away, banked the unmistakable shark-like silhouette of a Pucara, apparently turning in our direction. The mist obscured it almost as quickly as it had appeared, but the alarm had been raised. The rest of the party, some burdened grotesquely with the bulbous missile cases, broke into a stumbling run for cover. Not far from where we stood, a missile-laden marine gasped towards us. We ran out to assist him into the shadow of the rocks as the sound of engines intensified. All of us were trying to help him uncase the beast, fumbling, cajoling, cursing at the buckles and straps. But it suddenly became apparent that we were labouring under a major delusion; he was one of the protection party. He had no more idea of how to operate this system than I did! Fortunately the clouds settled even lower. Another squall blew in, and eventually the sound of engines receded.

Taking advantage of the deteriorating weather, we set off round the shoulder of Mount Kent. At least now we were screened from direct observation to our right, and the boulder-strewn surface offered some cover, even if it was hard going. As we ascended, taking turns with the crushing missiles, I noticed with approval that Max still retained his. Already we were climbing into an increasingly vicious wind which would probably be at gale force on the summit. When we got there, it was indeed so strong that we could barely stand outside the shelter of the crags. The half-frozen members of 'K' Company who were not on sentry duty huddled amongst them for shelter and warmth. Their suffering was distressingly evident, yet nothing could be done to alleviate it, for the present at least. With luck Sea Kings would be able to lift in sleeping-bags and cooking fuel within a day or so, otherwise resupply would have to be manpacked.

The men of 'K' Company described how their cautious climb through the darkness had finally ended at the abandoned Argentine positions we could see all around. These had obviously been evacuated extremely hastily, judging by the amount of equipment left lying around. Halfway down the northern slope, which descended to the track leading towards Murrell Bridge, there was another tented camp. At dawn, Peter's snipers had winged a couple of luckless stragglers and captured some prisoners there, before the rest had run off down the valley. When the fugitives reached Estancia House they would run into a footsore 3 Para, so we did not rate their chances of survival too highly.

A sweeping panorama lay revealed to us as the visibility improved. To the north-west, 6 kilometres away down a wide sloping valley, could be seen Estancia House, with the shimmering sweep of Teal Inlet running away behind it into the far distance. The fenced pastures and scattered flocks of sheep suggested hill farms in the Lake District, while the brown shades of heather, speckled with grey boulders and glinting with streams, reminded me so much of my own Dartmoor. To the west and south rose the high, undulating features of Smoko Mount and Mount Challenger. This was altogether a harsher terrain than that to the north-west, a landscape of bleak, jagged ridges slashed by sharp re-entrants or encrusted with jumbled stone runs. Between us and the Challenger ridge lay the open, serrated plateau that unfolded eastwards for about 5 kilometres to the long slopes of Two Sisters Mountain. This particular feature had come to be regarded almost as the last bastion of Stanley – gazing across at those exposed approaches rearing up towards the separate pinnacles of granite we could see why. To the south of Two Sisters was a spine of rock that bisected an open ridge like a porcupine's quill. This was Goat Ridge, from where the ground sloped upwards again to dark, gaunt crags that had been compressed to form the sharp crestline of Mount Harriet.

The most riveting view of all, however, could be glimpsed slightly forward of the summit. There, to the east, we could see Port Stanley, 15 kilometres away. It seemed almost unreal, like a travel film for which any of us could have written the commentary. We had long ago committed the layout of the town to memory, from countless briefings and map studies on board *Canberra*. There was Government House, red roofs, conservatory and all. Along the waterfront stood the seaplane hangar; there was the whaling jetty; that was the Cathedral – surely those were white fences along the race-course? Beyond, in the haze, lay the airfield, from which several aircraft could be seen to be operating.

Beside me, Corporal Adams began to comment upon the battered appearance of Moody Brook, his erstwhile barracks. Back in April, the Argentine invaders had attacked this first, thinking that the Royal Marine garrison would still be asleep there. In fact it was empty, for Mike Norman had long since deployed his small force elsewhere. Now we could actually see some sort of military vehicle driving along the road towards the barracks. Through the blast of the wind I observed Peter Babbington in earnest discussion with his artillery observer, Captain Chris Romberg RA. The other officers seemed keenly interested in the outcome, and were consulting maps and measuring distances. I went over to them, and discovered that the idea was to bring down some salvoes of 105-mm 'charge super' on to Moody Brook. This charge boosts gun range to its maximum of 17,000 metres, but rapidly wears out the barrels, and so must be sparingly used. The Battery Commander, David Brown, would evaluate the gun-wear aspect of things, but I would have to decide whether it was really prudent to show our hand in this way. Our orders had not addressed this possibility because it had seemed so certain that we would be calling down artillery fire from the outset. On the other hand, last night's activities on and around Mount Kent could hardly have gone unremarked, while in a few hours' time another whole company group would be flying in.

A few artillery rounds would demoralize the occupiers of Stanley, said Rose. Cheer up the British inhabitants, declared Peter. Make history, urged Max. Kill some bloody 'spics', growled Corporal Adams. David Brown radioed his agreement from the landing-site. Chris Romberg predicted that he could spot on to the target. There seemed to be no point in consulting anybody else who wasn't there with us, so the gunner party commenced with that radio jargon which reaches back through the haze of battles to the days of limbers and mounted gun teams: 'One, this is Three-One. Fire Mission Battery. Fire Mission Battery – over ...' The guns went into action.

As he had promised, Romberg straddled the road outside Moody Brook with his second salvo. It was a most satisfying sight as the conical puffs of smoke blossomed in the air, long before the distant 'crump' of the explosions reached our ears. Everyone in Stanley must have heard them, loud and clear. Months later, I read in an American magazine of an Argentine soldier who confirmed that these first shells had created consternation amongst their number. For home consumption, Max Hastings recorded a short but dramatic commentary, which was relayed over SATCOM that night, much to the chagrin of his rivals back at San Carlos. With everyone's morale considerably raised by this episode, we said our farewells to 'K' Company and started the long trudge back to the LS in the gathering twilight.

That night, 31 May, 'L' Company flew in without interference, endorsing Julian Thompson's bold decision to seize such a key feature within enemy-held territory. Later, captured documents would show that an Argentine company had been lifted out of the area, at minimal notice, to reinforce.Goose Green during 2 Para's attack two days earlier. The SAS surveillance that detected enemy redeployment had identified the chance for an immediate *coup de main*, instead of a difficult and costly attack later. It had proved to be a fleeting opportunity, well taken.

3 Commando Brigade now took full advantage of their new initiative. As soon as 45 Commando and 3 Para had recovered from the epic 'yomp', they both moved up to consolidate around 'Four-Two'. Then Brigade HQ, with some vital logistics, embarked in the assault ship HMS *Intrepid* for a daring overnight dash round the north coast to Teal Inlet. The move demonstrated once again how amphibious shipping can decisively improve tactical options.

Meanwhile, the unit began to consolidate and move forward onto the ground from which it seemed obvious that we would eventually assault the enemy. At first we wondered if our objective might be Two Sisters, since we were more or less opposite that feature. Brigade HQ, however, was naturally anxious to secure the flanks as soon as possible. Since we were closest, 'Four-Two' was soon tasked to exploit as far south as the Mount Challenger ridge. David Wheen and 'L' Company achieved that in one overnight move, finding only abandoned enemy positions before going firm on the saddle. But it was obvious that Commando HQ would have to move because 'L' Company was now more than 6 kilometres away. Tac HQ moved from the original, increasingly noisy, LS without too many regrets, and joined up with Main HQ behind a ridge roughly midway between Mount Kent and Mount Challenger. The guns, now a complete battery, moved up with us, thus ensuring that our new location would not, after all, be a complete haven of tranquillity. On 2/3 June, 'J' Company were relieved of their responsibilities for POWs from Goose Green, and flew directly to the new Commando HQ by Chinook. By now I had visited 'L' Company in their lofty fastness, from where their patrols had already penetrated as far as the eastern extremity of Challenger, aptly named Wall Mountain. Again, no contact had been made with the enemy, so Brigade HQ agreed that we should leapfrog on, to establish another company further down the ridge.

At this stage the Commando held the right flank of the Brigade's crescent formation confronting the main enemy defences along the ring of mountains encircling Stanley. On the left, 3 Para had moved up onto the high ground above Estancia House and opposite Mount Longdon. In the centre, Andrew Whitehead's 45 Commando had come forward into roughly the area we had just vacated. Brigade HQ had already established a tactical headquarters behind those positions. I was assured that before any attack, 'K' Company on Mount Kent would be relieved, to rejoin the main body of the Commando. It was becoming clear that Mount Harriet would be 42 Commando's objective. From now on, that gaunt ridge of crags became our preoccupation, the sole object of our unfriendly attentions.

Southwards from their position on Challenger ridge, the men of 'Lima' Company looked out over the narrow coastal plain to the choppy blue waters of Harriet Sound, with Bluff Cove clearly visible to the south-west. Immediately below them, the steep southern slopes of Challenger and Harriet mountains were skirted by the Stanley-Goose Green track. This was in plain view, and was still being used at night by the enemy. Looking eastwards down the ridge, Wall Mountain reared up into a jumble of rocks about 3 kilometres away, glowering across a deep ravine at the bleak western face of Mount Harriet. The distance between these features was less than 2 kilometres as the crow flies, although if there were any of those birds in the islands such a trip was likely to prove hazardous for them from now on. North-east of 'L' Company, an exposed valley of stone runs extended for about 5 kilometres to the slopes of Two Sisters. Enemy observers on that mountain could detect movement on Challenger, particularly by helicopters, whose landings usually brought down harassing artillery fire on the company position. As if to emphasize this, there was a graveyard of burnt-out Argentine helicopters in the middle of that rocky wilderness. Before we came ashore at San Carlos, SAS patrols had called down air strikes on the area after they had detected a camouflaged landing-site.

The men of 'J' Company were looking tired and pensive when they reached us on 2 June. The aftermath of the battle for Goose Green had proved harrowing. Before marshalling and guarding the large numbers of Argentine POWs, they had been exposed to the dead and wounded of both sides, often at very close quarters. Everyone could find a counterpart among 2 Para's casualties, for death had not discriminated between officers, NCOs, or soldiers. Among the enemy's casualties there had also been ghastly sights of the victims of blast or burns. Many of the Argentine dead lay where they had fallen and could not be removed until some while after the battle, by which time their bodies presented an even more disturbing spectacle. The company had also been made aware of the enemy's superiority in numbers, and of his substantial stocks of arms and ammunition. The overall feeling was that although the Argentines – particularly the inexperienced conscripts – were clearly vulnerable to determined attack, they nevertheless possessed formidable means of defending themselves. Their positions would be infinitely harder to breach in mountainous terrain. Mike also told us of the devastating potential of the Milan missiles for 'bunker-busting', as 2 Para had used them to marked effect. But he worried me with the information that there had been a considerable stock of napalm bombs for Pucaras on the Goose Green airfield. However, the mass of POWs had seemed reassuringly docile, with no apparent resolve to prolong any resistance: 'Once you've cracked them they're like sheep – just waiting to be penned!'

That evening, 'J' Company set off with two guides from Commando HQ on the long plod across slippery slopes and rocky re-entrants to reach 'L' Company. They were then to bypass David Wheen's positions and move on, through a series of checkpoints placed out by 'L' Company to help guide them onto their final positions, further down the ridge. The weather was as malevolent as ever, bringing impenetrable mist and fierce showers of sleet or rain. Communications, however, were good. We monitored progress by listening on the radio to the designated nicknames of the objectives being passed to indicate progress. Once or twice I stepped outside the Command Post, trying to sense the conditions they were enduring. I felt a helpless concern for those soaking, heavily burdened figures squelching blindly through the murk, desperately hoping that their leading element would get them speedily to the end of this endurance test. Fortunately there are almost fourteen hours of night in the Falklands at that time of year, so the cover of darkness provided generous protection.

But darkness does not last for ever, even in the Falklands. The move was beginning to run ominously behind schedule, and as the situation deteriorated we became more and more anxious. If 'J' Company had not linked up with 'L' Company or their checkpoints, then they could have strayed off course into the low ground in front of Two Sisters mountain. Here was no man's land, with all the hazards of minefields, enemy ambush, or strong fighting patrols from both Commandos which might mistake 'J' Company for the enemy. I held some increasingly tense radio conversations with Mike Norman. He was handicapped by his total lack of familiarity with the ground, and so had understandably relied upon his guides. They, however, had clearly become disorientated. The 'L' Company screen began firing flares and bursts from their machine-guns as markers, but these were either obscured in the mist, or were indistinguishable from the noises of harassing artillery fire in the area. With time inexorably running out, we redoubled our efforts to restore the situation by firing single 105-mm shells into pre-arranged areas, hoping that 'J' Company could take a bearing on these. But even this failed to clarify their whereabouts in the sinister blanket of fog. An obvious alternative was to order them to turn back. But what then? By now, the time and movement calculations indicated that if we could not vector them onto Challenger soon, then daylight would expose over a hundred men to lethal observed artillery fire or directed air strikes.

Uncompromisingly, this war had created a dilemma that I would have to resolve. In peacetime, one would merely have suspended the exercise on safety grounds. Here, a crucial decision to change direction had to be made immediately. I spoke to Mike Norman again on the radio link. Sounding weary but calm, he declared that he and his men must have by-passed 'L' Company unknowingly, and were now beyond them along the Challenger ridge. This, however, did not explain the failure to link up with the screen of David Wheen's patrols, or the fact that Mike could not pinpoint any of the recognition devices we had fired. Besides, if 'J' Company went too far down that ridge, they could stumble onto Wall Mountain, which we suspected was still occupied by the enemy.

I could prevaricate no longer. The company was ordered to turn 180 degrees and march west until it reached a defensible position with cover. About an hour later, we received confirmation that this had been done, which partially relieved our worries. But I wondered what further dilemmas daylight would bring. Perhaps I should have kept 'J' Company with Commando HQ until conditions had improved and the junior leaders were orientated to the area? But time was precious, and progress had to be maintained. The rain lashed against the frail command post, dripping depressingly through the groundsheets. We dozed fitfully against the background buzz of radios interspersed with the fast, high-pitched chatter constantly monitored by the signallers on duty. Danger and uncertainty were making it hard to maintain confidence in one's own decisions when the consequences of a misjudgement might be so disastrous.

As dawn broke, we were joined by Phil Wilson and the RSM, both of whom knew that this would be a crucial moment. 'J' Company began to report that the mist was lifting in their vicinity. They reckoned that they were below a ridge, facing west above a bowl-shaped valley. Now they could make out a major feature to their right, silhouetted against the horizon. Yes, and beyond that in the distance was what seemed to be an expanse of water. Wait! Now they thought they could discern movement about a mile or so below their positions. There were shapes down there that could be camouflaged vehicles. Or perhaps they were tents? No, they were something else, they were guns ... In fact, they had just fired! As we listened to the crash of our own battery a few hundred yards away I wondered whether to laugh or rage.

Afterwards, of course, bystanders muttered about map-reading and compass bearings, estimating distance, following contours, and so on. As every experienced hill-walker knows, however, once one is diverted from a route that involves changes of direction, then completing the proverbial circle is all too easy in bad visibility. Compound that with broken terrain, back-breaking loads, filthy weather and the constant worry of bumping into the enemy, and it seemed only a huge relief that 'J' Company was more or less back where they had started. That, anyway, was how I chose to see it!

Some days later, the particular difficulties of navigation across the monotonous Falklands terrain were re-emphasized dramatically when the RSM and I visited 'J' Company, now finally established in their new position. It was a clear, cold evening with a copper sun setting over the bleak hills. We were enjoying a brief respite from the prevailing blizzards. It was outside the usual air-raid time-scale, and welcome resupplies had been flying in by support helicopter to the Commando HQ several kilometres behind us. As we stood talking with Mike Norman in the shadow of some rocks, we heard the approaching rumble of an incoming flight from San Carlos. To my consternation, instead of contour-flying out of sight into the HQ, these helicopters appeared flying high in formation over the ridge behind us and on across the open ground towards Two Sisters. For an optimistic moment or two we assumed that they were going to circle back over our positions, or 45 Commando's, or even Brigade HQ; anywhere but straight on towards annihilation! But it swiftly became obvious that these pilots were making a most unusual error of map-reading. They headed on inexorably for the ridge of hills beyond our forward positions and straight towards the main enemy.

Every radio set within earshot suddenly burst into spontaneous hysteria: 'Whisky Leader. Whisky Leader. Emergency. Emergency. Emergency. Turn back now you are inbound enemy positions ...' 'Zero, this is Nine. Turn those sodding Whisky callsigns back *NOW*. Use every bloody channel available ...' Predictably, my language deteriorated under stress as I called Commando HQ, although I could hear a calm Corporal Adams passing an immaculate sitrep to Brigade HQ on our other set. It was all going to be too late, however. Travelling at a ponderous 60 mph, the arrow-head was already halfway to the Argentine positions. We watched dumbfounded, incredulous with rage and frustration, as the helicopters throbbed past us and on towards Two Sisters, ignoring the flares fired desperately towards them.

Behind me someone began cursing monotonously: beside me, a horrified troop commander looked as though he was going to cry. Once they were in range of the enemy, these lumbering airborne mules with their underslung burdens would be blasted from the sky by missiles or machine-guns. There was nothing any of us could do except watch helplessly.

Once again, St Jude seemed to intervene. In a demonstration of crass stupidity and indiscipline, the Argentines opened fire at least a kilometre too early. As the tracer arched out towards them, the pilots were granted their reprieve. Wobbling convulsively in understandable disarray, the aircraft banked about and headed back to safety. I wondered what their own radio net sounded like! Indeed, why had they not been switched to ours?

Later it emerged that these were newly arrived anti-submarine pilots, accustomed to monitoring their air-raid warning system as a priority. After that incident, however, ground-to-air communications improved dramatically, as pilots asked to be vectored into the various landing-sites. This terrain of endless ridges, re-entrants and stone runs was as difficult to navigate over as it was to map-read across. It was amazing how seldom, rather than how often, anyone got lost.

At about the same time, in the twilight of another murky day, I was sloshing around the waterlogged, makeshift shelters constructed amongst the rocks on our perimeter. There off-duty marines rested stoically, like badgers in their setts, resisting the all-pervading dampness and the shifting winds, carefully conserving their energy and body warmth. Just then a light helicopter landed in the re-entrant below us, and an indistinct but familiar figure emerged clutching a bundle of equipment. It was Guy Sheridan!

I had become resigned to the fact that he would not succeed in rejoining us for the main battle, although word had reached me that he was trying. It was a marvellous relief to have him back, to provide the advice and encouragement for which I increasingly felt the need. Although I knew full well how strong and loyal was my support, the age-gap between myself and the Commando HQ team was more than ten years. They needed to have confidence in my judgement, confidence which could not be risked by my revealing too many reservations, or seeking too much reassurance. Detecting the lines of strain on their weathered faces, I knew that they were grappling with enough problems without taking on mine.

Now, however, I would have someone to confide in, a partner to worry with, a counsellor from whom to seek comment. Guy was a tried and patient friend, one who sensed my moods and could detect when physical strain was exacting a price.

In particular, he understood about my back. We had covered many miles together over the years, and he had sometimes seen my endurance frustratingly eroded by the strain of the old injury. Now I was especially glad of his presence, for the problem was becoming more acute. The cold and wet were seeping into increasingly cramped muscles. If only I could have eased them by resting on a flat surface, instead of the humps and holes we lay upon in precarious shelters. To make matters worse, I was constantly carrying a load of equipment that dragged down upon my shoulders and restricted lateral movement from the hips. At any time a slip in the slime, or a stumble while negotiating boulders, could wrench the knotted sinews into spasm, which would necessitate casevac and treatment. If that were to happen it might be disastrous for unit morale. How much credibility could an ailing leader expect on his return in these circumstances?

But salvation was luckily at hand. Early one morning, a day or so later, accompanied by the QM bearing mail, dry socks, new gloves and cigarettes, our beloved 'Bandwagons' (BVs) rumbled into sight. It was an amazing spectacle to see those compact tracked vehicles yawning through the slush, their articulated trailers glissading as they thrashed remorselessly up the slope. We were unbelievably fortunate that the BVs could make equally good going over glutinous mud as they could over snow and ice. The Commando's six vehicles would now guarantee improved and secure communications, and a weatherproof, camouflaged command post from which Commando HQ could maintain infinitely better control over the unit. It also had my own independent 'Rover' vehicle, from which I could discreetly monitor events on the radio nets without interfering, unless it proved necessary. I could also talk to the Duty Officer on a telephone. The number of trips that this would save me, cursing and splashing through the darkness from my sleeping-bag, guaranteed better rest and drier feet at night.

Best of all, I had the bliss of a hard, flat bench on which to straighten. No monk could have cherished his solid pallet more than my own distorted frame would appreciate that 'Bandwagon' during the long days to follow, while we completed preparations for battle.

9

SURVIVING ON THE MOON

In the early stages of the Falklands War, Major Roger Blundell, a long-standing friend, had to brief a team of high-ranking planners at Northwood about the difficulties that would follow a successful landing. It became clear that there was little understanding among his audience of the Falklands wilderness, where, away from the scattered settlements, movement or shelter from the elements are major problems. Roger advised them to regard the project as though it were the moon. The area would be barren of facilities, and the landing force far removed from the UK infrastructure that would have to provide replenishment. A few weeks later, when some members of that originally sceptical staff were purposefully chartering tankers to ship out drinking-water for the troops, he felt he had made his point.

The surroundings in which we now found ourselves were indeed a wilderness in the biblical sense. At times the terrain bore an eerie resemblance to the high moors of England, but at home the water-table does not lie just a few inches below the surface. In the Falklands during winter, almost all the high ground is sodden with brackish water, rather than drained by fast-flowing streams. Digging for cover creates a water-filled ditch. Drinkable water is almost non-existent. Provisions for survival all had to be brought ashore, then transported to the troops. But there were no roads beyond Stanley, and the connecting settlement tracks were passable only to tracked vehicles or civilian tractors. On the higher ground, the steep, slippery slopes, the swathes of jumbled boulders, or the buttresses of crags along crestlines, made movement for laden men desperately exhausting and difficult, especially at night. Helicopters were the only alternative, and their use had been a fundamental planning assumption from the beginning. The four Chinooks and six Wessex helicopters on board *Atlantic Conveyor* were to have taken on that logistic burden – until an Exocet missile put paid to that concept in one devastating impact. Similarly, the lack of total air superiority over the beach-head severely inhibited use of the limited number of helicopters already ashore. Re-supply was therefore often inadequate, and sometimes haphazard, as priorities for ammunition, reinforcement or rations had to be allocated among widely dispersed units. When supplies did arrive, usually at twilight, they had to be manpacked out to the positions before dawn. For our three rifle companies this meant a long, hazardous march to Commando HQ, followed by a harrowing load-carry back out again, trudging through the night, eroding the marines' strength more and more. We desperately needed shelter and dry clothing. But ammunition and rations used up the available helicopter lift, no matter how sympathetically the logisticians perceived our plight.

It would all have been so much more tolerable without the infamous South Atlantic climate. Over the centuries, mariners have logged the Furies in these latitudes, and for the next three weeks it seemed that they were concentrating to overwhelm us. Each day brought blizzard, squall and downpour in relentless sequence. A particular curse of the area are the fierce katabatic breezes, which perversely change direction after a short time, continually defeating any effective siting of shelters from their wind chill. Occasionally the sun would break through, providing temporary warmth and a precious chance to dry out sodden sleeping-bags and clothing. But these respites were brief. On other days the damp mist enveloped everything in a clinging blanket, which stifled sound and reduced visibility to a few feet. The ground underfoot became a spongy morass in which boots could give no protection from the wet.

Inevitably, therefore, it was our feet that suffered most and soon began to deteriorate. After the war some critics suggested that most of the 'trench foot' injuries arose from inadequate boots, but in my view this was not so. Some of us in 'Four-Two' wore the Greenlander, a special mountain boot (or other types which do not cover the ankle), but there were marines with almost every variety on the market. As long as equipment was of military standard and texture, those who had paid good money were allowed to use improved articles in the field. But no matter the footwear, we all had soaking feet almost all of the time, because boot leather became saturated and then porous, however it was treated. On the move, blisters and abrasions usually followed from wet boots. But protracted immobility as a sentry, or in ambush, reduced circulation and could cause cold injuries which became so painful that in extreme cases an individual simply could not walk. The antidote was to dry and powder the feet whenever possible, before cherishing them in a dry pair of socks inside a warm sleeping bag. These last critical conditions became increasingly hard to sustain, although everyone appreciated their vital importance. That precious pair of dry socks was only worn at rest, then carefully protected from getting wet until the next time. It was a depressing preliminary to each day to steel oneself to pull back on the sopping, dank, odorous alternatives inside cold boots, but successful survival is mostly a matter of know-how, and of having the will-power to implement it. The majority of the unit soldiered on with their foot injuries until the end of the campaign. Nevertheless, we were beginning to see an ominous trickle of 'casevacs' in the last days.

Apart from their effect on our feet, wet and cold conditions increasingly threatened our survival prospects. A fit, trained man can endure both discomforts indefinitely only if there is dry shelter for recuperation, and nutritious food to restore warmth and energy. Each pack of our dehydrated arctic rations contained more than 5,000 calories, but water and cooking fuel were essential in order to reconstitute them. We were usually short of at least one of these ingredients, with the result that many of the troops suffered from diarrhoea or dehydration. This was particularly worrying when great physical demands were being placed upon them.

On top of all this, dampness insidiously spread from the wet clothes worn normally, into those hoarded for resting. The 'green slugs', as sleeping-bags were known, became correspondingly contaminated in turn. They were, in any case, often soaked from outside, despite their waterproof bags, by rain blown into the shelters. This was depressing, as well as debilitating. The dangers of indifference and apathy now became very real. Yet they did not prevail because the junior leaders, particularly the corporals, prevented that. Constantly encouraging, chaffing, or directing their sections, they warily monitored the state of their young marines, ensuring that rations were eaten, and feet dried out, whenever opportunity arose. It was so heartening to see that when a patrol returned from some arduous mission, an officer or NCO would quickly check the marines' mental and physical well-being, as well as seeing that weapons had been cleaned and the sentry roster understood.

The backbone of our perseverance was provided by the Sergeant-Majors. Respected for proven leadership, acknowledged for their professional experience, these influential veterans could galvanize activity, dispel confusion, instil confidence. Like their scarlet-coated forebears, they steadied the troops in battle, and maintained their standards and discipline between times. There was little that they had not seen in the service, even less that they could not improvise when necessary. They were the Company Commanders' mainstay, and the Commanding Officer's reassurance.

Senior amongst them was WO2 Dave Greenough, our only veteran of the Limbang landings, the most recent 42 Commando battle-honour. A drill instructor by trade, his field experience was matched by a reputation for uncompromising standards on the parade-ground. He had remained with Dennis Sparks at the resupply echelon to direct the unceasing working parties at the stores stockpiles, which meant that we needed a substitute in Main HQ. The gap was filled by the unlikely substitution of the Chief Clerk, who had cajoled me into bringing him forward as a command post watchkeeper. WO2 Len Cook's clerical expertise was matched by a strong frame and a vigorous personality. On the way south he had been elected as the President of the combined Sergeants' Mess Committee where, among the 400 SNCOs from assorted units, his Scots shrewdness and evident impartiality created much-needed harmony. His younger brother, also a clerk, was now in a rifle section with 'J' Company.

'L' Company Sergeant-Major was WO2 Cameron March, an imperturbable ex-policeman whose maturity and sound judgement were both a balance and reassurance to his bustling company commander – even in small things. Although David Wheen did not smoke, he had a compulsive craving for liquorice allsorts. Amid the myriad needs of 'log reqs' (logistic requirements) for Wheen's ever-increasing company on Challenger, CSM March eventually managed to obtain even some of those.

In 'K' Company, WO2 'Dusty' Millar, another hardy Scot, maintained a calm and steadying influence on everyone. An impressive figure, with a courteous manner, he could praise inspiringly or rebuke with devastating effect. Most of the time he tactfully left the dynamic leadership to Peter Babbington, providing instead a paternal encouragement to the lame and weary.

When we formed 'J' Company, WO2 Fred Cummings was diverted from his vital responsibilities as the senior physical training instructor. Until we sailed from Ascension he had remorselessly driven the unit fitness programme which, we were finding, now counted for so much. A small, unassuming man, he was a Black Belt at judo and an accomplished all-round sportsman. Although dwarfed by the bulk of Mike Norman, the two of them adapted compatibly into an effective partnership, which is the key ingredient for achievement between company commander and sergeant-major.

My memories from Commando HQ are of cheerful, bedraggled individuals who alternated between watch-keeping in one of the control complexes, and taking their turn on the perimeter for sentry duties. The HQ was vulnerable to air attack, artillery bombardment and enemy patrolling at night, so contingency reactions had to be prepared and practised. Everyone had a prepared trench, or 'sangar', for cover. There was a strong perimeter defence, which the RSM constantly reviewed and refined. And, as our main strength lay in defensive artillery or mortar fire, there was a ring of lookouts on the high ground above us. At night we pushed out listening-posts to provide early warning of hostile approach.

By now, Main HQ had sent Matt Sturman and Tony Miklinski to rejoin us and provide the watch-keeping back-up we so badly needed. However, they also brought with them more radios, which had to be manned, with additional logs to be kept and maps to be marked-up. The secure-speech radio link, which allows an operator to speak 'in clear' without danger of the enemy listening in, also proved a mixed blessing. In theory, it speeded up planning discussions, or the passage of urgent information. The Argentines were known to monitor our normal radio nets, making open speech too dangerous and forcing us to use time-consuming codes. British officers are notoriously verbose, however, and soon as much time was being taken up with trivia as was saved by protected dialogue.

I had no secure terminal in my BV, so would stand for hours in the command post, fuming, impatient to break through the waffle of others whose problems seemed infinitely less important than my own!

It was now that we also began to see increasing numbers of prisoners. They were either captured by our patrols, or sometimes just found wandering, apparently eager to give themselves up. The marines were more intrigued by their enemies than actively hostile to them, but could not resist some gentle mockery: 'Hey, José – who cries for Argentina now, then ...?' Most of the captives seemed very young and bewildered, although some of their so-called Special Forces troops inclined to arrogance, a posture swiftly punctured by the caustic wit of our own hard-bitten NCOs. The prisoners' wonder at the high morale of our troops and the rapport between officers, NCOs and marines was very evident. There was much laughter on one occasion, brought about by the FN automatic rifle with which a marine had presented me on Mount Kent. I had kept the weapon, largely because it was handier to carry than my Sterling submachine-gun. A rather cocky Argentine sergeant asked if this meant that the British rifle was inferior to the FN, to which I replied that there had not been a chance to use it yet. 'But', chipped in one of his escort, 'We have really been waiting for someone like you who could run fast enough for the CO to find out ...' It was rare for them to speak English, however, so we pushed them quickly on back to Brigade HQ, where there was one of the very few interpreters who had been brought out with the Task Force. Before the prisoners left, however, we were able to see for ourselves that the press speculation about starvation or widespread exposure amongst them was rubbish. It was all too evident that they were better off than we were for material comforts.

As we patrolled and plotted the options of the inevitable attack, another personality emerged upon the field of battle. Major-General Jeremy Moore had unexpectedly come back, and was now taking an important load off Brigadier Thompson's shoulders. He did so by shielding the commander of 3 Commando Brigade from the distractions of communicating personally back to UK whilst also striving to direct operations forward. Despite this responsibility, General Jeremy flew up to the mountains as often as he could to visit the troops. They appreciated his affable concern for their circumstances, and were reassured by his evident confidence that the attacks would be successful. With tactful judgement, he had selected a neutral head-dress for this mixed force of Royal Marine Commandos and Army battalions. In his Norwegian Army forage cap he cut a distinctive figure, reminiscent of wartime silhouettes from the Afrikakorps. It was good to see him amongst us – even without his familiar green beret – and I hoped that he was as impressed with 'Four-Two' as we were pleased to see him.

My own routine was divided between visiting the companies and planning for our eventual attack on Mount Harriet. Brigade HQ was established in a farmhouse at Teal Inlet, and one morning I flew down there for a briefing on future intentions. The farm's owners, the Bartons, turned out to be closely related to family friends who had visited us in the United States the year before. It was still a small world, even in this lunar landscape. This sort of excursion into civilization was a rare treat, where small personal habits like washing one's hands in a basin could be indulged in as if they were a gourmet dinner. There was, of course, another obvious, if more intimate, bodily function that I would have appreciated just as much were I not such a creature of habit. Throughout my childhood, the family regime had decreed that the day should begin with purging the system, and somehow the habit persisted. As a result, even on exercise in Norway my metabolism would confront me with the need for an abrupt progression from warm sleeping-bag to cold, alfresco crouch. This routine persisted even in the Falklands. As other memories of that war fade, one that will not is the misery of pulling on clammy socks and wet boots to squelch off into the dawn mist to my particular set of crags. There I had found a deep crevasse down which I could dump waste matter, rather, I believe, as mountaineers do. It was probably not as satisfactory as doing so from the North Face of the Eiger, an action graphically described to me by one of my friends, John Barry. But it made me feel better and I liked to imagine General Galtieri was down there at the bottom.

Our clothing was simple and functional. Next to the skin I wore a set of Leefa underwear, extending from ankle to wrist, which was comfortably light, but provided excellent insulation without inducing sweating. Needless to say this was not an issue item. It is, however, very popular with Scandinavian athletes, which is why so many of us preferred it. Above that came my Norwegian army shirt, light but extremely warm, with a high collar that could be zipped up to retain body heat, or opened to let it out when necessary. Outwardly I conformed to the established rig of camouflage-pattern windproof suit, undoubtedly one of the finest foul-weather garments anywhere. Although densely woven to defeat wind chill, it does not absorb much water and will dry rapidly in the breeze. In 42 Commando, we invariably wore our green berets when moving, so that even if we had had to put our windproof hoods up, they could be pulled back, revealing the beret, for instant recognition when necessary. Complementing my ensemble were the varieties of wet and dry socks, two types of glove, a USMC scarf, and an inelegant but beloved pair of gaiters which kept my lower legs gratifyingly dry and warm. Sadly they could not do much for my feet. Dressed like this, I was as light as a bird and almost as well insulated; this was what was worn, however, and not what was carried.

Of the burdens borne by 'Four-Two', mine must have been one of the easiest. In addition to a fighting-order of pouches assembled on a belt, many of us carried the Norwegian army patrol pack in preference to the British equivalent. The Norwegian pack is a comfortable single sac of canvas, having some strap-on potential on the outside. Within it I could cram a heavy sweater, spare shirt, washing gear, waterproof suit, light shoes, cooking gear and fuel, all fitted around the main item, which was my contribution to Tac HQ. This was a heavy, crank-operated battery-charger, which Corporal Adams frequently needed in order to revitalize the batteries that we could only rarely exchange. Never before can an inanimate object have absorbed such malevolent regard! Together with rations for forty-eight hours, ammunition, an entrenching tool, binoculars, steel helmet, sentimental pewter mug and my 'Argie' FN, the weight I bore must have been around 80 pounds. In a rifle company, or particularly Support Company, it was often well over 100 pounds. And here was the real cause for complaint about the equipment we were using. That 'GIO Pattern' web equipment of belt and pouches had been developed in the early 1960s and universally condemned thereafter. The design was such that loads were unbalanced, the load capacity was inadequate, the webbing itself inflexible. Because it was absorbent, it often froze. In the Falklands War it proved exasperatingly uncomfortable and quite useless for its task. We deserved better from twenty years of peacetime research and development.

For Guy and myself, the command BV became our workplace and our shelter. Although it was extremely cramped with two of us in there, we could share the monitoring of the radio, as well as co-ordinate our problems much more easily. During the day we hardly saw each other. Guy concerned himself with logistic and administrative preparations, while I was usually away. Occasionally we had to have 'O' Groups with the company commanders, but we kept these to a minimum for obvious reasons. By squeezing up like sardines, all the officers except Phil Wilson and Mike Norman could just fit inside the BV. Those two were so burly that they had to remain outside, peering cheerfully over the back of the vehicle. Although its canvas screen could be draped over their shoulders, the rain and wind lashed at their buttocks. In the dim red glow of the battle-lights, I could glance round at the fierce, blackened faces, bristling with stubble, drawn with fatigue, and imagine myself among some desperate band of cornered brigands. Then someone would make a characteristic aside, we'd all laugh, and suddenly they were transformed back into the officers of 'Four-Two' whom I knew so well from Orderly Room, mess parties, parades in ceremonial dress. Beneath those grim faces the humour and mutual trust remained untarnished. It was so very important for us all to be reminded of that.

It would have been nice to have had 'a glass of comfort' on these occasions. But such things were wistful memories, until one day we were visited by Tom Seccombe. He struck a majestic figure as Deputy Brigade Commander, dressed distinctively in his own choice of field gear, which included Wellington boots and a blackthorn stave that would have done credit to Little John in Sherwood Forest. He tramped around the positions dispensing gruff encouragement and hilarious observations in appropriate doses, much to the delight of the marines, who knew him well and appreciated seeing him. After putting to me some shrewd suggestions for improving our lot, he turned to leave, heading for his helicopter. 'Oh, by the way, Nick ... I think we should exchange water bottles,' he suddenly said. I goggled at him utterly mystified. 'Come on, here's mine,' he went on, slightly impatiently. I handed over my battered, half-empty bottle and received a new and very full one in exchange. Only after I had saluted as the helicopter took off did I realize that this was certainly no ordinary bottle of water. The next 'O' Group gave me the chance to share 'Uncle Tom's' kind consideration with the others ...

Brigadier Julian, of course, visited 'Four-Two' as often as he
could, and he and I looked at Mount Harriet together from
various vantage points. We knew little enough then about the
enemy strengths, but the position was obviously being held in
order to prevent a British advance along the track from Goose
Green to Stanley. We also concluded that there must be some
form of mine barrier, although only patrolling could determine the
answers we sought. The Brigadier, however, was obviously more
worried just then about whether 42 Commando could survive in
its present positions long enough to accomplish such patrolling.
Then, a day or so after we had last seen him, one of his staff visited
us for the first time. It was a ghastly day of wind and rain, and
Commando HQ looked like a shipwreck with the survivors
stumbling miserably about in the murk. I was not too surprised,
therefore, to be told later in the day that the Brigade Commander
was coming up again the next morning. Julian Thompson asked
me, with sensitive concern, whether I agreed that the Commando
should be withdrawn for a 'drying-out period'. Every effort would
be made, he promised, to bring us back into the line for the main
attack. He left me with twenty-four hours in which to think it
over ...

It was clear that how I answered would be one of the critical
decisions of 'Four-Two's' war. By now there was evidence of real
suffering among the troops in the rifle company positions. I could
see that if we endured too long in these mountains, we might not
be capable of a major attack at the end of that time. Moreover, our
patrols were now going to have to fight for the intelligence we
needed to plan the main assault. That would require leadership,
initiative, aggression and stamina, from increasingly weary and
weakened junior leaders and marines. The self-confidence and
determination with which we had landed were now being eroded
ominously. Morale and fitness are like bank accounts – incessant
withdrawals must be compensated for eventually. The initial time
that 'K' and 'L' Companies had spent on Mounts Kent or
Challenger, without the contents of their large packs, was now
exacting its price.

But withdrawal smelt of failure, and spelt obscurity. Whoever
took our place would certainly attack Mount Harriet, since they
would have patrolled and planned for it. If we came back at all, it
would be as a reserve or flanking unit. This was precisely what I

sought to avoid. If we must go to war, then 'Four-Two' surely deserved the chance to fight a proper battle. I believed that this was the collective view. All the same it was only fair to give each company commander the same option as the Brigadier had given me. I ordered them all to consult their subordinates. To a man they turned the offer down, decisively and with confidence. 'Nobody wants out of this mountain, Colonel,' said David Wheen. 'We just want to hurry up and get onto the next one ...' My other sensor of the Commando pulse, the Regimental Sergeant-Major, was equally positive about the will to remain for a fight. I told Julian Thompson. It was clear that he was as relieved by the reaction as I had been.

10

INTO NO MAN'S LAND

I suppose it is certain that never again will any of us spend so much time studying the map contours, or observing the slopes, of a single, bleak feature like Mount Harriet. In any other context it would have rated no more than a passing glance on the map; posed merely an obstacle to avoid, rather than cross, on a march. Instead we measured the distances, plotted those heights, traced the contour lines, and shaded in the cliffs and crags. David Brown's gunner teams calculated crest-clearance for our shells and mortar bombs, while the Intelligence Staff plotted possible routes and likely enemy positions. In the companies, all this information was refined into compass bearings to march on, or scrutinized to identify which concave slopes provided the best cover for a night approach. By day, eyeball and telescope evaluated Mount Harriet constantly from several observation posts. At night the viewing devices were changed, but surveillance remained unbroken.

Our special frustration was that there were no air photographs, even old ones that might reveal unseen topography, let alone a recent series to pinpoint enemy dispositions. We accepted that the few precious Harriers could not be risked even had they been equipped for photo-reconnaissance. But it did seem incredible that, during all those years of garrisoning against invasion, no photographic survey of the islands had ever been made. 'There's nowt for it but bimble out there to find out for ourselves', declared Sergeant Millard, the Intelligence Sergeant, sombrely. We were going to have to do this anyway, because domination of the buffer zone between occupied positions is a basic preliminary to success. I

141

was confident our patrols could achieve that domination but it would have helped to eliminate so many imponderables if we could have seen what lay beyond our sight.

With the traditional superstition of campaigners, the code-names for our objectives were inspired by distant loved ones, in the hope that this might bring luck as well as security. Whether my daughters' Russian and Irish names would do so remained to be seen, but I certainly felt that they would confuse Hispanic radio interceptors. Mount Harriet had therefore become 'Zoya'; Mount Wall, our granite 'crow's nest', was now 'Tara'. Almost as soon as the names had been promulgated, we almost lost 'Tara'!

In all the frustrating circumstances of this near-disaster, my own judgement of one aspect was less than sound. Once again, I was furious with myself. On the morning before 'J' Company flew in, the Brigadier had summoned Andrew Whitehead and myself forward to a spot from where we could observe our objectives and discuss boundaries, routes and co-ordination. The call came unexpectedly, while Tac HQ was wearily 'brewing-up' during an all-too-rare pause between our rounds of the positions. As the RV was clearly visible less than half a mile away, I decided that it was unnecessary to deprive all the heavily burdened radio operators of their rest, and set off with only the ever-ready Corporal Adams. Although we could still communicate with most of the Commando, the Mount Wall team was on a separate radio link to Main HQ. Our own gunners, with one of the operators I had now left behind, providing mobile communications for me into that link. Away at the RV with only Corporal Adams, I therefore could not get in touch directly with the Mount Wall patrol.

As we approached the crestline, the sound of a small-arms and artillery exchange from the direction of Mount Harriet began to reach a crescendo. Almost at once, Adams handed me the handset plugged into his PRC 352 radio (this enabled me to listen or speak even while we kept pace with each other). An excited dialogue was in progress between David Wheen and the Reconnaissance Troop Commander, Chris Mawhood, on Mount Wall. Some of Recce Troop had been discreetly patrolling forward of their isolated observation post when they had detected an Argentine patrol approaching. There was no alternative but to engage them at once, before the fire-fight involved the observers behind and those resting off watch. Four of the enemy were instantly killed in a withering burst of fire, and a fifth man then went down to a head shot by one of our snipers as he scuttled vainly among the rocks. But two or three Argentines escaped back down towards the road. Retribution, in the form of a vicious artillery fire mission on 'Tara', was now being exacted.

While I watched the oily smudges mushroom around her crags, a more alarming dimension arose. Main HQ intervened, relaying an unconfirmed message that an enemy company was deploying from transport on the road below Mount Harriet. The situation began to deteriorate rapidly. But, to my fury, the orders needed to restore the situation could not be passed, because we had no direct link with Mawhood. It was also becoming increasingly difficult for me to break into the busy Commando net.

Every instinct told me that the enemy would be most unwilling to risk a company in the open and in broad daylight, having had several devastating experiences of our artillery already. Furthermore, it would take them at least an hour to ascend the precipitous slopes and get anywhere near our positions. Meanwhile I could hear David Wheen on Challenger calling for a fire mission on the road, and prudently ordering forward his machine-guns from the rear positions, to strengthen the defence against an enemy advance. The situation called for decisive direction, which I should have provided from Tac HQ, but could not. The final disruption came when our RAF forward air controller, up with Mawhood's troop, judged that his highly classified aircraft direction equipment might be captured. He therefore destroyed it, in accordance with strict standing orders. This seemed to convince everyone that their situation was desperate, and I was informed that the position was being abandoned, even while I was attempting to pass on the order to hold firm for the moment.

It was a most unfortunate development. Suddenly we had lost an invaluable vantage point, which the enemy must now be expected to seize in strength. A much-needed and expensive piece of equipment for directing accurate air strikes had also been destroyed. Last, but very damaging from our point of view, half of Recce Troop and two fire-control teams had lost most of their kit. My frustration was not lessened by the thought that if the radio links had been better I might have been able to dispel the confusion. From that moment on, it was clear that Tac HQ must always move with me, however short the distance, or whatever the personal inconvenience to others.

Fortunately, the loss of 'Tara' turned out to be only temporary.

'I should like you to get back up there just as soon as "J" Company is established,' said the Brigadier mildly, within a few minutes of the withdrawal. Tactfully, he did not query the apparent confusion of the withdrawal in the first place. I was pleased to be able to report that Tony Hornby's troop was back up there within twenty-four hours of 'J' Company reaching Mount Challenger. Astonishingly, the Argentines had made no effort to occupy Mount Wall, a feature that stared straight across at them, although they had pinched most of our gear. For the second time they had avoided counter-attacking to seize back obviously vital ground. It was becoming obvious that tactical boldness paid off handsomely.

By 1 June 3 Commando Brigade confronted its objectives from a crescent-shaped curve of high ground. Around Mounts Longdon, Kent and Challenger were grouped 3 Para, 45 Commando, and ourselves; with Brigade HQ and an increasing logistic stock-pile at Teal Inlet. Five gun batteries were to be deployed in support of us all for the attacks, but for the moment their ammunition expenditure was rationed. The highest priority was placed on flying forward 105-mm shells to build up a reserve for the batteries. 500 rounds per gun was the estimated requirement, and bringing that forward would need more than 300 Sea King sorties.

Among the front-line units, we were closest to our objective from Mount Challenger, although the distance to Mount Harriet from Commando HQ was more than 5,000 metres. However, the shortest route between 'Tara' and 'Zoya' was actually the most hazardous. It lay across a deep, boulder-strewn ravine, overlooked by Argentine strong-points established in the eastern crags of Mount Harriet. On our right flank, that is, south of the two features, ran the Stanley-Goose Green track, which had obviously been a main Argentine supply route. They now clearly expected the main British advance to be made along this, and we had already spotted freshly dug earth on either side. These workings were being noisily extended each night. Between the track and the coastline lay several kilometres of flat, marshy plain, criss-crossed by farm tracks and cratered with ponds and lakes. These would inhibit movement without providing cover. On the other flank, to the north of 'Tara', was the rocky plateau on which, a week earlier, I had feared 'J' Company might have become lost. Looping across it, then ascending through a maze of stone runs, was a route onto the saddle between both Commandos' objectives. There the shallow bowl was ominously bisected by a slab-sided, razor-backed quill of crags. This was called Goat Ridge, which, to keep my girls company, we code-named 'Katrina', after an American cousin. Goat Ridge had already been designated as the inter-unit boundary, although responsibility for its capture would be ours. The ground between 'Katrina' and 'Zoya' was largely out of sight, so we could make no detailed observation.

The map indicated that this ground would be open, but probably difficult to cross. Whichever way one viewed the area, however, Mount Harriet predominated, threatening our approach. Harriet is also a natural fortress, as is graphically described by Julian Thompson in *No Picnic*:

> The tops of the high features were crowned with great, craggy castles of rock, which stood up like the spines of some vast prehistoric reptile. These crenellated bastions, with deep fissures, sudden sheer drops and great buttresses, provided excellent defensive positions.

For generations, British military staff instruction has leaned heavily on the 'Tactical Exercise Without Troops' (TEWT). In these, aspiring commanders have to resolve tactical and logistic problems based upon marked maps of ground actually before them. The crucial preliminary is the 'Appreciation', in which 'Factors' are identified and then analysed to deduce the 'Courses Open'; the best of these is then identified. Now I would have to do this once more; not for practice, or qualification, or promotion, but to manoeuvre within a brigade attack at night against a real enemy.

Much to our relief, Brigade HQ had long since declared that we would seize our objectives in darkness. Given the odds against us, and the dominating ground to be surmounted, this made absolute sense. Since Goose Green our troops had convincingly proved their superiority at night against an inexperienced enemy. Even so, I did not believe that 'Four-Two' could attack along the axis of that straight, flat, almost luminous track which ran along the south side of Mount Harriet. We would have to make a flank approach, but only by sending out probing patrols could we identify from which direction that should come.

As if to emphasize the more covered northern approaches, a disconcerting event focused everyone's attention on the south. In broad daylight on 3 June, HQ, 5 Brigade landed 'A' Company, 2 Para at Fitzroy. 3 Commando Brigade had received no prior warning, and consequently the soldiers were assumed to be enemy, especially as the helicopter was a Chinook, which both sides possessed. Initially, our gunner regimental HQ accepted this as an artillery target. I listened to David Brown tasking his battery while we awaited further confirmation from Brigade HQ. Their urgent cancellation came after they had double-checked with Divisional Headquarters. But only a few seconds before the misunderstanding became a tragedy, which would have led to great and unnecessary loss of life.

That night, the first patrol, from 4 Troop, 'L' Company, was sent to investigate whether a culvert bridge across the track below had been blown. They were then to attempt an ambush of the stragglers and working parties we knew moved around there. The patrol was led by Acting Lieutenant Ken McMillan, a self-confident young officer only just out of training. He was well aware of the danger of minefields, which we already suspected might not be marked. Our worst fears were soon realized, when Marine Mark Curtis was blown into the air even before the patrol had crossed the track.

> I felt down my leg. My boot had been blown off. The numbness started spreading. I realized something was wrong, so I put morphine into my thigh. Cuthell was shouting 'What the fuck happened?' I told him 'I think my foot's been blown off ...'

It had, and only the resolution of Lance-Corporal Garry Cuthell and the remainder of the patrol saved Curtis's life. They had to carry him back through stone runs and up precipitous slopes for more than seven hours before reaching safety. Much of the time his cries of agony pinpointed their whereabouts. They feared that they were being followed, and were shelled spasmodically in diabolical weather which precluded any hope of helicopter casevac. Perhaps the key to the wounded marine's amazing survival was the presence of Leading Medical Attendant Hayworth, whose expert treatment with drips and drugs kept him alive in the darkness and searing sleet.

In the Commando units, we were lucky to have such uniquely qualified Royal Navy 'medics', who accompanied all the fighting patrols from their affiliated companies. What we didn't have, however, as we now began to appreciate, was a functional stretcher for this sort of emergency. All that first-aid training on *Canberra*, and yet no one had foreseen the requirement! Indeed, why did the infantry not have an effective, collapsible stretcher after all these years ...?

The following night, we used our attached 2 Troop 59 Independent Squadron RE, with our own assault engineers, to clear and mark a path down from 'Tara' to the track. But there was still so much more dangerous territory to be crossed.

We endured fewer hazards in Commando HQ, although the Argentine 155-mm guns were well within range. These should long ago have located the battery within our perimeter and subjected it to counter-bombardment. On most nights we would lie in our sleeping-bags and wait, with some trepidation, for the unmistakable boom of big guns firing from the mountains near Stanley. This would be followed shortly by the rapidly increasing wail of an express train rushing through the sky, before a roar and reverberating crash signalled arrival at the destination. Fortunately, that was never where we were, although the shells landed close enough on occasions. 7 Battery, of course, was constantly engaging the enemy. The high-pitched screech of our own shells whistling out towards the enemy created an entirely different sensation. One night around this period we were bombed with air-burst shrapnel from a high-flying Argentine aircraft. This was disconcerting, but once again reassuringly inaccurate.

My personal *bête noire*, however, was still the precariousness of flying. I avoided doing so whenever I could, even if it meant long, tiring marches out to the companies. But time was usually too precious. On one foggy, unpleasant day, I found myself en route to Challenger in a Gazelle flown by new aircrew who had just landed with 5 Brigade. The pilot was a fast-talking young Sergeant who assured me that he knew the way through the billowing mist, while his crewmen kept gesticulating at the map and declaring that we were nearly there. Because Corporal Adams and I were bundled together in the back, it was impossible to check ... but I had increasing doubts. Eventually, as we hovered in towards a dim mass of rocks, a rift in the mist revealed the ground dropping steeply, and the fleeting glimpse of a curving track below. There was only one place that could be, which was east of Mount Wall and in full view of Mount Harriet. Both sides would surely engage us if the fog cleared. Mercifully, it did not, and we hover-taxied sullenly back along the crestline until I recognized 'J' Company positions. There we dismounted, briskly and without reluctance, to complete our visit on foot.

The next important patrol went out on the night of Sunday 6 June. Once again, 'L' Company provided the main group, which was 5 Troop led by Sergeant 'Nev' Weston. His Troop Commander, Lieutenant Jerry Burnell, was literally *hors de combat* with hypothermia, brought on as much by supervising the survivability of others at the expense of himself, as by the fact that 'L' Company had not received a ration resupply for five days. Included in this strong fighting patrol was Sergeant 'Jumper' Collins with three men from 'K' Company, who were to conduct the first deep probe into the area south of the road. Although it was very open ground there, I wanted to discover whether we might be able to loop round in a right-hand curve without being detected. With so much Argentine activity all around that area at night, this small group would need 5 Troop as protection to fall back upon if they were 'bumped'. Normally, such a probe would have been a Recce Troop task. But Mawhood's marines had been temporarily evacuated to the Echelon at Teal Inlet, because no one could last for long in these mountains without sleeping-bags or the survival equipment they had lost on Mount Wall.

The patrol set off at 1945 hours, and moved down our cleared path before crossing the Stanley-Goose Green track. As ever, movement across this terrain in these circumstances seemed excruciatingly slow, but there was no alternative if the patrol was to avoid detection. We had enjoyed exceptional communications ever since the BV202s had arrived, so I was able to monitor the patrol's progress, and even speak to Sergeant Weston if I wished. At about 0100 hours Marine Kevin Patterson from 5 Troop trod on a mine, which blew off his foot below the ankle. Because some of the escort had already set up a base near the track, the remainder began to retrace their steps towards them, carrying Patterson as best they could. Although he was a much smaller man than the 15-stone Curtis, the terrain was sometimes so rough that, with unbelievable stoicism, he hopped along on one foot while his comrades supported him. The 'ministering angel' on this occasion, MA Collins, had the unlikely nickname 'Snow Ferret' ...

The weather was as foul as ever, but Brigade HQ informed us that a Scout helicopter would attempt casevac provided that we could identify a safe landing spot. Commando HQ's communications, more powerful than the patrol's, were best equipped to co-ordinate this hazardous manoeuvre. So while the pilot, Captain Nick Pounds RM, thrashed through the gusting rain and stygian gloom towards enemy territory in which exhausted, wary men strained to hear his approach, we relayed their terse queries and directions from the light and shelter of Commando HQ. Against all odds, a pick-up was made on the track itself, amidst pressures one can only imagine. Nick Pounds's only comment to me later was about the cheerful courage of Patterson, who had joked over the intercom as they flew straight to Ajax Bay and the surgical expertise that would save him.

After the casevac had been completed I spoke with Sergeant Collins on the radio. We had a critical decision to make. Although there was now a very serious risk of his patrol being compromised, we must go on seeking a route through the minefields. Unless one could be found, an attack from the right flank would be impossible. They understood that already, Collins told me calmly; he and the other three were ready and willing to carry on.

Not long after setting out again, when roughly opposite the enemy positions at the western end of Mount Harriet, Collins and his men had another desperate experience. Suddenly they realized that their patrol had been spotted. A large group of the enemy loomed out of the darkness and began to move down towards them from the track. Collins retreated rapidly with his group, until he fell into a water-filled peat cutting. The rest of the patrol threw themselves on top of him. After struggling up for air, he realized they would have to make a stand or be captured. The four of them hastily adopted a somewhat optimistic defensive position. At that point, the Argentines went to ground as well. For the next – excruciatingly cold – hour or so, nobody moved! Then, despite the acute tension, Collins turned to Lance-Corporal Steven Sparkes, who lay beside him, and whispered in the troops vernacular, 'How's your bottle, then?'

Unhesitatingly, Sparkes replied that it had 'gone pop' a long time ago. This apparently reduced all of them to uncontrollable fits of the giggles, proving once again that, even in dire straits, humour can prevail over other emotions. Meanwhile, Sergeant Collins had surmised that the winners of this 'Mexican Stand-Off', as he called it, would be the experienced professionals, and he was eventually vindicated. Exasperated and by now unsure of what they thought they had seen, the enemy soldiers stumbled back to the road, shouting insults or invitations before moving back into their positions. It seems possible that they may in the end have concluded that the four men were Argentine stragglers from Goose Green.

Making careful note of these newly identified positions, the patrol gingerly made their way back along another route. They reached 'L' Company lines just before first light, where Guy Sheridan was waiting to debrief them. They had achieved an outstanding feat of fieldcraft, which now encouraged me to persist in seeking an approach along the right flank. We savagely shelled the newly pin-pointed enemy positions the next night.

CO and 2/IC now worked to a continuous but quite separate routine, which meant that between us we could keep in touch with far more of the 'sharp end'. Remaining apart was also an insurance that both of us were not knocked out simultaneously. While waiting for Collins's patrol, Guy had spent most of the night sitting amongst the rocks of 'L' Company HQ where, earlier, he had been chatting with David Wheen and Kim Sabido, the IRN reporter. One of them inadvertently set off Sabido's tape-recorder on which, that morning, he had recorded a particularly vicious barrage over the position. At the full-volume screech of an approaching salvo, somebody yelled 'Incoming!' Everyone hurled themselves under the nearest sheltering rock. To this day, Guy isn't sure whether the incident was a 'bite' or not ...

David Wheen may have had the last laugh then, but Commando HQ had been vastly amused earlier on, before artillery fire became a way of life for us all. Wheen had complained to the BC that the adjustment of defensive fire around his new positions on Challenger was too close. 'Understood' came the polite reply, 'but all I can suggest is that you keep your head down. We're not firing at the moment!'

On 7 June, 'K' Company was withdrawn from Mount Kent and moved down to join us at Commando HQ. The Brigadier now believed that the attack could be mounted within a few days. It was vital, therefore, to rehabilitate the marines as much as possible after their ten-day ordeal by exposure in that lofty wilderness. Lashed with rain, sleet, and snow, battered by katabatic winds that reached hurricane force at times, 'K' Company had endured temperatures below 12 degrees, creating a windchill sometimes lower than minus 30 Centigrade. The men were gaunt, soaking wet, and very tired. But the pitiless South Atlantic weather gave them no respite with us, as the rain hissed down onto the pathetic shelters they had constructed amongst the rocks. That evening, the RSM and I slithered around these 'grots', conversing with anonymous hooded heads just protruding from sopping bags. How were they? Better than before, thank you! Was everyone completely soaked? 'Well actually, Sir, I think my left bollock might still just be dry.' How did they feel? 'A little bit annoyed with the Spics for dragging us out here from leave.' Could they keep going? 'For as long as it takes to chase the bastards off this patch!'

On the following day, Frank Allen, who had just been brought up to join us at Commando HQ, wrote in his diary:

> The place we're in is extremely wet, windy and unpleasant. The view though is impressive, with the line of the valley sweeping up to the rocky peaks where we crouch. The whole area is veined with 'stone runs', an amazing phenomenon – literally rivers of stone in flow patterns from the hill tops.
>
> Bang – another salvo!
>
> My function here is to try and co-ordinate the rather haphazard supply forward, dependent as it is on weather and helicopter availability.
>
> This situation is horrible! I'm filthy, damp and cold – we all are. Mercifully the day has been dry because when the rain starts the discomfort is awful.
>
> I can't write any more now as my hands are too cold ...

After repeated attempts, Frank had finally managed to bring forward the Commando's large packs. For a brief, carefree spell the atmosphere was reminiscent of opening presents at Christmas, with weather-beaten marines gleefully extracting 'dry sox and clean nix', caches of 'nutty' (chocolate), even the odd battery-powered razor. My pack was not among them.

On the morning of 8 June, I flew to Challenger again for a meeting with Sergeant Collins near 'Tara'. Other fighting patrols, which we had sent out onto the saddle below 'Katrina', had convinced me that was not the route for the Commando to take. Enemy machine-guns on 'Zoya' covered almost all the low ground that side, and there were other Argentine positions north of the main feature. If the Goat Ridge crags were reinforced from Mount Tumbledown, then we could be enfiladed. And I was also conscious that in this operation 45 Commando would be manoeuvring under fire close by, which created the danger of costly confusion in the darkness.

It was a clear, cold morning. Collins led me to a ledge with panoramic views of the whole south side of 'Zoya', the track, and the plain of his previous adventures. By now, he must have realized that he would be asked to venture out yet again, but he showed no sign of it as he calmly identified map features on the ground. The longer I considered the options, the greater my conviction that a surprise right hook into the enemy's rear was the answer. But first Sergeant Collins would have to navigate a feasible route through the minefields and other obstacles. Afterwards, we could consider how to travel that route undetected.

While we pondered over the view, I became increasingly incensed at the sight of an enemy working party calmly laying mines alongside the track, about 2,000 metres away. Strolling provocatively up and down the road beside the labouring Argentines was, unmistakably, a pair of their officers. They were obviously meant to be supervising and encouraging, rather than indulging, as they were, in that well known officers' pastime of gossiping together. What seemed particularly intolerable was that one of my SNCOs was actually having to watch the mines being laid that might cost him his life that night. I called up David Brown at Commando HQ who agreed, exceptionally, that a few salvoes could be made available. The FOO on 'Tara' was told to get on with it. A few minutes later the first rounds spouted just short of the left-hand working party. With understandable alacrity, the Argentines downed tools and hared for the roadside ditch. The 'management' however, appeared unimpressed, gesticulating imperiously at the conscripts to get back. Seconds later, they were vapourized by the next salvo, which neatly straddled the road. That seemed to put paid to work for the day, as well as evidently cheering up Collins, who went off purposefully to prepare for his next mission.

Later that afternoon, the RSM and I were still visiting positions on Challenger when Corporal Adams routinely informed me of an Air Red Alert passed on the Brigade net. We had not ourselves seen hostile aircraft for more than a week, but knew that the enemy still made occasional sorties against San Carlos or ships off the coast. However, the general view seemed to be that the Argentine air threat had been largely eliminated. Only such a conviction could have explained the NATO-exercise scenario below us at Fitzroy, where two LSLs were leisurely unloading a mix of 5 Infantry Brigade's troops and stores into landing-craft.

All this activity was clearly visible from Mount Challenger, 5 kilometres above Bluff Cove. There was no means of talking to them, because each brigade maintained separate integral communications, with a direct link only through Divisional HQ. Just the day before, someone among us had speculated whether Rapier anti-aircraft cover had been established down there. We had concluded that it was inconceivable, given recent experience, that valuable ships would be risked in an undefended anchorage.

I was deep in conversation with a Sapper about mine-clearing when Mr Chisnall seized my arm in a vice-like grip. Such informality from him was so unusual that I knew something must be wrong, even before I heard his urgent direction: 'Look over there, Colonel – down along the coastline. Just look at the bastards!' Skimming down the shore of Harriet Sound were four A4 Skyhawks of the Argentine Air Force. Even as we watched, helpless with horror, they rose upwards, and then swooped down upon the unsuspecting ships. A myriad of malevolent flashes preceded the great booming explosions with which we were all too familiar. We watched the aircraft make two passes. On the second, the left-hand ship, *Sir Galahad*, erupted in flames and billowing clouds of smoke.

It was a sickening scene for impotent spectators, although 'L' Company fired a Blowpipe missile which might have intercepted a Skyhawk, had one turned our way. For a while we could make out the frantic activity of helicopters and boats evacuating survivors. But soon the scene was obscured by an oily black smog, which hung like a shroud over the area in which 5 Brigade's troops had been landing. It was obvious that they would not now be moving forward for a while, which must delay our own advance as well. But it was not until the next day that we learned of the magnitude of the disaster.*

That night, we sent a strong fighting patrol from 'K' Company back to the area of 'Katrina'. It was led by Lieutenant Mark Townsend, a university graduate who had just completed his Commando training. The purpose was twofold. First, Brigade HQ had tasked us to escort an eight-man patrol of the Mountain and Arctic Warfare Cadre into a covert position. The Cadre's special expertise includes long-range reconnaissance, and on this occasion

---

* *Sir Tristram* was hit and damaged; *Sir Galahad* was set on fire and gutted. The Welsh Guards lost thirty-six men killed with many more wounded, of whom two died later; eighteen other soldiers and sailors also died.

their patrol was to 'lie up' on Goat Ridge for the whole of the following day. As a diversion, while the M and AW Cadre men were inserted, Townsend and his lads were to harass the enemy's forward positions, attempting to draw their fire and expose the defences. By now we had pinpointed a series of strong-points and machine-gun nests with this tactic which, although dangerous, invariably spooked the enemy's inexperienced conscripts into firing wildly into the darkness. Already we knew that there were at least two companies holding the area, one at either end of 'Zoya'. Now it seemed increasingly likely that there were even more Argentines in the vicinity. After our ventures to the south, I was also keen to keep up activity on both flanks, in order to avoid giving any indication of our intended axis of attack.

1 Troop had a stimulating night out. They killed six enemy and wounded several more, forcing the Argentines to abandon at least one position. Best of all, they spread panic and confusion throughout the area. Marine Graham Fisk unexpectedly had to demolish one wretched defender with a 66-mm rocket at close quarters: 'There was nothing left of him from his kneecaps upwards ...'

Each time we terrorized the defenders of Mount Harriet, their confidence would be eroded. At the same time, we must seem increasingly ferocious to them. This patrol also managed to pin-point three more machine-gun positions before returning unscathed, under impressively close cover from a series of thunderous barrages. These, we hoped, had punished the defenders as much as they depleted our reserves of gun ammunition. The next day, 'K' Company's morale was sky-high after such a successful 'blooding'. Confidence in Chris Romberg as their artillery controller was also firmly established. Somewhere in all the excitement, the M and AW Cadre patrol had slipped undetected on to 'Katrina', from where they made invaluable sightings throughout the next day. It had been a good performance by all concerned.

While all that was going on, the redoubtable 'Jumper' Collins and Lieutenant Colin Beadon, the Milan Troop Commander, with three other marines, were painstakingly feeling their way through the maze of obstacles across that naked plain south of Mount Harriet. They were no doubt grateful for the chaos beyond the crestline as a distraction for the enemy above them. After some hours they penetrated to the track junction opposite 'Zoya's' western extremity. At this point, Beadon had seen what he came for – sites for his Milan firing-posts down the track towards Stanley, along which the enemy could counter-attack with his armoured cars. Collins, however, had one more task, which was to check on a fence that I had hoped could be used as the start-line for our attack. Alone and unarmed, in the interests of stealth, he slipped across the track and crawled off into unseen ground among enemy positions. Half an hour later he was back. The mission had been accomplished.

On Thursday 10 June, I flew to Brigade 'O' Group below Mount Kent. Already Ian McNeill had passed our outline plan to the staff, who now knew our attack would be 'right-flanking'. We had asked for a dispensation from the silent-attack policy because harassing gunfire might be necessary to distract enemy lookouts across the plain. It was reassuring to be told that this would be available 'on call'. But I was thoroughly unhappy to hear that the start-line would be secured for us by the Welsh Guards. They had reorganized after their disastrous losses in Bluff Cove, and were to come forward below us after 42 Commando had seized Mount Harriet. My reservations were simply that all the problems of liaison, co-ordination and communication with a different formation now had to be dealt with, when we could have done it independently. Just before the 'O' Group I met Johnny Ricketts, the Welsh Guards CO, as well as David Chaundler, now commanding 2 Para after parachuting in from the UK. There was, however, no opportunity for detailed discussion.

Then, for the second time, with simple, but comprehensive orders, the Brigadier inspired us commanding officers with the confidence to launch our units against a long-established and numerically superior enemy holding formidable defensive positions. Despite the logistic setbacks, the ferocious elements, the unforeseen consequences of enemy air attacks, the conflicting interests within the Task Force, and the diverting pressures from the home base, we were ready. Many of his problems were those that commanders in war have always had to face. But some could also be ascribed to twentieth-century communications and the scope that they provided for armchair campaigning. Regardless of all this, Julian Thompson never lost his aim, which was to attack where he chose and when he was ready. Which would be on the following night – Friday 11 June.

11

MOVING ON STAGE

An end to frigid bivouac was upon us. But suddenly we were running out of time in which to complete our preparations for battle. There was so much to be done as pressure mounted within the unit. One particular dilemma had been whether to move 'K' Company onto Challenger two nights before the attack, or one. The additional twenty-four hours would have given them rest the night before and the chance for junior leaders to spend a day observing their battleground. It would, however, mean a further concentration of troops in that area, which would inevitably increase the risk of giving the game away. And, for the same reason, our vulnerability to artillery or air strike would also be increased. Now the whole problem was resolved. 'K' Company would have to march all night, recce, rehearse and prepare on Challenger the next day; then move straight into battle.

Before leaving Brigade HQ, I spoke to Ian McNeill on the radio, to alert him that 'Four-Two' must now initiate all the concurrent activities of preparation for battle. A warning order went out to all sub-units, giving timings for orders, where to group up, when to move forward. In Support Company, Phil Wilson began to deploy the mortar line to the rear of 'Tara'. The Milan missile teams dispersed to their designated rifle companies. The Company Quartermasters dispensed reserves of ammunition and rations.

The heavy and cumbersome support weapons, with their stockpiles of bombs or missiles, could be flown forward only as far as the rear depression on Challenger. Beyond that point, everything would have to be manpacked stealthily forward to 'Tara', more than 3 kilometres away along Challenger's jagged ridge. In Support Company, many loads exceeded 120 pounds.

Most of 'L' Company covered that distance three times, each man humping six 81-mm bombs, weighing 9¼ pounds apiece, onto the mortar line. All of this had to be done under cover of darkness.

On the logistic side, Dennis Sparks at Teal Inlet now began the replacement of stores and other items which might be crucial in the battle. The problems were almost insurmountable. Only a handful of helicopters was available to resupply each unit with a wide range of stores that had become depleted. They could not possibly all be moved in time. Not only had we been short of rations for some time, but we had lacked many other essentials as well. Drinking-water had become virtually unobtainable. Cooking fuel was so scarce that marines were no longer able to boil the liquid they got from the brackish puddles. As a result, increasing numbers of them were suffering from diarrhoea, or 'Galtieri's Revenge' as they called it. Everyone had given up shaving many days before. In his diary entry for that evening, Frank Allen wrote:

> The clear weather today allowed more supplies to be got forward; some clothing and sacks of sheep's wool for drying boots. We went through the large packs in Commando HQ and requisitioned all the two-man cookers and overboots, which we sent forward. The cookers are to ease the situation with hexamine tablets [solid fuel], which are extremely scarce. These petrol burners went forward with the last of our fuel and the news is that there's none available for at least 36 hours. Once our generators stop for lack of petrol we will be unable to recharge radio batteries, let alone cook food.

As soon as I returned from Brigade HQ we plunged into detailed planning for the Commando 'O' Group the next morning. Decisions had to be made, movements co-ordinated, timings adjusted. Delegation of responsibilities was now essential, for anticipation or reaction from junior leaders would be crucial. From now on the complete infrastructure of this fighting unit had to function spontaneously.

During the advance, David Brown would control our most powerful and crucial asset. He had been at the Brigade 'O' Group with me, but we had also discussed beforehand the outline plan of 'Four-Two's' attack. David could now prepare a separate complex sequence of fire missions onto a selection of targets, to cover the various manoeuvres necessary in our assault. He would co-ordinate our requirements with his Regimental HQ, as well as with Support Company, since the mortar troop constituted an important ingredient in our supporting fire. We had also been given other gun batteries in support.

As Operations Officer, Ian McNeill would have to prepare the detailed co-ordination of groupings, tasks, routes, boundaries, timings, logistics and administration. Assisting him would be Lieutenant Hank de Jaeger, the Intelligence Officer, and Charlie Eggar, our Signals Officer. Both these subalterns would prepare annexes for the written orders which collated the latest intelligence on the enemy, and designated the radio nets required by the unit, with call signs, frequencies, and codes. Somehow, we found time to construct a large briefing model, and to mark-up a series of maps for issue at the 'O' Group. Commando HQ, meanwhile, remained vigilant, a team permanently on duty in case we had to counter enemy action.

Before Ian's 'number crunching' began, I had a brief tactical consultation with him about some refinements I wished to fit in. Surprise was a fundamental requirement of the battle plan, but it would be lost if we were detected during the approach. Apart from harassing fire on call, we needed some additional distraction to divert Argentine attention from the plain we would be crossing. Another worry was that preponderance of the enemy's heavy machine-guns covering the early part of the route. I was also concerned about reorganization on the objective once the enemy had been dislodged. Mount Tumbledown was only 3 kilometres behind 'Zoya'. The Argentines could swiftly mount a counter-attack from that area, and we knew that they possessed a heliborne reinforcement capability. Our artillery radar had recently reported several enemy troop helicopters manoeuvring over 'Katrina' at night. Finally, we still had to decide where Tac HQ should be during the battle. We would need to be as far forward as possible – ideally between the leading rifle companies – but command and control can only be exercised with effective communications. Both David Brown and Charlie Eggar were doubtful that these could be maintained from down on the plain.

A diversion had already been planned with a secondary purpose. As part of the preliminary deployments, a Milan detachment would be moved forward from 'Tara' until it was in range of the threatening machine-guns. The moment we suspected that our movement on the plain might be detected, the ragged cliff-top dwellers on Mount Wall would stage a simulated patrol clash. The explosions, lights, shouts and screams should irresistibly lure the trigger-happy enemy gunners into joining in with their fusillades of .5-inch tracer. At this point, the mortars would illuminate the eastern face of 'Zoya' where, although our Milans did not have night-sights, their operators should now be able to aim through those amazingly accurate eyepieces over a distance of about 1,000 metres. In theory, this devastating missile might achieve what artillery, mortars, and naval gunfire, using HE, airburst and phosphorus, had so far failed to do – eliminate those machine-guns concealed amongst the crags.

We also decided to form a composite group made up of those not normally in the assault element. Cooks and clerks had long since gone to the 'sharp end' with 'J' Company, where they were now indistinguishable from their riflemen equivalents. Now, the Adjutant and RSM quickly amalgamated an assorted group of drivers, technicians and storemen with Surveillance Troop who, until then, had maintained long-range observation over our flanks and rear. Led by the terrier-like Sergeant Brian Evans (who sardonically dubbed his charge 'Porter Troop'), these thirty ranks were to follow closely in rear of the assault, carrying the awkward sustained-fire conversion kits for the machine-guns and as much ammunition as possible. In this way the rifle companies could fight 'light' (if 50-75 pounds can be called that), knowing that the long-range firepower, essential for breaking up counter-attacks, would be brought up at the earliest possible moment.

In the end I bowed to prudence and technology, accepting that Tac HQ must stay on high ground from where we could communicate and observe. But I was unhappy that we should not accompany the advance. It remained a decision that was hard to make and disturbing to live with. There can be no question that, in battle, commanders should be forward whenever possible. There they are seen to share danger, can sense instinctively the changing circumstances, are able to react decisively when necessary. Ian McNeill pointed out, however, with inexorable logic, that the assault companies had little enough room to manoeuvre as it was. The CO and all his entourage plunging about in the darkness on top of them could create distraction, rather than provide encouragement. David Brown also reminded me that if we could not communicate from the plain, we would have no control of our artillery and naval gunfire support. They were both right, of course; particularly if something were to go wrong. A Commando HQ that was not embroiled in a crisis would be much better placed to resolve it.

I was left one more major task, which was to write my own part of the orders. The opening statement must be the 'Mission', or aim of the attack, declared twice to emphasize its crucial importance. Within the subsequent 'Execution' paragraph would come the designation of tasks to sub-units, and the allocation of assets for completing those tasks. In effect I was explaining the plot, and the players' roles within it, to the assembled cast. McNeill, as producer, would then clarify sequence, timing, 'props' and orchestration.

Obviously we had to have a reserve, either to call forward as reinforcement, or to fall back through. 'J' Company was in the best position to provide that, since they confronted the nearest Argentine positions. As we now knew there were two enemy strong-points at either end of 'Zoya', I decided that 'K' Company would attack first against the eastern positions. Because these were the furthest away, surprise should be the more disconcerting. If the diversion on 'Tara' had not been needed during the approach, then it could still create confusion at this crucial moment. The enemy nearest to us would also feel vulnerable to attack from behind and isolated from reinforcement. When 'L' Company subsequently began their attack, that too would also come in from the rear.

The approach across the plain would have to be as quiet as possible until 'K' Company had reached its objective; it was vital to keep the possibility of confusion if things went wrong to a minimum. Movement of the two companies was therefore separated by an hour, as both had to use the only marked route through the minefields. This time-difference did mean, however, that when deploying for the assault each company could use the same forming-up position and start-line.

The arrangements for securing the start-line, for which the Welsh Guards had been tasked, remained a nagging worry. It was here that we would be most vulnerable to interference, as the companies moved forward into the assault. Our own Recce Troop was now back having been re-issued with equipment taken from casualties, but Brigade HQ was reluctant to stand down the Welsh Guards. Frustratingly, we had not managed to discuss the project with them in any detail. Although their CO had flown up from Bluff Cove on one occasion I had been away on 'Tara'. Now we were told that the Guards might not be able to send anyone to our 'O' Group. I therefore decided to send them a liaison officer with a radio, to move with their Battalion HQ. He would have to fly down to Bluff Cove after the orders tomorrow. Whatever happened, it was essential that we remained in communication when our leading elements reached the start-line, so close to the enemy.

That night, Guy and I repacked our kit in the back of the cherished Bandwagon. What a difference its flat, dry bench had made to my back, and how effectively we had been able to plan and write upon its hinged table. We were now leaving such luxury for rocks and ponchos again. The vehicles could come no further forward. We drained the remnants of a bottle of vodka that someone had left us, and warily discussed the plan for tomorrow. It was my plan and not Guy's, although he would have to implement it if something happened to me. Nevertheless, it would have been unfair to have sought reassurance for my own decisions and worrying to have sensed a lack of confidence in his reply. This then must be the 'loneliness of command' – maintaining a solitary self-confidence. I rolled myself gratefully into the comfort of my 'green slug'.

I lay awake, having deliberately not written a last letter home. That would have been tempting fate too far! In any case, I had sent one off only a day or two before; perhaps the next would be written from Stanley, if the enemy cracked quickly. We were all gambling on that. But if the defenders hung on and absorbed our initial assault, then the Brigade would be left precariously far out on a lonely limb. I thought of those who would be leading 'Four-Two's' assault – Collins, Weston, McMillan, Beadon, Babbington, Wheen. Then I decided to worry no more!

Brigadier Julian came up the next day to wish us well, walking round the tense Commando HQ, puffing cheerfully on his pipe and radiating self-confidence. But for the first time I realized that he was anxious about the defences we were taking on, and the casualties we might suffer. He reminded me that the Welsh Guards, now augmented by two companies from our comrades in 40 Commando, were ready in reserve. 'Try not to get bogged down, Nick – maintain the momentum for as long as you can.' I knew what he meant, and later I would pass on similar sentiments to Peter and David. The gaunt frame of Max Hastings was also among us, looking as warlike and weatherbeaten as the rest. Knowing his knack of judging where the most exciting action would be, I was uncertain whether to be flattered or frightened by his presence. But he seemed to have brought us luck on Mount Kent, where he and I had last seen each other. It was good to forget the tension for a moment or two in a swift conversation about the outside world and its happenings. Another 'hack' was Kim Sabido from Independent Radio News, who came to me for my permission to accompany 'L' Company into the assault. I was very dubious about that; not only from concern for his safety, but also for fear that he could inhibit, even endanger, those around him. A company attack in the dark, across steep terrain and under fire was going to be a hazardous undertaking demanding total concentration from all concerned. No one would have time to safeguard a 'civvy', or look after him if he got into trouble. 'Fully understood', said Sabido courageously. As David Wheen was happy to take him along, I let him go.

Throughout the morning various advisers and controllers appeared, each of them adding another string to our powerful bow. They included Captain Nigel Bedford RA, a Naval Gunfire Support Controller who had already lived dangerously in this war on a series of Special Forces operations similar to the Pebble Island raid. Bright and entertaining by nature, he contrived to look smooth and relaxed whatever the circumstances and the pressures. For this attack, he would be directing the fire of HMS *Yarmouth*, a Rothesay Class frigate whose accurate twin 4.5-inch guns could provide the equivalent of a battery of artillery in support. Another adviser was Lieutenant Andy Newcombe from 3 Commando Brigade Air Squadron. The squadron had already lost several aircraft in action, and we were all aware how vulnerable his two Gazelle helicopters would be on the following day. I planned to hold them back until dawn, when we should be able to fly Blowpipe forward on to 'Zoya'. But casevac or crisis could change all that.

Early that afternoon, everyone was assembled for the 'O' Group with the company commanders in the front row, ranged in alphabetical order from left to right. Behind them sat David Brown with his FOOs, the Forward Air Controller, other advisers, officers from Commando HQ, the RSM, the Adjutant, and a few others, including Max Hastings. It was a numbingly cold, grey and cheerless occasion. I was only too conscious that I must convince these exhausted, anxious professionals that we had a sound and workable plan. For a moment my self-confidence wavered. What would they think when the hazards of the approach became apparent? How difficult would it be to fight through those precipitous crags along the crestline? Could we really reorganize in time against counter-attack? Why wasn't Tac HQ with the assault? ... But a glance along the line of familiar faces reassured me that they wanted to believe in this enterprise, to commit themselves to it. There seemed no hint of confusion or scepticism – concentration appeared absolute, expressions receptive, notation unhesitating. After a while I noticed that one of the sentries had fallen asleep among the rocks behind us. It seemed a good omen that he could feel so relaxed about plans for his own destiny.

In *Battle for the Falklands*, Max Hastings recalled that I concluded the 'O' Group by emphasizing that we would be fighting the decisive battle of the war. The truth of that needed little emphasis. We all knew the plan had to work. There could be no second attempt on the same scale. One of my incidental recollections is of a semi-humorous plea for conservation of the anti-tank ammunition, in case we were attacked by the enemy armoured cars. The tale of Marine Fisk's exploit with the 66-mm rocket had now done the rounds, and there were clearly many who wished to emulate him ... Later, when Guy described the orders in his diary, he began:

> *FRI 11 JUN*   'K' Company moved up to Challenger last night. 'J' Company also moved forward to Wall Mountain Pass by dawn and the CO gave his 'O' Group at 1400. It was bitterly cold with a heavy frost ... The 'O' Group was a cold factual affair with the realization that people were going to be killed tonight. The orders were as follows:
>
> *GROUND*   Hank de Jaeger (IO) described the ground on a model.
>
> *SITUATION*   This included attachments, detachments, and Brigade Orbat (also given by IO).
>
> The CO then came on:
>
> *MISSION*   5 phases, preceded by preliminary phase as follows ...

After Ian had clarified the intricate co-ordination of arrangements, I dealt with the reassuringly few and simple queries that arose. When would the diversion on 'Tara' be activated?

Unless the approach march seemed in danger of detection, the diversion would be withheld until 'K' Company was crossing the start-line. What if mines had been laid on the approach route during the last forty-eight hours? An advance party of sappers under Lieutenant Beadon would detect them and find a way through. Who was responsible for blocking enemy reinforcement from Stanley? Again, Colin Beadon would deny the enemy any advance down that road, using the advance party, 'Porter Troop', and a Milan detachment. There was also the Welsh Guards held in reserve. What about casevac? This was more difficult to answer. In peacetime, we were accustomed to giving priority to casualties, whether on training or in Northern Ireland. Here that could not apply. 'If you find yourselves in a minefield, remember that you *must* go on. Men must not stop for their "oppos", however great the temptation. They *must* go through and finish the attack, or it will cost more lives in the end.' So Max Hastings recorded my answer. I had to stifle my own instincts, asserting and then re-emphasizing that the assault must roll on remorselessly, come what may, until the men these officers would lead were amongst the enemy ... 'I believe that, once we get in among them, they will crack pretty quickly. We want to end up with "Argies" running all the way back across those hills to Port Stanley to show the others what is coming to them!' Grim smiles all round, as the cold and cramped 'centurions' gathered their maps and notes together and quietly wished each other luck.

But during this council of war, tragedy struck on the mortar line, now sheltering under the crestline of 'Tara'. Speculatively, or by a malevolent coincidence, the enemy launched a 155-mm salvo which overshot our observers on 'Tara', but crashed amongst the crags behind them. One huge, 95-pound shell somehow tipped over the edge. It burst among the men of Mortar Troop as they were consolidating their base-plate positions. Several marines were horribly injured, including Corporal Jeremy Smith, a charming and intelligent young section commander, and Marine Hagyard, a vociferous and robust member of the 'Four-Two' rugby team. It seemed initially that Hagyard was the most seriously hurt, because he had literally been split open from pelvis to collar-bone. But as the casevac choppers swooped in, despite the incoming barrage, it became apparent that Corporal Smith was mortally wounded with a splinter in his heart. He died on the flight out, our first, forlorn, fatality in the preliminaries to the night's battle. No

one needed reminding that this was going to be a serious business
– we all knew it now. I was terribly depressed by Smith's death.
My undeclared hope had been that 'Four-Two' could quickly
overwhelm the enemy's apprehensive troops with minimal action.
Yet, before we had even begun, a fine young man had lost his life,
and others had been severely wounded. We shouldered our gear
and sombrely took off in Wessex helicopters to the rear of
Challenger.

There we would have to remain until it got dark, lest the
movement forward of a large group festooned with aerials alerted
the enemy to our intentions. I was so concerned to avoid warning
the Argentines that we had prepared a series of bogus radio calls
which indicated no change to our locations or logistics for several
days to come; these were now sent out on the various nets. The
signallers also made vain attempts to contact Lieutenant Tony
Allen, who should by now have been with Battalion HQ of the 1st
Welsh Guards, acting as our liaison officer. Other messages sent
through Brigade HQ also failed to connect us to him, which
boded ominously for co-ordination on the start-line. Even more
disturbingly, a sub-unit of troops from Bluff Cove now began to
move eastwards across the plain towards the area of our
forming-up position. Inevitably they attracted the inaccurate
attention of Argentine artillery. But what worried us was that this
movement must focus the attention of enemy observers on 'Zoya'
onto the very last area we wanted them to notice. More plaintive
calls to Brigade HQ gained us sympathetic concern, but had no
success in preventing the unwelcome movement. I munched
gloomily through a Marine Green version of the Last Supper,
missing Guy's culinary expertise which, in quieter times, would
have surmounted these bleak surroundings.

With an hour or so of daylight left and our preparations to
attack apparently proceeding as planned, Phil Wilson proposed that
he and I should walk the two kilometres or so forward to the
mortar line. There we could try to reassure the shocked and
saddened crews. I readily agreed, toying for a moment with the
idea of leaving my pack behind. But there had been too many
sharp lessons on that score already, and so we left in full regalia.
By the time we got down to the mortars, I realized how much
heavier that was than the patrol load of recent weeks. At the
mortar line, the men had been stunned and subdued by what had
happened, but the Mortar Officer, Lieutenant Dick Rafferty, and

his NCOs had restored morale by galvanizing the troop into strengthening its protection among the rocks. Both Troop Sergeants, Geoff Rudland and Ian Robinson, were displaying particular resolution as, cheerfully but sensitively, they diverted the younger marines from a decline in spirits. (By a cruel twist of fate, these two SNCOs would survive the war only for both to die, one of a residual brain tumour, the other of a heart attack, within two years.) By the time Phil and I had got back up to our original position, it felt as if we had yomped far enough for one day. In reality, the proceedings had only begun.

As twilight settled along the ridges, cloaking us with misty invisibility against distant observation, the Challenger feature seemed to stir and mutter as if awakening from a deep sleep. Like skeins of geese gliding slowly into their night feeding-grounds, the distant silhouettes of laden figures converged into snaking files, tramping silently past towards the sunset. Armed, bowed, blackened, with only eyes glinting from sidelong glances, teeth flashing in an occasional grin of recognition, they moved inexorably on. Occasionally the muffled 'chink' of weapons, or a stifled curse on stumbling, rose above the moist squelch as hundreds of boots crushed acres of tussock, and equipment softly rasped against clothing from the endless movement. Inextricably linked in purpose and manoeuvre, the Commando prowled slowly along the darkening ridge towards the unsuspecting enemy.

On a moonlit night a few weeks before, as the eerie greenish light of the Aurora Borealis flickered across the sky, the RSM and I were standing together by an ice-bound wooden bridge. The rifle companies had glided past us shrouded in white, their skis crackling on crystallized snow granules, as they swished gracefully away across the Arctic landscape. It was a memory that would last for a lifetime, the culmination of twenty-five years of commitment. I had felt so very fortunate then. Here, on this dark evening, each man was camouflaged, burdened with bulky equipment, festooned with deadly weapons. Among them were officers, NCOs and marines whom I knew by name and could recognize instantly. But the gloom now masked personalities with a sinister anonymity. Violence and fear would soon confront each individual. In anticipation, their corporate mass reeked of aggression. Tonight I felt even luckier to be on the same side as them ...

12

OUT OF THE DARKNESS

Eventually it was the turn of Tac HQ, now more than twenty strong, to move on down into the saddle behind 'Tara'. Already grouped and waiting there, the three rifle companies had dumped their large packs and sleeping-bags, which would be flown forward on the following day once our objectives were secure. In the blackness, commands had to be relayed by word of mouth, and men held on to each other's belts as they moved slowly forward. Earlier that day, we had each sewn a white strip of rifle-cleaning flannelette onto our left shoulders, for recognition. This was already beginning to pay off. The weather forecast predicted intermittent moonlight later on. But, for the moment, we shivered in icy darkness, listening gratefully to the distant sounds of an enemy fire mission on someone else.

Although 'Juliet' were reserve company, each troop had a separate, essential task, while Mike Norman and his Company HQ had several, to be performed in sequence as the attack progressed. The first was to organize the assembly area, which he described afterwards in a letter:

Everything then happened at the rush: it seemed that no sooner had I hiked forward to the new Company position, explained the various tasks, than the first of the unit started to arrive as the daylight faded. Organising an assembly area is an easy task; getting other commanders to comply with your plan when they arrive with their own preconceived ideas is another matter. In addition, all our clientele were engrossed in thoughts of their forthcoming battle and couldn't, or wouldn't, get over excited

169

about troop dumps and straight lines.

'K' were the first Company in and the first to go, but even a cool operator like Babbington was obviously troubled by his thoughts and was putting off that initial step of leaving. I found an apprehensive Peter in deep and dilatory thought. I asked 'Have you got everything?' 'I think so', he replied – together we did a quick finger check off, then just stood very close facing each other. I grabbed his hand, shook it and said 'I'll see you at first light at the top, then.' He said 'I'll be there', and disappeared into the darkness with his company. I knew what he'd been thinking because we'd had a very quick word at the end of the 'O' Group. I'm not a particularly religious man, but I offered a silent prayer for my very good friend, but then cursed him soundly as I realised he'd gone without his Milan Section and that I would have to tell the CO we'd screwed it up already! [They caught up at the track.]

Timings to move out had already been given, so radio codewords would merely confirm progress at various checkpoints. Colin Beadon and his advance party had already set off down to the track below. Guy and Phil Wilson were ensconced in the Mortar Troop HQ, where they would remain, unscathed, we hoped, in case they had to take over command. On the Brigade radio net, a staff officer was plausibly and convincingly explaining, in clear speech, that fuel shortages would delay movement forward for several days ...

Immediately after the Commando 'O' Group, Matt Sturman had taken me aside to urge that he should be allowed to go with 'Porter Troop'. There were, he argued, enough officers of the required experience in Main HQ, and so he could be far more useful forward with this untried organization, which we had created to defend against counter-attacks. It was a characteristic request from a dedicated officer who had volunteered to accompany the Commando in the first place, and whose calm professionalism might prove decisive in unforeseen circumstances. I said that he could go. Soon he would begin to lead 'Porter Troop' off down 'Tara's' rough slope, a tactical distance behind 'K' Company, who had begun their move as soon as Beadon had reported that he had crossed the track.

Now that the concentration area was clearing, Tac HQ could also move out on to its chosen vantage point high on 'Tara's' southern shoulder. We were not the first to appreciate its tactical dominance, for the Argentines had obligingly constructed a spacious peat bunker there around a stone sheep-pen. Whether it would have withstood the impact of a 155-mm shell was doubtful, but it gave a little shelter from the piercing wind, and some convenient platforms on which to lay the radio sets. From there we had a panoramic view of the plain below, with the track winding a ghostly trail around the base of the Challenger and Harriet features. In the distance the sea shimmered and foamed, although the gloom of the ground below us seemed reassuringly impenetrable, except where those pale lakes and paths could be discerned. But there was already the faint, luminous hint of light behind the clouds as the moon began to rise over the horizon.

The advance party, consisting of 9 Troop from 'J' Company, with engineers and anti-tank elements in support, was already behind time: the Milan teams could not sustain the pace as they struggled over the rough going under their crushing burdens. There was nothing to do now but wait as patiently as possible, monitoring progress, reacting to the unforeseen, praying that our luck would hold. As if to emphasize the last aspect, I found myself whispering quietly with Albert Hempenstall, the Chaplain, while we gazed out over the plain on which so many lives were now being hazarded. The 'Padre' was popular within the unit, and always present in adversity, while his transparent sincerity made him the approachable figure his appointment demanded. The marines also respected him for his long experience with the Green Beret: 'That vicar's slept in more dank bivvies than you've had hot dinners, my son', I once heard a section commander declaring to some new intake. How much solace and compassion would Albert need to draw upon later?

About an hour after 'K' Company had crossed the track, a silvery three-quarter moon sailed provocatively out from behind serried banks of cloud. The effect was most disconcerting. Light and shadow were harshly accentuated everywhere, but at that distance we could detect no movement from the direction we knew our troops to be. However, enemy patrols or listening posts in the area would be a major hazard, although none had been detected there previously. Shortly afterwards, when the Advance Party had just reached the lake in the centre of the plain, the Argentines suddenly put up several starshells. If it had been possible to 'freeze' more rigidly, then we would have done so. David Brown and I deliberated urgently, before our own vengeful salvoes wailed

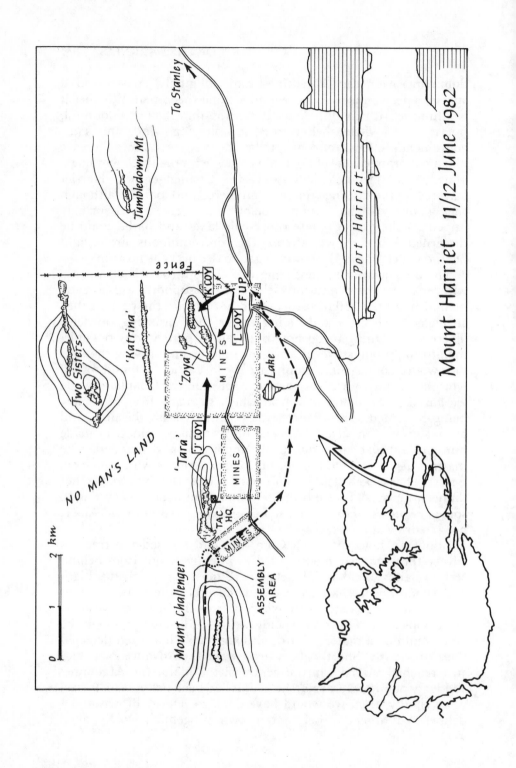

Mount Harriet 11/12 June 1982

above us, to burst among 'Zoya's' nearest crags. For the past two nights, the Argentine defenders there had been regularly harassed with gunfire, so that this sort of diversion would not now seem unusual. Beadon and Babbington reported themselves on the move again, but we held David Wheen's company on our side of the track for the time being. There was silence everywhere else on the 3 Commando Brigade battlefront, although hundreds of commandos and paras were stalking through the darkness towards their objectives. This time the assault would come in the middle of the night, instead of being the traditional dawn attack.

'L' Company had already had their share of problems. In the blackness of the concentration area someone had accidentally fired his rifle. Such an accident is always a hazard, although the risk of detection at that distance from the enemy was luckily not a worry. Nor, by a miracle, was anyone hurt. But the company had been unsettled by the incident, and the marine concerned would have to go into battle knowing that he would later be charged for the offence and heavily fined for negligence – providing he survived. Then, on the way down the track, the Sergeant-Major had begun to sense that all was not well in one of the leading troops, and had gone forward to check. In a rear section he came upon a laudable but extreme manifestation of the 'buddy' system that is emphasized throughout the Commando course. A marine who had joined us just before sailing had somehow completed his training despite a congenital defect which prevented him from keeping his balance over uneven ground in the dark. With misguided loyalty and resourcefulness, his mate had rigged up a length of cord between them, pathetically attempting to provide a handhold when he stumbled. The cord was severed and the encumbrance left behind with the large packs.

On two more occasions the dreaded starshells cast a baleful glow over this wilderness, on which two rifle company groups and assorted teams of supporters skulked in the shadows. Each time we invoked retribution in the form of artillery and naval gunfire support. The shells burst in vicious conflagrations along the crestline, 105-mm with a lurid, red flash, the 4.5-inch shells with an evil greenish glow that seemed to rise up from the stricken target. It was odd to listen to the calm, almost casual exchanges between Nigel Bedford and HMS *Yarmouth*, nearly ten miles out to sea. Under his direction she could put down a devastatingly accurate weight of fire at minimal notice. No sooner had he passed the target co-ordinates than the horizon flickered, a prelude to the sound of the salvoes howling in from the sea. Despite this increasing disruption to the night, however, we did not seem to have been detected, and no enemy machine-guns or artillery sought to interfere with our progress. 'L' Company crossed the track and set off, an hour or so behind 'K'.

Not long afterwards, Colin Beadon reported that he had reached the forming-up position. This was important news. It indicated that the original route was still clear, and that 9 Troop had now marked it for the rifle companies following. Beadon would now secure the area and deploy his Milan firing posts covering the route from Stanley, before moving off in search of the Welsh Guards on the start-line. We had heard nothing from them as yet, nor had our liaison officer managed to get through to us on the radio. The various delays were frustrating both company commanders. They were understandably under pressure, and some crisp dialogue had already taken place about holding up the advance and maintaining the separation between sub-units. I heard Max Hastings chuckling in the background at one of the more explicit sallies. The 'Four-Two' command net was known for its volatility, which was clearly amusing him. There was no point in suddenly becoming tactful and sympathetic now – that might really have created alarm and despondency!

Beadon reported no sign of the Guards along the fence we had selected as a start-line. In the event of failing to communicate, we had agreed a rendezvous time with them, but this had long since passed. Soon Peter would be approaching the forming-up position, where I was anxious he should not have to linger. 'Shall we secure it ourselves?' asked Colin. 'Yes!' we told him swiftly. There remained, however, the imponderable threat of that missing Guards group bumping into either ourselves or the enemy at this crucial period. We spoke to Brigade HQ, imploring them to try and contact 5 Brigade, find out what was happening, and order the Welsh Guards to recall their Recce Troop.

While this was happening Colin had secured the start-line with our own people, and was moving back down towards the FUP. Suddenly he detected movement on his left. Peering through his image intensifier, he observed a small group of men in amongst the rocks several hundred metres away. Their hoods resembled British windproofs, but they were west of the fence line, so he was wary of confronting them from the enemy's direction. After a circuitous approach he got close enough to be reasonably certain. Bravely stepping forward with his hands raised, he found to his relief they were the Guardsmen. The sighs of relief must have been audible in Stanley. But there was no more time to be lost. 'K' Company had by now been stalled in the FUP for some time. We told Colin to hold where he was, and released 'K' Company. Beadon wrote later: ' "K" Company filed past us one by one, led by Sergeant Collins from out of the darkness. It was an awe-inspiring sight! I could not help noticing the amazed expressions of the Welsh Guardsmen ...'

Meanwhile, we had been shaken by a different and even more worrying development. 'L' Company suddenly came up on the air to declare that they had strayed off the route. They were still confident of maintaining direction towards the FUP from the silhouette of the mountain, but crossing this unknown ground would be desperately dangerous. One detonation amongst the tip-toeing troops would signal the horror that one of our companies was trapped in a minefield. The area might then be saturated with artillery or mortar fire, although there at least they were furthest away from those machine-guns. For the moment, 'Lima' Company was casting about to see if it could retrace its steps to the marked track. We waited in numbed tension as the cold deepened and the moon began to reach her zenith. Already we were well behind time. Any minute now, 45 Commando and 3 Para should start their attacks. Brigade HQ had accepted that we would be late, but were concerned that our surprise might be lost when the others clashed. The first firing had just begun from the direction of Mount Longdon when David Wheen informed us that he was back on track, and within striking distance of the FUP. There would be just time for 'K' Company to move out to make room for them.

This was also the moment to activate our deception because, on the far side of 'Zoya', 45 Commando had closed with the enemy on Two Sisters.

'Three-One, this is Nine. "Vesuvius". I say again, "Vesuvius". Over.' 'Three-One. "Vesuvius". Wilco. Out.' As this exchange crackled across the frozen air waves, a spectacular *son et lumière* was enacted above 'Tara's' eastern crags. Explosions, lights, small-arms fire and blood-curdling yells riveted attention in that direction. Almost immediately, these provoked the gratifying sight of Argentine tracer arching out towards the source of disturbance.

Next moment, night turned into day as our mortars illuminated the western end of 'Zoya'. In synchronized sequence the parachutes floated down, their accusing arcs of light lingering over the sources of enemy fire. Agonizing moments later, several Milan missiles 'whooshed' up from below and streaked towards their targets. Milan seems to have an almost leisurely time of flight, the missile twisting disconcertingly as the computer corrects it onto the point of aim. That never seemed more nerve-racking than now. Surely the enemy machine-gun teams would cease firing and take cover? Or were they mesmerized by those thunderbolts approaching them? But even if the missiles homed in, we were uncertain that they would prove effective amongst the crags.

Our doubts proved unfounded. The magnitude of the explosions was overwhelming, even from where we stood. For an instant some tracer cartwheeled across the sky, before fading away. Then the chatter of those weapons was stilled. It was a great moment, and as we passed the news to the mortar line I could hear their shouts of excitement in the distance behind us. Later, I was reminded that each Milan missile cost the same as a Renault 17 TL estate car. Cheap at the price – although most of 'Four-Two' couldn't afford to buy a new car themselves!

Now the tension became almost unbearable. 'K' Company had crossed the start-line and was ascending the exposed half-mile or so of steep uneven slope. At the top, long established in their rocky fastness, were numerous enemy soldiers whose alertness and determination would remain uncertain for only as long as surprise could be maintained. The earlier 'K' Company was detected, the more costly it would be for them as they closed with the defenders. We did not believe that this approach from the rear was mined, because our original patrols had observed enemy movement there. But a separate concern was whether wire obstacles protected the actual position, since these would seriously impede our final rush forward. Yard by yard, like some Nelsonian leadsman chanting the depth from the bows of a man-o'-war, Peter Babbington began to murmur their progress into the radio: 'One hundred metres, nothing to report. Two hundred ...' After 500 I began to wonder if the enemy might have run away. At 700 metres, the silhouette of Mount Harriet's jumbled ridge began to loom over 'K' Company. Suddenly adrenalin raced with the words everyone had been waiting for: 'One-Nine. Contact. Wait. Out.' Peter, retaining the initiative, had decided to engage some enemy to his front seconds before the Argentines would inevitably open fire ...

At last, the fight was on! In Tac HQ we could only monitor the radio nets and observe the myriad of explosions and tracer now erupting from that area. During planning, we had discussed how the rifle companies could most effectively maintain radio control. They had opted for having everyone down to the section commanders on the same net; there were, therefore, far more stations than usual talking to each other. But on the other hand everyone knew what was going on, which is vital in these circumstances. Monitoring 'K' Company's command net now provided a vivid impression of the vicious, close-quarter fighting in which they were engaged:

'One-Nine. Three. Go left. Go left. They're bugging out behind you! Use grenades. Use eighty-fours ...'
'Sharkey. We're pinned down, for Christ's sake get a gun group here ...'
'... I've lost a section commander! One of my corporals is down ...'

On the Gunner net the urgent, precise voice of Chris Romberg could be heard constantly designating new targets for our guns. Their fire was being brought down with unerring accuracy almost onto the assaulting groups of marines. Afterwards, none of us doubted the decisive role our gunners had played in this battle. Over 1,000 shells or bombs would fall on 'Zoya' alone that night, all of them instantly, precisely laid to cover movement, suppress defensive fire, break up resistance. They gave us an overwhelming advantage, only too evident from the shattered enemy strong-points, the twitching, cowed prisoners so terrified of their own incoming artillery.

Peter Babbington told me what was going on when he could, passing crisp, taut sitreps that could not disguise his excitement. Later, he told us how he and an elated Romberg had sat upon a prominent rock directing their battle, with the signallers in cover below them. After a while, Babbington had impatiently demanded more microphone lead. He was told stridently that the signallers considered themselves to be under heavy fire and certainly did not feel inclined to expose themselves any further. He commented modestly: 'This is where I think people end up getting awards, because they don't actually realize they're doing anything particularly brave – they're just doing their job, and this means they get exposed to fire.'

The marines of 'K' Company were wreaking havoc among the enemy positions. In the darkness they flitted amongst the crags keeping staccato contact by voice and radio, reporting their movements to each other and warning which weapon was being used. The 66-mm and 84-mm anti-tank shells provided the shock action upon which they could close with a dazed enemy. Already Argentines were throwing down their weapons and raising their hands. But some were shot by their own side as they threw down their arms. Where this occurred, 'K' Company meted out swift and ruthless retribution to those Argentine officers or NCOs trying to stiffen resistance. From the beginning, we had said that the enemy must be allowed to surrender, or he would fight more desperately. In these crucial minutes the momentum of the rifle sections never faltered as, urged on by eager troop officers, they began to overrun a confused and faltering enemy.

Inevitably, 'K' Company's casualties began to mount. Corporal Lawrence Watts, a most professional young NCO, was shot through the heart as he led the rush onto an enemy strong-point. Corporal Steve Newland was hit in both legs as he single-handedly took out a heavy machine-gun position. The Company second-in-command, Lieutenant Chris Whiteley, was scythed down by shrapnel. It was, of course, what we had expected, the junior leaders taking the brunt of the casualties as they led from the front. Quoted in Max Arthur's book *Above All Courage*, Corporal Newland's initiative and courage epitomizes that of them all:

I thought, 'Shit, I'm on my own!' So I sat and had a quick think. Then having made up my mind I picked up my SLR (rifle), changed the magazine and slipped the safety-catch. I then looped the pin of one grenade onto one finger of my left hand and did the same with another. I was ready. So I thought, 'Well, you've got to do something.' I pulled one grenade, WHACK – straight at the spics. I dodged back round the rock and heard two bangs. As soon as they'd gone off I went in and anything that moved got three rounds ...

Peter Babbington now confirmed that his company were sufficiently established for 'L' Company to cross the start-line. This they did with text-book alacrity, hardly pausing to change formation. There would be no silent approach for them, though. The enemy on 'Zoya' were thoroughly alerted, and almost immediately the company moved into a deluge of machine-gun fire. Several casualties went down in those first few minutes, including the second-in-command Ian Stafford from the Argyll and Sutherland Highlanders, and Julian Pusey, one of the troop commanders. Kim Sabido of IRN was alongside Ian when he was hit and stayed with him for a while to try to help, all the time coolly recording the clamour of battle about them.

At Commando HQ, we listened anxiously as it became clear that 'Lima's' suppressive fire was threatening 'Kilo's' advance down the ridge, but both company commanders resolved that by decisive co-ordination between them. Then David Wheen began a steady advance towards his objective opposite Tac HQ's position, as Captain Nick D'Apice, his FOO, brought down a series of surgically accurate fire missions. Under their cover 'Lima's' advance gathered pace. Casualties lessened, although they were to face through the night a series of close-quarter engagements against a forewarned and more resolute enemy. In the end I had to reallocate the capture of 'Katrina' to 'K' Company, because at dawn 'L' Company was still fighting for its last objectives.

Visually, this tableau of twentieth-century infantry in battle was electrifying. The moon, appearing from behind scudding wisps of cloud, cast a chill pallor upon the black-etched silhouette of the bombarded mountain. Raining intermittently upon its summit were concentrations of red and yellow flashes, afterwards obscured in thick smoke or incandescent clouds of phosphorus. The naval shells seemed virtually to drop in the same hole each time, round after round, with a shower of sparks as though there was an iron foundry on the hillside. Rising above the chaos, Argentine flares burst almost hysterically, as if hoping to dispel the fog of battle and freeze the combatants. Red tracer floated aimlessly across the sky, sometimes bouncing abruptly upwards like sparks from a firework display. In the pool of darkness, in which we had our box at this amphitheatre, muffled, shivering figures peered incredulously out towards the inferno. From there, the disembodied voices in our earphones calmly reported progress.

The climax of this spectacle stole upon the scene almost unnoticed. A small white light began to move slowly seawards from the direction of Stanley. Totally absorbed in our own affairs, I distractedly assumed that it must be a helicopter. Then suddenly, as the angle of refraction changed, this light became a streak which accelerated out to sea at ever-increasing speed. Suddenly we realized that it must be a missile. 'My God, it's an Exocet!' someone cried, as we remembered with horror that intelligence had warned that the enemy might have some of the missiles mounted on vehicles. Nigel Bedford instinctively sensed the target and began urgently warning the bombarding ships. But there were only seconds left. As we watched, the doomed target reacted with a desperate release of two of her own missiles. Against a star-spangled background, the glowing red retaliation of HMS *Glamorgan*'s missiles confronted, then by-passed, the racing flash of the Exocet just before it struck. For one unforgettable instant we saw the shape of a warship emblazoned against the darkness. Then there was a distant explosion as she went off the air and disappeared from view. All of us were certain that we had witnessed the sinking of a second Royal Navy destroyer.

We reported the dismal event to Brigade HQ, and were reminded that time to complete our reorganization on 'Zoya' for the next phase was running out. If each unit had gone firm on its objective by first light, the plan was to continue the attacks onto the next Argentine positions. In our case, the next objective would be Mount William. But I doubted whether we could now be ready, and said so. For the moment, it was imperative to get Tac HQ and 'J' Company moving up to 'Zoya', or we would be overtaken by the dawn before we had got there. David Wheen could at last confirm that the enemy opposite on 'Tara' were too preoccupied to interfere with movement below them. The cumbersome, vulnerable Tac HQ was urgently assembled and we lumbered down the mountainside, with Mike Norman and 10 Troop, 'J' Company, providing protection. The 'Strolling Players' of 11 Troop, who had staged such a successful diversion, would hold on to 'Tara' until we were established on 'Zoya'.

On the way down, I realized that we weren't going to reach the far end of 'Zoya' by daylight if we followed the cleared route across the plain. For a time I kept this to myself while the risky alternative raced through my mind. Eventually I revealed the stark option to Ian McNeill, hoping that he would talk me out of it; 'Yes, Colonel, that's what we'll have to do', was how he replied. He then reminded me that our assault engineers, who could clear mines, were in the FUP with Colin Beadon. Next I tried the RSM. 'Very good, Sir. Presumably 10 Troop will provide protection in front of us?' was all he said. At the track Mike Norman was waiting, so I told him too. Was it my imagination, or did that massive bulk seem to sway momentarily? But he asked only: 'Are you sure that's what you want to do?' 'Yes, we must,' I said reluctantly. 'Right!' he replied in ringing tones, 'I'll lead a buggers' rush down the road and we won't stop for anything.' Before anyone could argue, he was off. We all followed in varying degrees of trepidation. Halfway along what seemed to be an illuminated race-track, I realized Marine Green did not appreciate that the road might be mined. It would have been cruel to have spoiled his blissful ignorance; I merely hoped others were equally unaware. Above us 'L' Company's battle raged noisily on. It was becoming very obvious that 'Zoya' was now being heavily shelled by the enemy as well as ourselves.

Breathless but unscathed, we arrived at the original forming-up position where confusion seemed to reign. Amidst the lightening gloom, a mass of dishevelled, bemused figures meandered listlessly about at the edge of the road. It took me a moment or two to realize that they were prisoners, but not much longer to recognize that they outnumbered us! A marine swathed in a poncho and seated on some rocks, smoking casually, seemed to be in charge. The RSM stalked indignantly over, to find that it was the irrepressible Corporal Newland. He had been carried down by some of the POWs, and was now constructively awaiting casevac ...

Even as we stood talking to an elated Matt Sturman, urgently sending 'Porter Troop' forward up 'Zoya' and co-ordinating the evacuation of casualties off her slopes, more and more prisoners surged on to the road. But here they could be rounded up by Sergeant Shiel, revelling in his responsibilities as Provost Sergeant. Eventually 'Four-Two' would take nearly 300 POWs. The escape route was now blocked for an enemy confounded by surprise, and overwhelmed by the momentum of 'K' Company's attack. Somewhere among them, although I did not realize it at the time, was my counterpart, Lieutenant-Colonel Diego Alejandro Sona, the CO of 4th Infantry Regiment. He was later flown back to Brigade HQ, where I eventually read the report of his interrogation:

... The CO looked utterly crestfallen and shattered by the events of the night. A search revealed two diaries, the first being one which detailed his activity on the Falkland Islands since he arrived in early April. It even included the dates when he had been able to have baths at the Upland Goose Hotel and when he made telephone calls to his wife Susanna in Buenos Aires ... His regiment had walked to Mount Wall where the troops had suffered considerably from the approaching winter. It had been difficult to dig in because of the rocky earth and therefore the soldiers had built sangars. At the beginning of April the Regiment had been withdrawn to defend Mount Harriet ... Lt. Colonel Sona said that his troops had experienced great difficulty in building good defensive positions and earthworks not only because of the rocks but also because of the patrol activity in and around the features ... Lt. Colonel Sona was shaken by the loss of his Regiment but he remained dignified and aloof, refusing to answer any questions on Argentinian deployments. He said he had not expected to be attacked in such force and in such a subtle manner ...

Someone who did have a direct experience of involuntary surrender an hour or so later was Marine Andrew Timms. 'J' Company was taking over from 'K' Company on the eastern end of 'Zoya'. Intent on relieving himself before first light and the expected counter-attack, Timms slipped behind a large boulder. He found himself confronting ten armed Argentines who immediately surrendered to him. Afterwards he wryly observed that the only reason he didn't throw down his own weapon was because the Argentines were quicker. Had he understandably done so, Timms would have been a unique statistic – the only man to have been taken prisoner twice in this war. (His first experience had been at Government House!)

In chilling contrast to the satisfying spectacle of columns of dejected POWs, the RSM led me to a shallow quarry where several rows of recumbent figures forlornly lay. These were our wounded, already nearly a dozen, eventually to be almost twice that. Most of them had been hard hit by bullets or shrapnel, so their proximity to death would have been measured in millimetres of ruptured tissue, split seconds of explosive impact. Now their prospects of recovery depended upon immediate stabilization, followed by timely casevac. Already Ross Adley, the doctor, and his medical team were descending down to the track from 'Tara'. These casualties could be moved back once the Regimental Aid Post had been set up beside the track to give immediate treatment. Afterwards they would be flown out as soon as the helicopters could come forward.

It was a harrowing sight. We stepped carefully among the wounded men, crouching down to talk with those who were conscious. Marine Vincent of 'K' Company was engaged to the previous RSM's daughter. I made some pathetic remark about her wheeling him down the aisle soon. Chris Whiteley, who had shrapnel in both legs, was in considerable discomfort. His morphine had not yet taken effect. But Ian Stafford was as high as a kite on his pain-killer, making jokes and complaining that Highland dancing and skiing wouldn't be so easy from now on. For others, it seemed that merciful oblivion had insulated them from pain and shock. I will always recall, however, a pair of desperate, hollowed eyes staring into mine from the pallor of a white, sweating face. As if to intensify the wounded men's agony, Argentine artillery fire began to fall ever closer to the road. It seemed so callous to leave them now, but we must press on or Tac HQ would never reach the top by first light. 'J' Company had been sent on already, so that 'K' could fight through on to 'Katrina'. We began our weary ascent.

For the first time in this war I began to worry about my physical endurance. During the night everyone else had seemed to be shivering constantly but, for once, I had felt indifferent to the cold. Obviously this must have been because of my total preoccupation with the attack. Now I seemed drained of energy following our gallop along the track, which had proved quite arduous. Perhaps it wasn't too surprising, because the attack had now been going for ten hours and, like most people, I had had several jarring falls in the dark on the way down. As our pace slackened I feared that this time it was not just an overloaded signaller slowing us down. Ian reassured me that everyone was flagging. This encouragement was then compromised by the indefatigable Chisnall, who paced up beside me to offer to carry my equipment as well as his own! He probably could have done, but such selflessness goaded me to press on through what had suddenly become a swirling blizzard.

.As the slope steepened into the rocky outcrops of 'Zoya's' upper ridge, we seemed like pilgrims wandering in some biblical wilderness. Out of the swirling murk we would suddenly come across small groups assisting disabled figures to stumble down the mountainside. Sometimes they were Argentine, made all the more macabre by their dark, flapping cloaks. All too often it was 'Porter Troop' bringing back our own wounded. Beyond the snow flurries, shells howled and crashed among the crags. Small-arms fire crackled continuously in the background. We began to come upon abandoned weapons and equipment, which meant that we must be entering the defensive positions. Not much further on this was confirmed when we found the first bodies huddled grotesquely outside rock sangars.

Unexpectedly the jubilant voice of Peter Babbington called down to us from what seemed to be a fifty-foot cliff. For so long he had been an insubstantial voice from the chaos of battle that it seemed unreal we should meet again now. A last, sinew-tearing scramble, then there he was, standing jauntily on a humped ridge that ran off on both sides into the darkness. 'Colonel', he said, 'I reckon we've done it ...'

I ought to relate that we shook hands, danced a jig, drained an Argentine 'dram', or slapped each other on the back. The fact that we didn't shows how jaded I must have been, because Peter and his team positively glowed with energy and aggression. They had 'a real buzz on', as he subsequently described it. This seemed to override completely all the fatigue and strain of their protracted approach and the vicious fighting.

'J' Company was now firm at this end, while 'L' Company had pushed the enemy off the positions facing 'Tara', although there was still some resistance from the depth positions towards Two Sisters. I couldn't see any last-minute resistance stopping 'K' Company now. So we released them and they swarmed off towards 'Katrina' like hounds from the meet. Mount Harriet was ours!

13

SURRENDER

While darkness paled into dawn, a weary calm temporarily settled over our mountains. Snow flurries died away with the diminishing artillery. The frosty panorama of last night's battle gradually began to emerge. 'Katrina', in silhouette half a mile to the north, etched an image of Stonehenge buttresses laid end to end. Beyond those serried granite battlements that separated us, we could observe 45 Commando consolidating on the twin peaks of Two Sisters. A mile or so beyond them, we looked down into the saddle and forward slopes of Mount Longdon. There 3 Para was skirmishing even now, as the distant crackle of small arms and crump of explosions testified. Ominously, it was also apparent that the Argentine positions on Mount Tumbledown, directly opposite us, actually overlooked them. The sun silhouetted Tumbledown's dark crags, two miles away across an open, boulder-strewn valley. I felt relieved not to be out there with 45 Commando, attempting to maintain the momentum of a second attack. We could never have reached Mount Tumbledown before dawn. Instead, we would have been caught, weary and exposed to a fresh enemy protected by another formidable feature. That mountain, however, now became the vital ground. It had to be seized as soon as possible, because all our new positions were vulnerable to harassing fire directed from its vantage points.

Our immediate surroundings filled me with admiration for what the rifle companies had achieved in close-quarter fighting along the length of 'Zoya'.

The spine of Harriet is a jumble of crags which provides a natural fortress for defenders, and an endless series of obstacles to an attacker. Strewn amongst the rocks were weapons, equipment, ammunition, clothing, blankets. Here and there, a grey-clad body lay huddled. Upturned rifles, each supporting a helmet, indicated others. Further up the ridge, towards 'Tara', the burning tentage that had attracted so much enemy fire during the night still smouldered sullenly. Not far away there was the astonishing sight of a new and undamaged Mercedes-Benz jeep, fitted with leather seats and a tinted windscreen. Everywhere there was filth. In particular, there were heaps of foul-smelling ordure, where Argentine soldiers had apparently dropped their trousers on impulse. We were to discover this disgusting trademark in all the positions we occupied, and found it incredible that the enemy seemed to avoid widespread disease. After the war some journalists suggested that deliberate fouling had been an Argentine policy. That may have been so in Stanley, but out here there had been no time for such futile contamination. Marines can hardly be described as fastidious beings at the best of times, but we were all revolted by what we found. There was, however, no choice but to remain for protection among the enemy's old positions.

Prisoners were still a major headache. Many frightened defenders had prudently crawled into the rocks, where they remained hidden until daylight. Then, dazed and apprehensive, they tentatively revealed themselves, or were rooted out by the searching marines. 'L' Company had consolidated on the furthest strong-point opposite 'Tara' by dawn. WO2 Cameron March, their indomitable Sergeant-Major, was brewing himself a well deserved drink of hot chocolate when, through the steam and gloom, he noticed a group of marines returning to Company HQ. They appeared disorganized, and were sky-larking about with captured helmets. Without diverting himself from his long-awaited brew, he delivered a crisp rebuke on the fatal risks of complacency, and of being mistaken for the enemy. Only when the group remained hovering round him did he peer more closely. The 'marines' were actually Argentines! They were subsequently sent on down towards Commando HQ, where more than fifty had now been assembled. All were extremely nervous of us, and obviously terrified of the shell-fire which ranged malevolently round 'Zoya'.

Eventually the irresistible urge of an RSM to take charge overwhelmed David Chisnall. He confronted the enemy rabble with mime: 'Walk slowly down to the road and all will be well', the charade said. 'Run and these machine-guns will be turned upon you.' The reaction consisted of anxious murmurs, followed by gesticulations of despair. Then the prisoners began to mill around in increasing panic. Clearly communication had not been successfully established, so the Provost Sergeant now tried out his Costa Brava patois. He discovered almost immediately that the POWs believed they had been ordered to run – before being shot! They were reassured by their amused captors, with some difficulty, that nothing so sinister had been planned. But it was quite obvious that these conscripts had been told to expect no quarter from the British. Later, a similar tragi-comedy was enacted at the road below. Albert Hempenstall, wearing his Padre's 'dog collar', benignly approached a group of enemy prisoners. Almost immediately some of them began to weep pathetically in evident anticipation of the last rites. It all made me wonder what our own prospects might have been had we been the vanquished.

Meanwhile, Tac HQ was preoccupied with reorganization and the precautions that would have to be taken against counter-attack. 'J' and 'L' Companies were firmly in position at either end of our mountain feature. But reinforcement with support weapons, and their registration on to predicted defensive fire targets, was an urgent requirement. Guy had managed to get up to join us not long after dawn. He now undertook the complex arrangements for replenishment of ammunition, replacement of damaged or missing equipment, and the flying-forward of sleeping-bags. It was desperately cold in the windchill, and the exhausted marines would be particularly susceptible to exposure now we were static again. Brigade HQ had already warned that there would be no move in the next twenty-four hours.

The main enemy threat came obviously from the direction of Mount Tumbledown. 'J' Company, at that end, must therefore have priority in supporting fire arrangements. Luckily Mike Norman was another specialist in this field, and he now put his knowledge to real advantage by utilizing the captured weaponry as well as our own. Once it was light enough the Argentine heavy machine-guns were re-sited. When, shortly afterwards, a group of enemy stragglers appeared on the track below Tumbledown, these guns were given a most successful 'user trial' by a gleeful Sergeant Shiel. An equally unexpected advantage was the captured concentration of four 120-mm mortars, with a stockpile of several hundred HE bombs. These heavy and cumbersome tubes have a range of more than 6,000 yards, and so could be brought to bear on to all the likely enemy approaches. The alert sentries had already pinpointed a mass of Argentine troops inside some quarries about two miles down the track. We decided to disperse these before they could get up to any mischief. Mike Norman cheerily invited me to fire the ranging shots. I found this extremely exhilarating, because the huge bomb's time of flight was so extended; having pulled the firing lever, one could dash up onto the crest in time to observe its impact. After a few near misses the nerves of the irresolute enemy gave out and they retreated in disarray towards Stanley. All of which provided a cheering diversion for the chilled, wearied, but still smiling marines of 'J' Company and Commando HQ.

Leaving Guy with the Battery Commander to consolidate the defensive arrangements, the RSM and I moved on to see 'K' Company. They had been withdrawn from 'Katrina' after clearing that area, which was then handed over to 'L' Company. Now they were in reserve halfway along the ridge. Peter Babbington gathered them together in a protected hollow amongst the crags, where I could say a few words to them.

'K' Company was a moving sight. Weatherbeaten, grimy and dishevelled, the marines formed a ferocious semi-circle around us. Swathed in bandoliers of bullets, festooned with grenades, they leaned lightly on their weapons, inhaling wearily on captured cigarettes. Some had minor injuries covered with khaki field dressings. Others were cloaked against the cold in the heavy Argentine blankets they had captured. Inevitably, one's concern was focused on two overwhelming impressions. The first was their pathetically sodden feet, shifting ceaselessly in the slush. The other those red-rimmed, hollowed eyes that glowed from blackened faces. I really cannot remember what I said. No doubt it echoed so many similar occasions, when exalted commanders have commended exhausted troops for achievements beyond all expectation. I do remember that I envied them their now-exclusive brotherhood. That belongs only, but always, to those who fight at close quarters alongside one another. Each rifle company would retain that special bond for ever. But, if you hadn't been there with them, you could never be a part of it.

Concluding my inadequate few words, I glanced up along the ridge behind us. To my surprise, two low-flying aircraft were just pulling up into a steep ascent about half a mile away. Even as I recognized them as being friendly, each released what seemed to be a massive black canister, which then began to glide down towards us. Never notorious for poker-playing, my face clearly betrayed consternation. A number of men glanced apprehensively behind them, before the whole company hurled themselves to the ground as cries of 'Air attack!' and 'Incoming!' rose up. Only Chisnall and I remained upright. This was not through fortitude (although he might have stood firm), but because by this time it was obvious that the bombs would pass well over our heads and fall on Mount Tumbledown. It was all over in one breathtaking moment, quickly restored with blasphemous humour as someone called out: 'Off your knees, lads. It isn't really Him after all – this one's too small!'

With that alarm over, we then enacted a rare military custom. Rare because it can only take place on operations. Normally promotions to substantive (that is, paid) rank must be authorized through the official pay and records organization, although a CO can grant local unpaid rank in certain circumstances. However, when casualties amongst NCOs must be replaced urgently in battle, a 'field promotion' can be authorized then and there. It was a poignant occasion, the first time any of us had taken part in such ceremony. I promoted Lance-Corporal Steven Sparkes to Acting Corporal to replace his fallen Section Commander Lawrence Watts, with Lance-Corporal Christopher Sheppard in place of the wounded Corporal Newland. Their pride in increased, and very real, responsibility was matched by the obvious approval and support of the rest of the company. That simple, significant ceremony remains another special memory of Mount Harriet and 'Four-Two'.

Next, Tac HQ walked on along 'Zoya's' ridge towards 'L' Company. The natural bastions of rock seemed to provide impenetrable protection, as well as allowing almost complete surveillance of the open ground below. To our consternation, we twice found large image-intensification devices which had been abandoned. They would have given the Argentine defenders a much better chance of detecting our approach had they been assembled, but both were still half unpacked. Earlier, the RSM had spoken to a captured enemy officer who refused to believe that we could have moved as we had done without individual night-viewing devices. Which was all the more reason for them to have constructively used the sophisticated surveillance equipment they possessed and we did not.

Eventually we came upon the machine-gun nests in the outcrop of crags facing 'Tara'. The Milan missiles had certainly wreaked real devastation here. Each gun had been shattered or twisted by the blast, as indeed were the wretched gunners there with them. The fields of fire dominated all approaches from Mount Challenger, as well as routes along the track. Significantly no guns had been sited against an approach from behind, which accounted for the welcome inaccuracy of some of their shooting against 'L' Company in the later stages of the attack. When we reached David Wheen, however, it became obvious that the company had experienced even greater problems than could have been gleaned from the radio. 'Lima' had come under heavy fire from the outset. The Company 2/IC and two marines in Company HQ were shot within 100 metres of crossing the start-line, while a further eight men fell before the summit was reached. Although we had managed to neutralize the machine-guns with Milan, snipers using night-sights had taken a heavy toll. And, for once, the Argentine use of artillery had also been effective. Even after taking eighty-four prisoners, 'L' Company had still been held up by a strong position half way to 'Katrina'. This had to be attacked in strength twice before it was overrun.

By the time we got back to our own positions, the haphazard shelling had settled into a regular and dangerous series of fire missions directed quite accurately into our positions. Casualties began to occur among the companies. Marine Stephen Chubb from 'J' Company, who had taken part in the spirited resistance at South Georgia before capture and repatriation, was seriously wounded by shell splinters. Casevac was now extremely dangerous for the helicopters, which had begun flying in ammunition and sleeping-bags, but were soon forced back to operating from the track below 'Zoya'. Peter Babbington and a working party from 'K' Company had gone down there to pick up stores when he sensed danger. Suddenly they were bracketed by incoming 105-mm shells:

> I told the boys to hurry up as I could feel that a fire mission was coming in on us. Too late, it arrived so we took cover. Meanwhile two marines were moving down towards us from the top of 'Zoya': I remember watching a shell explode between them and they disappeared. Eventually one reappeared and, encouraged by the marines down in the FUP cheering him on, staggered towards us with shells chasing him ...

Later Frank Allen, who had flown forward to co-ordinate this fly-in of stores, had an equally unpleasant experience:

> Shells began landing in the open ground between our position, in a sort of open quarry, and Mount Harriet. Marines from 'J' Company were carrying rations up to the feature and were caught by the shells in the open; two were wounded almost immediately. The shells then tracked down towards us and were landing less than 100 metres away. I had grabbed an Argentine helmet and was moving from hole to hole in the opposite direction from the last explosion ... It was very frightening indeed and the awful dilemma after each explosion was whether to stay put or move.

Five casualties had to be evacuated on this occasion, but there were many minor injuries and some narrow escapes. Notable among these was that of Marine Geoffrey Power in 'K' Company. He was lying in his sleeping-bag alongside his equipment, which included three 84-mm shells. A 105-mm round landed right beside him, exploding the 84-mm and blowing his sleeping-bag clean away. Apart from being a little deaf, Power was completely unhurt, and soon indignantly voluble about the loss of his 'green slug'. There were, too, many fine examples of courage and selflessness. WO2 Fred Cummings, our relentless PT instructor and later Sergeant-Major of 'J' Company, brought in two wounded marines under the heavy barrage that had just injured them.

We soon realized, however, that we were fortunate compared to 3 Para on Mount Longdon. Often most of the long open ridge which they had fought so long and hard to capture was obscured by mushrooming clouds of smoke from savage 155-mm and 105-mm harassment. Over the Brigade radio net came distressing reports of casualties, with constant requests for casevac.

At around midday, Guy considerately urged me to get some sleep. Reorganization was complete, but we had already concluded that it was just too dangerous for both of us to remain together on 'Zoya'. Before dark he and Lance-Corporal Paul Childs, his radio operator, bodyguard and constant companion since South Georgia, would have to withdraw to Main HQ. Sleep was a crucial requirement for all of us, or we should cease to function, so I should rest while he could cover for me. Despite the cold and noise, once rolled up in my USMC poncho under a rock the strain and discomfort slipped away into welcome oblivion. When I awoke, 11 Troop was rejoining from 'Tara', to make us complete. Tac HQ had also been told that the Scots Guards attack on Mount Tumbledown was postponed by twenty-four hours until the following night. Their start-line would be immediately in rear of the 'L' Company positions, and 'Four-Two' was to provide supporting fire. There was also a warning order about a full Brigade 'O' Group which would task us for the next series of attacks. I tried hard to stifle premonitions that the unit couldn't be so lucky next time. The intermediate hours of darkness were spent with Ian McNeill and David Brown in our new and spartan CP, a cleft in the rocks protected by a tarpaulin.

That night it was bitterly cold, with a hard frost and some snow by dawn. In the soft, purple Falklands light the mountains seemed almost inviting under their white shroud. The impact of shells on Mount Longdon, however, followed by the noise of our own counter-bombardment passing overhead, soon dispelled that attractive illusion. I wandered round Tac HQ and 'J' Company during the morning stand-to. How gaunt many people looked now. Often this was those of larger frame and fuller face, rather than the lean or small. We seemed to shrink proportionately like wizened children. Almost everyone was suffering from some sort of problem with their feet, which had been constantly wet and cold for nearly three weeks. No one had changed their clothes since the landings. Shaving had ceased once we had moved forward from San Carlos. As we left Challenger, we had decided that 'personalized' sleeping-bags were a luxury we could no longer afford. They had been dumped centrally, away from the packs, in case only minimal loads could be flown forward. Unpopular though that was, it turned out to be realistic. All that most sub-units received on 'Zoya' was an underslung net-load of sleeping-bags, which could be rotated amongst those allowed to rest. Most smelt absolutely foul and were depressingly damp. But they gave some protection against the chill winds that never ceased to blow.

Later that morning came the unexpected treat of mail. Guy had brought it up as he rejoined for the day. We decided to celebrate with a dram of Argentine Scotch from one of their officer's ration packs. I sipped it appreciatively while reading a humorous despatch from my friends across the Atlantic. The letter had been written while celebrating in that same bar we should have met at, until the abrupt summons to war. Jim Goldsworthy, who joined the Royal Marines the same year as me, was a colonel on the NATO staff in Norfolk, Virginia. He would have traded anything he possessed to be in this war with us. Typically, that was not allowed to show in his light-hearted urgings to sort the problem out decisively and return to keep my social engagements. A 'Raven' napkin, provocatively imprinted with lipstick kisses from his fiancée, jolted memories of that other world of love, laughter and security. Further nostalgia was dispelled by an icy blast that whipped the flimsy pages away from numbed fingers. Ian McNeill came to say that a helicopter was inbound to fetch me for the 'O' Group ...

As Mr Chisnall, Corporal Adams, Green and myself trotted briskly back along the crest, vicious salvoes of enemy fire began to crash on to the more open ground between 'Zoya' and 'Katrina'. It was decidedly unpleasant. By now we had become attuned to the tone of 'incoming' and could usually tell whether to take cover or not. On the way back from escorting me, however, the RSM was blown several yards into the air. He thumped down, dazed but unscathed, before the horrified gaze of the other two. We arrived opposite 'Tara' to the unexpected sound of a religious chorus over the gunfire. Albert Hempenstall and a large group from 'L' Company were holding a quick service amid the cover of some rocks. In rear of them, the Scots Guards were now dug in and making preparations for their attack on Mount Tumbledown the next day. It was a classic 'behind-the-lines' scene at which, sadly, I could not linger. The hovering pilot was clearly feeling nervous and exposed to the salvoes just over the crest.

On the way to Brigade HQ he told me that they had miraculously survived a large air strike an hour or so before. On arrival, this was all too obvious from the damaged helicopters, collapsed tentage and craters gouging long scars in the peat. A rather shocked Brigade staff officer showed me the briefing tent, which looked decidedly tattered. Our guardian angel seemed to have intervened again, because the original briefing time had been postponed earlier that morning. This extract from Julian Thompson's book makes it very clear how fortunate that was:

The briefing tent where the Orders Group should have been assembled, but which was empty at the time because of the delay in preparing orders, was shredded with splinter holes and many of the legs of the camp stools within were chopped off or mangled. The casualties inside would have been heavy, probably wounding or killing most of us, including all the Commanding Officers and key Staff Officers in 3 Commando Brigade.

The new orders clarified how both brigades would dislodge the remaining Argentine units from their defensive positions around Stanley. The Tumbledown and Wireless Ridge features had to be seized that night. Units involved would be the 2nd Battalion, Scots Guards from 5 Brigade, and 2 Para, now back under command of Brigadier Julian Thompson for their second major battle. 'Four-Two' was subsequently to take a series of objectives leading towards the airfield, some of which we hoped to approach by helicopter. The concept of operations was to by-pass Stanley and maintain momentum by harassing a demoralized enemy. With our superiority in artillery and the increasing availability of offensive air support, we should keep them on the run. Intelligence revealed that Mount Tumbledown was held by a marine battalion. That made me even more relieved that our advance had been held at dawn the day before. There is a sentimental bond between marines, to be set aside when necessary, but nice to preserve if possible. More importantly I had instructed Argentine marine officers on courses with the US Marine Corps. It was likely that these troops would fight more resolutely than the rest.

When I got back from Brigade the Scots Guards were beginning to group up and assemble their stores. It was not the moment to divert their CO with good wishes. His Support Company Commander was already with Captain Phil Wilson on 'Zoya', where we were providing observation, additional communications, and advice based upon our recent experiences. Once the attack began our own mortars and captured weapons would also provide additional fire support. Since we were so obviously involved in this attack, Guy would now remain with Tac HQ to control our own defence. This left me free to monitor the progress of the battalion in case we could react in any way to assist the Scots Guards.

For almost all of that night I listened in on their command net, experiencing a conflicting range of feelings as the long-drawn-out ordeal took its course. To listen as someone else directed, encouraged, supported and manoeuvred his companies was riveting. The Scots Guards fought a desperate struggle, taking numerous casualties at a series of formidable obstacles. I could not help feeling relief at the ordeal we had been spared this time; admiration and sympathy for those enduring it now. The battle for Mount Tumbledown was prolonged and bitter because the enemy was alert and determined. Only a series of close-quarter assaults dislodged them from their strong-points, and these demanded a high price in courage and casualties. One impression that will never fade was the timeless, Oxford English dialogue on the Scots Guards' command net. This was quite different from the crisp, varied tones of 'Four-Two', or the parachute battalions with us. But the Guards officers spoke far more than their radio operators, and always in those measured, courteous terms. In a sense I could have been eavesdropping on the 2nd Battalion, Scots Guards advancing to the attack half a century ago. Sadly, a tape-deck to record it for posterity was not at hand.

During the night, 13/14 June, it snowed again. Dawn at 1030 hours was another freezing ordeal, as we stood-to on crackling ice and slithery rock for our next move forward. By then the Guardsmen had won the day and the battered survivors of the 5th Argentine Marine Battalion were falling back into Stanley. Some of the Scots Guards radio operators in our Fire Control Centre were jubilant at the battalion success. But when I commiserated with them on their losses, it became clear that they only partially comprehended the extent of casualties. As is often the case in combat, their own responsibilities had insulated them from the battle picture. A melancholy example of unawareness which can be an advantage at the time.

Brigade communications now chose this moment to deteriorate sharply, adding to the general air of uncertainty and excitement. All units remained poised for the 'off'. Our own move forward would be after 45 Commando, and might be by helicopter, depending upon the situation. I became preoccupied with remaining in touch with events. We were at one hour's notice to move. The hard-pressed signallers were given a difficult time. As usual the Gunner net seemed to be working better than ours. We turned to David Brown for a running commentary.

He must have been the first to utter that emotive word 'surrender' (presumably in response to a radio message). At that stage it was unconfirmed. A rumour? An exaggeration? Wishful thinking? Whatever, at this point I was deeply suspicious. To slow down the adrenalin of these aggressive young warriors prematurely might be very dangerous indeed. Canute-like, we attempted to confine the suggestion within Tac HQ. But there were nearly half a dozen different radio nets in the Commando, several with 'out-stations' amongst the companies. The sound of cheering and sights of vigorous back-slapping spread along the ridge of Mount Harriet. 45 Commando came up on the net to ask if it were true. I rebuffed a friendly journalist who sought some quotable comment ...

Another one, Patrick Bishop, began his own book (*The Winter War*) like this:

> It was a while before anyone realised that the guns had stopped firing. We were standing on a rock ledge on the east face of Mount Harriet looking down towards the town. The crags around were chipped and smashed by the fighting of the last two days and the pathetic debris of the Argentinian defenders lay strewn all around. At 3 pm we heard some uncertain cheers from the Marines on the rocks above. 'That's it,' one of them shouted, 'They've surrendered.' One of the officers, Captain Mike Norman, who had been captured and sent back to England by the Argentine invaders ten weeks before, laughed and shook hands with an officer standing next to him, but the rest of us wanted the news to be true too badly to rejoice until we were sure.
>
> The Commanding Officer, Colonel Vaux, went over to the radio and called up Brigade. 'It's not confirmed', he said. 'It's just something they got from the fleet.' It started to snow again. Colonel Vaux went back to the radio. 'They're falling back from Sapper Hill!' he said. 'There are white arm-bands and flags all over the place.'

Once it was obvious a retreat was in progress Brigade HQ put us at instant readiness to move. At that point Guy and I decided to indulge in some private irresponsibility. All through this war, every step of the way, our awkward, heavy, uncomfortable helmets had bruised and rasped as they dangled awkwardly from our equipment. Nor had either of us ever worn them for long. Mine invariably gave me a blinding headache within minutes, while alarmingly diminishing any awareness of danger. (It was actually a twenty-year-old parachute helmet which should long ago have been replaced with the lighter version.) Furtively, like schoolboys pinching apples, we slipped into the rocks and placed them triumphantly on a prominent ledge. For all I know they remain there to this day.

Without warning, a flight of Wessex helicopters streamed in. Vague radio instructions were obtained from Brigade HQ to fly north of Mount Tumbledown. We were to disembark on the slopes overlooking Moody Brook and then advance towards Stanley. Suddenly Tac HQ was embarking. There was only an instant to glance back at this crucial place in my life. Then, lift-off, and a frenzied scrutiny of the map as we thrashed through the air on a new mission. The distractions now were whether we would find ourselves in the minefields, or how to deal with a fleeing enemy who had not yet surrendered. Guy remained on 'Zoya' to co-ordinate reinforcement and resupply with the reserves left behind.

The road from Moody Brook into Port Stanley is plainly visible from the shoulder of Mount Tumbledown. So also, that day, was almost all of the high ground for which the battles had been fought. Streaming off there now, towards an uninspiring collection of red-roofed wooden bungalows, haphazardly adjacent to dilapidated piers, were hundreds of distant dark figures. Altogether three major British units and several smaller ones were converging on Stanley. Behind us in the hills the remainder moved on round to encircle the harbour. These hordes were converging on what was then the most notorious small town in the world. It was hard to comprehend that this might be the end. That history was being made.

'J' Company, who would have spearheaded our next attack, carefully picked their way down to a muddy track. In front was 10 Troop, with almost all of the original garrison, returning now to the scene of their bravery and humiliation. It would have been poetic justice if they could have led the advance into Stanley. But such happy coincidence rarely occurs in war, and 2 Para, who had been closer, were almost there. As they had fought more battles than anyone else that also seemed rather appropriate.

We moved on down past some battered buildings around which were several burnt-out and riddled vehicles. The perforations in them were so numerous and tiny that it was puzzling. Someone explained that it was the result of the RAF's new cluster bombs. Later, Argentine prisoners were to describe graphically the devastation these caused, although there weren't all that many bodies around on this occasion. Further on we came upon a section of enemy 105-mm guns that had been completely destroyed by counter-bombardment. David Brown was pleased to see this. Throughout the war his observation officers, as well as those from other units, had painstakingly reported bearings of enemy gunfire, together with estimated times of flight for the shells. When several reports had been collated at Brigade HQ it was sometimes possible to pinpoint a gun position and hit it with counter-battery fire before the enemy moved. Clearly that had worked in this case.

Next we passed Moody Brook barracks, the home for Royal Marine garrisons since time immemorial. Even without having served there, the tales of others had made it seem familiar. Now, however, the buildings had been virtually razed to the ground. In the past, the Corps had struggled fruitlessly with bureaucracy to have the authorized rebuild carried out. Annually we had been defeated, at the last minute, on being informed that the vote for works services had been exceeded for the financial year. Weeks before we got to Stanley, we had been told of Julian Thompson's signal to London, drafted in anticipation. The text declared triumphantly that the administration could no longer evade rebuilding Moody Brook, because his gunners had been obliged to destroy the place! In fact, this ultimatum was never sent. The Argentines did not occupy the barracks, having severely damaged the empty buildings during their invasion. Apart from a bomb-proof shelter only one building was left standing, so Corporal Adams informed me, and this was the greenhouse. Like many marines from previous garrisons, he had an affection for the place, and was extremely put out to see how it had been ravaged.

As we moved on his indignation turned into nostalgia. 'You know, Sir, I might ask the wife whether she would like to return. Once things are sorted out, we might want to settle down and make a life here in the Falklands.' I glanced at him incredulously; then told him not to be such a bloody fool! Absolutely the last idea in my mind was to remain in this miserable wilderness a moment longer than necessary. On the other hand, the islands had no previous associations for me. Nor was there any sort of family connection. My reaction had been superficial, while Adams's came from the heart. I tried to make amends by suggesting that he rebuild Moody Brook as a holiday camp ...

Eventually we came on to the 'main drag' to Stanley, a muddy, broken and narrow strip of paving raised above the mud and slush

on either side. The nearer we got to the town, the more desolate
the scene. Damaged guns and vehicles were tilted grotesquely off
the road, abandoned equipment, weapons and tentage heaped
everywhere. The stench of smouldering refuse and rotting
carcases rolled over us, arising mainly from the slaughterhouse,
where the freezers were no longer working. A radio message was
passed, requesting us to stop at the hospital. I asked Corporal
Adams where that was. 'In the middle of town,' he told me. That
made no one the wiser. In every direction could be seen buildings
painted with the Red Cross. It was the most flagrant violation by
the enemy of the Geneva Convention, which must have
endangered their own wounded by its indiscriminate absurdity.

As we reached the outskirts, another radio message summoned
me forward to the Brigadier. Julian Thompson, looking incredibly
tired, was puffing cheerfully on his pipe and congratulating the
marines and paras on reaching their goal. He warned me at once
that no formal surrender had taken place.

His obvious concern was that if the situation deteriorated we
would be heavily outnumbered. At such close quarters we could
be overrun, unless troops remained alert and in secure positions.
As Tac HQ had walked forward, such gloomy thoughts had also
occurred to me – as well as some others concerning civilian
property, unit rivalry and, above all, the availability of alcohol.
Even as we spoke, the slurred voice of an early predecessor into
town could be heard in the background. He was wrangling with
an NCO in 'K' Company about who had got there first, or had the
right to requisition anything he wanted.

It was a time for the various units to stay separate and under the
firm control of familiar leadership. Tempers were short, nerves
frayed, violence a reflex. How shortsighted to test the patience of
these exhausted troops unnecessarily now! With little said on
either side, 'Four-Two' reversed course and withdrew to the
outskirts. 'L' and 'J' Companies shared a decrepit seaplane hangar
and 'K' Company moved into an empty cowshed opposite.
Commando HQ had to return about a mile down the road to a
derelict school. Even so, retracing those weary steps seemed worth
it if we could keep our distance from overcrowding and tension in
Stanley.

14

VICTORS AND VANQUISHED

There was no chance for victorious celebrations. Nor even any time to reflect upon the amazing rapidity with which events had gathered pace. The Argentine marines being driven off Mount Tumbledown had probably been the deciding factor. From there we would have had observation over all other enemy positions, including the airfield. By then, the enemy commanders were only too well aware of the devastating artillery and air strikes which would be directed on them from this vantage point. Whether the hordes of aimless stragglers knew that too is doubtful. The majority were just totally demoralized, without any further will to fight. It was a most singular display of military disintegration, which avoided becoming a rout only because British troops held back to spare further casualties.

After the war an emotional book was published in Argentina. *Los Chicos de la Guerra* alleges fearful carnage amongst survivors as they attempted to surrender to the 1/7th Gurkhas. But after all the self-delusion and propaganda perpetuated amongst Argentines previously, that allegation seems pathetic, as well as ungrateful. Fortunately for their conscripts, the cheerful little men from the mountains of Nepal never closed with any enemy; let alone drew their lethal kukris in anger for the Queen. After years of patient loyalty in peace and war, they were frustratingly deprived of the chance to display their legendary valour on this occasion.

Requisitioned vehicles quickly appeared, and I was able to visit the companies and sub-units without having to trudge up and down that desolate road again. In the fading afternoon everyone consolidated defence positions, established their boundaries and co-ordinated fire plans. For the moment a dividing line had been drawn across Stanley, beyond which British troops were not to pass. The intention was that the enemy would withdraw from there on to the airfield once a surrender had been negotiated. As long as they remained inside the town their proximity to the inhabitants was a hazard and an inhibition.

Entering the sea-plane hangar was like walking under a vegetable strainer. Everywhere narrow shafts of light speared the gloom through myriad punctures from a cluster-bomb strike. Inside was the anticipated squalor. It became quickly apparent that this would be worse than usual as the two companies began to clear up. A useful-looking wheelbarrow under a tarpaulin turned out to contain a dismembered corpse. On a balcony upstairs was a pile of amputated limbs from which the blood dripped down onto the floor below. Outside more bodies were piled together in the mud. We gradually came to realize that this had been a macabre makeshift mortuary. We decided it was too late to move again, but the decision to transfer to the putrid slaughterhouse the next day proved universally popular!

Across the road 'K' Company had already acquired three Mercedes jeeps and what turned out to be the only JCB in Stanley. They had also adapted an enemy water-carrier as a deep fryer and were soon enjoying their first chips from liberated potatoes. In Stanley, everyone could spend their first night for weeks under some cover. In the mountains, Main HQ and the various echelons were still surviving in the open. The next day renewed efforts were made to bring them down, although the competition for helicopter assets was formidable. Reports of several further minefield casualties meant that troops had been forbidden to try and walk out.

At some stage in my travels, information was passed on the radio of an 'O' Group at Government House that evening. An hour or so beforehand, Tac HQ asked whether I wished to fly or drive there. Pondering on this, I was prompted by the RSM that our affiliated pilot longed to cap his dangerous missions with a landing at this symbolic place. That seemed absolutely appropriate to me, too. In the deepening shadow of early evening we set off on what must have been the shortest flight of the war; all of three minutes, at the outside!

Hovering down on to terraced lawns unfolding from this handsome, familiar building was certainly poignant. Here this war had really begun, with the overwhelming of the garrison and the expulsion of the British Governor. Now we were back, and soon to restore him in his residence again. The Gazelle settled lightly about fifty yards from the house, as we savoured the moment with mutual satisfaction. 'Odd there are no marshallers or a guide for you, Colonel,' observed the pilot cautiously. 'Would you like me to shut down and accompany you?' I peered through the gathering gloom. Such solitude at a Brigade HQ landing-site was certainly unusual, but it seemed feeble to imagine some sinister implication at this stage. 'No thanks', I said briskly. 'They are probably all inside ransacking the cellar. Anyway, the other COs will be stacking up behind to land-on if we delay here ...' I jumped out, and he whirled away over Stanley Water. I began to walk towards the apparently empty, inscrutable house.

To alight in good order from a light helicopter is virtually impossible when burdened with equipment. The tangle of webbing, map case, weapon must immediately be sorted out and put on before moving off. In this case I didn't bother. After all, I was attending a triumphant 'O' Group following a victorious cease-fire. Behind the dark glass, shadows seemed to move as I approached. Then the doors on the right side of the elongated conservatory burst open and an armed group of shouting, gesticulating Argentines ran towards me ...

There was just time to shake free my Sterling submachine-gun, but it would have been futile. There could be no chance of loading it as well. The ironic, bitter, fact seemed to be that my luck had run out after the race was over. There was hardly time to be afraid before they were upon me, circling round in a sort of frenzied war dance and gabbling to each other in Spanish. Eventually it became apparent that there was an officer with them who was trying to communicate in English. After all my time across the Atlantic, I ought to have understood his Hispanic-American accent. But perhaps the distractions were too diverting for a moment or two.

A word like 'rendition' kept on being mentioned, as well as 'Generalissimos Moore and Menendez'. Suddenly it became gloriously evident that they were acknowledging my right to take over Government House as soon as the formalities had been completed! 'Con permiso? But when will your troops be here?' the immaculate little staff officer now disconcertingly asked. As I was agonizing over how to evade the question the group became excited again. They began pointing down towards the road at the bottom of the lawns. Rather later than I might have wished, St

Jude seemed to have returned to duty. Prowling towards us, well beyond the declared boundary, came a patrol of the Paras.

As plausibly as possible these were confirmed as 'my troops', who must now be provided with further instructions. The Argentines watched dubiously while I gingerly detached myself and descended towards the patrol. They, of course, must have been more surprised than anyone on seeing a confused-looking Commando officer emerge from this unexpected direction. With an apprehensive grin at the Corporal, I explained that in a moment I would leap over the fence and require his escort out of town. 'Watch out for the barbed wire, then, Sir!' was the dour reply. They glowered menacingly towards the group behind me, who retreated rapidly back into Government House.

Once over unscathed, apart from an ignominious tear in the trouser seat, my rage knew no bounds. Bloody Brigade HQ had nearly done for me! Now all the latent, unfair prejudice of fighting units for the uncaring staff overwhelmed common sense. Instead of retracing our steps from forbidden territory, we turned decisively right and marched towards the Secretariat, where I now knew the surrender negotiations to be going on. If Brigade HQ was not there, someone would tell me where it was. When I reached it, I would have something to say about sending misleading locations to vulnerable commanding officers!

We proceeded on through increasing throngs of bewildered enemy troops, mostly armed to the teeth, who subserviently moved aside as we approached. The squat, unimpressive Secretariat building stands upon a small rise, with a curved drive leading up to the main door. As we advanced up this, watched by hundreds of assorted Argentines, a military police officer moved to intercept us. Nothing could have been more provocative. His uniform was creased and clean, his boots shone, a shiny plastic belt gleamed. Covered in badges, tags and medals, with a coloured helmet adorned by tinted goggles, his sleek self-confident appearance was an outrage to our filthy, tattered state. He poked a gloved finger into my chest and declared that we could go no further ...

In retrospect, I like to believe that there was some dialogue, although it was certainly terse! Once it had been established that we could not pass, the Argentine MP somehow ended up overbalancing down the slope at the feet of my menacing, red-bereted escort. A muddy para boot emerged from the patrol and thumped satisfactorily into his chubby rump. For a moment circumstances seemed to be taking a more gratifying course until, suddenly and reverberatingly, someone cocked a weapon. For the second time that night I sensed that luck was evaporating away. The Paras' weapons would be cocked already, so this had to be an enemy bystander. He represented overwhelming odds, while we stood hemmed in on every side. The tension tingled ominously as everyone froze in anticipation of the next development.

When that came, it was so unexpected and bizarre that I still pinch myself for confirmation today. A door in the Secretariat entrance swung open to reveal a European lady in a dark dress. Whether she was young or middle-aged, large or small, I have no recollection. The memory is simply of a dynamic, angry person who crushingly reprimanded me in a Teutonic accent for jeopardizing the cease-fire. At the same time she was also berating the unfortunate police officer, still grovelling on the ground amongst my escort. The Paras were then firmly told to wait outside while I was sent grudgingly up the stairs to contact someone on General Moore's staff.

Utterly dazed by now, I ascended to the first floor and came upon the closed doors of what were obviously the executive chambers. Through them shone chinks of light, and murmuring voices could be heard. Sensing that this might not be the moment to intrude, I moved towards an open door on the other side. There I found myself confronted by several startled, senior Argentine officers, grouped around a baize-covered table. Each one was picturesquely arrayed in ceremonial uniforms of multi-coloured magnificence. Chalk and cheese, or chops in inappropriate temples, flashed swiftly through my mind. Sparing them further provocation at my distasteful appearance, I shuffled quickly on to an adjacent door. At last there seemed to be an ally, for here, talking earnestly into his satellite radio, was Colonel Mike Rose. He gazed at me in complete consternation, then excused himself respectfully to the person at the other end before coming over. 'Nick,' he said, very deliberately, 'I have no idea how you got here or what you want, but you must leave at once, do you understand?' I glanced around the room, where staff from both sides were earnestly consulting or drafting, and realized that I did. With my trusty escort, a brisk retreat was made to the dividing line. On the way back the Geordie corporal invited me in for a drink at their billet. There the Paras revealed to me that the lady of intervention apparently came from a Red Cross delegation.

Eventually, I did find Brigade HQ. It was no surprise to discover that the 'O' Group was long since over. After it, news of the formal surrender had been broadcast on the BBC World Service. That was the first confirmation for the Commander of 3 Commando Brigade and his staff that their war had been won. Ironically, for once the BBC had been neither premature nor indiscreet. A tired Brigade Major told me warily that the Brigadier was asleep. I would not be deterred. Stifling his protective instincts, he showed me upstairs.

If he had been asleep, Julian Thompson displayed saintly forbearance as he listened to the indignant and rambling account of my recent adventures. Soon exasperation was soothed into joviality. We ended up chuckling together over those bizarre events outside Government House and the Secretariat. A comforting dram, some thoughts for the morrow, and I was driven away to my own much-needed pallet.

Later that night sleep was disrupted by orders from the elusive staff. One company must be in place at Stanley Airfield early the next morning for the disarming of Argentine units. The POWs were to be concentrated there afterwards. It seemed an appropriate task for 'J' Company, especially as Mike Norman knew his way around. Even so, he had difficulty in locating Divisional HQ for a briefing, before discovering that they had switched to local time. This meant the company had arisen several hours early from precious sleep. The fog of war seemed to be thickening as the action receded ...

As soon as we could the next morning, Tac HQ drove out in the requisitioned Mercedes jeeps to witness this historic scene. All along the muddy road to the airport columns of dejected Argentines tramped. Weapons slung. Kit-bags shouldered. Many so fresh and clean that it was obvious they had not fought at all. The officers, in particular, were often immaculate in natty field dress. Their invariable pistols were holstered in smart leather-work, with binoculars or goggles very much the fashion. We found ourselves held up by another Mercedes displaying general's stars. Impatience turned to fascination when I realized this must be General Menendez himself. He was also en route to observe how we were treating his defeated army. We passed triumphantly by, before catching up with an orderly group amongst the rabble. These troops were marching briskly along with their regimental colours in the centre of a battle-stained column. Visions of those

hanging in the officers' or sergeants' messes occurred simultaneously to CO and RSM.

Eventually we reached the isthmus leading on to Stanley
airport, from which there was no exit. Here was the surrender
checkpoint. Every POW was being disarmed and searched there,
before being sent across. I confirmed with Mike Norman that
contingent commanders were being made to surrender formally to
him. Then quickly revealed that we wanted those colours. Even as
we spoke the column appeared in the distance. But, just as
someone was briefing me that these were the Argentine marines
from Mount Tumbledown, they halted. To our surprise and
chagrin the flags were swiftly burnt in petrol before we could
intervene.

At the time this was very galling. Later we conceded that it was
what we would have done ourselves. As they piled their arms, I
asked an officer if he knew we were the Royal Marines. He replied
tersely that they did. It was not the moment for regimental
camaraderie, although everyone acknowledged that they had
fought hard. Since that had been in conspicuous contrast to most
of their compatriots, we admired them for it. Later a very different
type of Argentine officer made a revealing observation to the RSM.
Referring disparagingly to his ineffectual conscripts, he compared
them unfavourably to professional commandos. Chisnall eyed him
contemptuously for a moment, before pointing out this was not the
significant difference. 'Look at him', he said, pointing to a gaunt
bedraggled officer, indistinguishable in appearance to surrounding
marines. 'Look at yourself. *That* is the difference!' The well
starched and portly major moved on rather sheepishly.

Mike Norman and I stood together for some time, marvelling at
the scene as piles of weapons and ammunition mounted at the
roadside. Nearby an endless line of POWs stoically waited to be
disarmed. How different their attitude to that of the marines who
had been ordered to lay down their arms at Government House on
2 April. In Max Arthur's book *Beyond All Courage*, Norman is
quoted: 'I compared their attitude to my own men, who when
called upon to surrender, a couple of months before, had been so
angry.' Then the defeated Royal Marines had been sullen,
truculent, intractable towards their captors. Here the conscripts
were meek, co-operative, so obviously relieved to be out of the war.

A 'small world' coincidence occurred at the checkpoint when
Marine Jeffrey Urand renewed a previous acquaintance.

With a few others from the original garrison he had escaped into
the mountains after the surrender. Subsequently they gave
themselves up for fear of reprisals against the islanders. Separately
from the remainder, they were flown to Argentina and intensively
interrogated. Although no physical violence was used, the
technique was aggressive and, at times, threatening. Their heads
were shaved and they were kept in solitary confinement, before
eventually being sent home. Now he suddenly heard the
unforgettable voice of his interrogator again. An officious
Argentine captain was addressing a company of forlorn conscripts
before dispersal onto the airfield. Urand strolled up behind and
tapped him on the shoulder: ' 'Allo, my darlin',' he said. 'Fancy us
meeting like this again.' The military police officer paled, gulped
and then slipped away into the ever-changing throng of POWs.

Next day, 'L' Company took over at the airfield and 'J'
Company returned to Stanley. A belated, but historic, event was
then staged at Government House, with the raising of the
Falklands flag. This was not the original, but one that Major
Ewen Southby-Tailyour had 'lifted' in 1978. Already other units
had hoisted their flags in victory here. All the same, it meant
something special to the original 'Naval Party 8901'; even if they
did have to postpone the wash and shave they had been longing to
enjoy for the past three weeks. The photograph of the scene turned
out to be one of the most famous images from the war ...

Two days later, Wheen was invited to supper by the Argentine
Marine Commander and the POW camp commandant. The
latter had formed a harmonious working relationship with David,
who provided much-needed facilities in exchange for a willing
workforce. On one afternoon when I visited, there were several
thousand POWs, literally sweeping the airstrip. The unexpected
hospitality was extended in a heated Portakabin where the meal,
served by stewards, began with a glass of sherry. Colin Beadon,
who was now 'L' Company second-in-command in place of the
wounded Stafford, also attended. Two other Argentines were
present. A mobile patrol controlled by Sergeant-Major Cameron
March lurked outside. Both David and Colin retained their
pistols.

For once, that legendary Anglo-Argentine accord seemed
plausible. Both British officers, fumbling with unfamiliar cutlery
after so long in the field, chatted amiably with their polite and
articulate hosts. One of the Argentines had been to an English

public school. The other had graduated from a university in Scotland. Conversation ranged across all sorts of topics, including the recent battles. The argument that well equipped professional soldiers can overwhelm inexperienced conscripts predominated. Argentine advantages in numbers and situation were considered irrelevant. Our ability to manoeuvre, particularly at night, was judged to have been decisive. Not surprisingly, the British logistic system was much admired. However, Argentine propaganda prevented these officers from comprehending that we had few helicopters for troop lift. Nor would they accept that our battalions were not equipped with a wide range of night-vision devices. British artillery was acknowledged to have been extremely effective, while the inferiority of their own observation and fire-control system was indignantly identified as a major handicap.

Exposure to the elements, even though there had been so much time in which to construct proper shelters in defence, was frequently mentioned. The point was made that their mountain warfare troops had had to be left on the frontier with Chile. Each of the Argentines emphasized that the British had never actually been expected to fight at all, let alone land on the other side of the island. Eventually someone conceded: 'We thought we knew about war, but you have shown us that we only knew about exercises.'

The consequences of the propaganda Argentina had so stridently created were very evident. These officers were still firmly convinced that HMS *Invincible* had been sunk with all hands including Prince Andrew. But they were deeply disillusioned that *Canberra* had not. Although mainland claims of Argentine air superiority had been exposed after a while, they were still largely unaware of their own aircraft losses. Resentment had set in after their controlled media had alleged counter-attacks in San Carlos Water, or claimed sustained resistance at Goose Green. By then they knew otherwise. Eventually the propaganda had become counter-productive. Now they were cynical about the whole conduct of the war, and bitter towards the military junta. It was obvious that misrepresentation, as well as ineptitude, had reduced the will to resist. Their conviction of the righteousness of their cause, however, remained undiminished. Wheen and Beadon were continually reminded:

'So we failed to recover our heritage this time ...'

'But the Malvinas are Argentine ...'
'This was only the first round ...'
'We shall be back ...'
The evening concluded with toasts to friendship. A light-hearted invitation for David to lecture on night attacks at the Argentine Staff College was accepted enthusiastically.

There was another instance of spontaneous regard early the next morning. At this stage 'J' Company was back on duty at the airport entrance. The thousands of prisoners were now assembling for their return to Stanley for embarkation to freedom. Mike Norman was awakened by Corporal David Armour, who told him there was an officer asking for him by name. 'What's his complaint?' muttered Norman. There didn't seem to be a problem, he was told, the officer simply had a message for him. Mike pulled on his captured 'wellies' and stumbled out into the gloom. An Argentine officer he did not immediately recognize greeted him with a respectful salute. Then apologized for disturbing him. 'Do you know who I am?' he asked. Mike Norman confessed he did not. 'I am the second-in-command of the company that attacked you on the 2nd of April at Government House. Now we would all like to say good-bye before we leave!' Norman followed him over to meet the commander and the rest of his company. There he was greeted like a long-lost friend before they wished him well and marched away. 'This had to be the end of a most remarkable three months, where the wheel had turned full circle ...'

On 17 June I flew off to visit our wounded on SS *Uganda*. The ship was steaming some miles off the island, as she had done throughout the war. This time the red crosses had been totally justified. Many of the Argentine wounded had been treated on board, before being transferred to their own equivalent ship, and some still remained even then.

I had feared that it would be a harrowing experience. But the wards were full of clean, cheerful young men, although many had brushed traumatically with death, before experiencing the pain and fear of casevac from the battlefield. Even now, most of them were suffering, while for some there was the haunting spectre of permanent injury and of being invalided from the Service. Yet it was one of the happiest places I remember from the war. Composed, cheerful patients conspired to keep one another's spirits up with bright, smiling nurses who radiated reassurance and efficiency. There was an atmosphere of optimism, as well as healing. It seemed that staff and patients had committed themselves to an instinctive partnership. Shock and pain were still evident, but confidence in recovery had been instilled in everyone. Already some of the 'Four-Two' wounded had been off-loaded at Montevideo and flown back to the UK. The ones I saw were too seriously hurt to be moved, or were recovering fast. Lieutenants Chris Whiteley and Julian Pusey certainly seemed to be on the mend. Their wounds were healing, and they both knew that complete recovery was virtually certain. Residual pain receded at the less fortunate circumstances of others. On the same ward, one of their counterparts in 40 Commando was having his foot amputated that day. In contrast, Marine Hagyard remained VSI (very seriously injured). Across his torso a jagged web of stitches criss-crossed around wounds still livid and suppurating. His sense of humour, however, was unimpaired, as he predicted cheerfully that soon rugby dressing-rooms would fall silent when he 'stripped off'. (I so hoped that would come true, and indeed it did.) There were also doubts that Lieutenant Ian Stafford would dance his reels again. His ankle bone had been shattered by a bullet, and the doctors' prognosis was gloomy. (These worries proved unfounded, too.)

In terms of creature comforts, life on shore now became progressively brighter. Main HQ and the echelons were all brought out of the mountains, and a reunited Commando HQ was set up in an empty building. Ironically this had once been used by imported Argentine workers who were employed by the European Space Organisation. Dennis Sparks, the Quartermaster, was contentedly established with Frank Allen, his assistant, amidst the ruins of Moody Brook Camp. Somehow they began to replace our losses and acquire all kinds of fresh rations for the unit. Guy, who was no slouch at this sort of thing himself, appeared one morning with a broad grin and a case of Argentine wine. I was even more amazed to hear that it came from South Georgia! Somehow he had contrived to bring it back to leave on HMS *Fearless*, before rejoining us in the mountains. We held our first 'dinner party' that night, and invited Paul Stevenson from Divisional HQ at Government House. As I recall, the menu included:

Pâté de Stanley (arctic rations meat spread)
Fresh Bread (a mouth-watering delicacy for us)
Curried Bully Beef (exquisitely cooked on a Trangia spirit stove)
Yellow Cling Peaches (canned in Argentina)

We washed all this down with some palatable claret, while Guy told us the story of the 'Argie' wine mountain on South Georgia ...

In the dining hall of the notorious scrap-metal workers, at the abandoned Leith whaling station, had been found several rows of empty wine bottles. Frustratingly, these had not been discovered until after the prisoners had been sent to Ascension. No full ones could be located within the labyrinth of old smelting-sheds, stores and warehouses, but Sheridan remained convinced that there must be a 'cache'. He reasoned that with around 1,500 empty bottles after four weeks of occupation, there must be a lot more somewhere to last the winter. Eventually, after an extensive search by the Reconnaissance Troop Sergeant, a shed was discovered packed with cases of 'plonk'. They were decreed legitimate spoils for the victors, and shared amongst the messes and guard ships. We raised a glass to 'M' Company, and hoped they were taking advantage when they could!

But there were less satisfactory recollections involving drink. On 19 June the Task Force was invited to 'splice the mainbrace' in the traditional style after a victory. It was obvious that there could not possibly be enough rum for each individual in the Task Force, but we were slightly disconcerted when the issue for more than 600 men of 'Four-Two' turned out to be six 7-centilitre bottles. It was the same for everyone, we were told. I therefore decided that each rifle company should get two bottles, since they had endured the most. But on the same day, Guy and I were in Divisional HQ when I observed one of their corporals with a 1-gallon rum container. On being asked, he explained that this was the ration for his own section that evening. Resentment was mollified in the conclusion that unhappy comparisons by 'teeth' towards 'tail' no doubt preceded gunpowder itself!

I seemed to visit Government House rather a lot in this period. To begin with, it had the supreme attraction of a 'sit-down-upon, flushing-water, almost-odourless loo'. That certainly encouraged a visit at the slightest pretext. On one of these I passed by a small room in which a morose-looking Argentine general was standing. It was Menendez again. I paused to ask him whether he was satisfied with the disarming of POWs on the airfield. He confirmed that he was. Then he asked me what my unit had done in the war. He grimaced when I explained that we had been reserve during the landings in case of counter-attack. He remarked that no move towards San Carlos had been seriously

General Jeremy Moore speaks to Captain Peter Babbington in front of 'K' Company

'K' Company march off to the South Atlantic. In the background, Tara Vaux (right) holds the 'Argies are tragic' banner

Cutting the surprise birthday cake.
Left to right: Albert Hampenstall, Dennis Sparks, David Brown, Frank Allen, David Wheen

'An original greetings card with a glorious "Argie" cartoon on it...'

'Every individual needed to test his own load and how he should pack it'—
Marine Casper Morehead of Mortar Troop

Colonel Tom Seccombe presents the author with the inter-unit sports
trophy—in the background are Kim Sabido and Robert Fox

The newly formed 'J' Company on fitness training

'The Beagle'

Concentrated fire across
Ascension Island

WO2 Paul Juleff, the Sergeant-
Major 'M' Company, stands
beneath the victorious flags of
Grytviken, South Georgia, with
RFA *Olmeda* in the background

40 Commando cross-decking into HMS *Fearless*

Dawn in San Carlos

'We began as we were to continue—with wet feet'

Digging in at Port San Carlos

Ian McNeill with Corporal Simon Aston—Port San Carlos

Guy Sheridan with Charlie Eggar, the Signals Officer (left), below Mount Kent

contemplated, because they could not believe that those were the main landings. In response to a question about his own future he looked even gloomier. I concluded that prospects for outmanoeuvred generals in South America were probably bleak. As I was leaving, a framed quotation from Samuel Johnson caught my eye:

THOUGHTS ON THE LATE TRANSACTION RESPECTING FALKLAND'S ISLANDS [1771]

...A few spots of earth, which, in the deserts of the ocean, had almost escaped human notice, and which, if they had not happened to make a sea mark, had perhaps never had a name? ... Beyond this what have we acquired? What, but a bleak and gloomy solitude, an island thrown aside from human use, stormy in winter, and barren in summer; an island which not the southern savages have dignified with habitation: where a garrison must be kept in a state that contemplates with envy the exiles of Siberia; of which the expense will be perpetual, and the use only occasional; and which, if fortune smile upon our labours, may become a nest of smugglers in peace, and in war the refuge of further buccaniers.

A happier occasion was celebrating the birthday of Prince William on 21 June, when General Moore presided at a dinner of the commanding officers and staffs of both brigades in the Governor's dining room. Most of us were still dressed in the clothes we had campaigned in. Only a fortunate few had achieved the luxury of a bath or shower on board a friendly ship. The previous evening, I had enjoyed a reunion with Max Hastings and John Shirley in the Upland Goose Hotel. During our supper, it had become obvious that my now well scrubbed hosts were trying to keep a tactful distance from their odorous guest. On this more historic occasion it seemed poetic justice that the cleansed should suffer the less fragrant. After drinking the Loyal Toast a signal of congratulation was composed amid merry argument. Not surprisingly, perhaps, it never reached Buckingham Palace.

Victorious we might have been, but the excitement and satisfaction of the surrender soon dimmed. We began to be menaced by lethargy and depression. Our surroundings were so indescribably filthy; the weather was so infinitely depressing; everyone was absolutely exhausted. Once the disarming was complete, 'Four-Two's' main function was to organize POW parties in clearing up the chaos in Stanley or on the airfield. To begin with I had worried that impatient young marines might harass the bewildered prisoners out of frustration. I should have known better. With that unique humour (which probably scored a half-century of additional years for the Empire), they established an easy-going authority which gained a grateful and positive response. '*Buenos dias, Señors!*' was a typical brief, overheard early one morning: 'Who knows how to clear a minefield, then? ... I see! Not feeling so macho today, are we? OK. How about some road-sweeping instead? That's more like it! Right, Carlos ...'

Such co-operation could only last a little while. Both victors and vanquished cared solely about how soon they would get home. Political prevarication over that would quickly rekindle animosity, and spread gloom and disillusionment. More than 600 miles away on South Georgia the situation was the same. On 16 June I had received an anxious signal from Chris Nunn seeking some indication of 'M' Company's future. It concluded typically: 'If there is no remission, please send length of sentence.' They clearly felt terribly cut off. How little we knew of their circumstances ...

15

THE FORGOTTEN COMPANY

Two days after Guy Sheridan had left South Georgia to join the Task Force, Chris Nunn led a small team from 'M' Company to site observation-posts around the perimeter. It was Saturday 1 May. In cold, windy weather they saw for the first time some of the precipitous and barren country around the settlement. They lunched in the old church at Grytviken. It was an eerie experience. The building was intact, the organ worked, and the last priest's cassock still hung in the vestry. On a nearby shelf was a complete library of books written in Norwegian. They were beautifully bound, and included among the titles most of the well known English classics. All this had remained untouched for the last twenty years or so. The two wooden Christmas trees in the vestry gave Chris an idea. The next day he decreed in company orders that if 'M' Company were still there on 25 June, the Southern Hemisphere Christmas would be celebrated. It was a festivity which he fervently hoped not to have to arrange. The prospect of being a long-term garrison while the rest of 'Four-Two' might be in action seemed very depressing. Their routine was soon well established. It received an early test, however, at about 0100 hours on 7 May, when an unidentified vessel was detected by the Hope Point and Brown Mountain observation-posts. 'M' Company stood-to as a dark shape showing steaming lights sailed into the bay. The vessel was challenged on maritime channel 16, but gave no reply. Nunn decided that she had to be stopped before rounding the point completely. Beyond that, hostile troops could easily be landed to compromise Grytviken. He ordered the mortar controller, Sergeant Day, to fire two rounds of 81-mm para-illumination. The nearest 84-mm Carl Gustav teams loaded their anti-tank weapons and prepared to fire on the ship.

The illuminating rounds burst directly above the vessel with the most startling effect. There was a frenzy of shouting and running about on board, followed by simultaneous transmission on the hitherto dormant radio! 'Don't shoot, don't shoot! We are the tug *Salvageman*' was broadcast in an unmistakable Liverpool accent. Chris replied that the ship was within an ace of being engaged by anti-armour weapons. Unless she hove to immediately she would be fired upon. This time the response was instantaneous. An anchor splashed into the calm of the bay, the rattle of the chain echoing around the hills in the still night air.

Although the tug was undoubtedly genuine, an irritated Nunn insisted that her captain should proceed ashore at best speed to confirm formal identification and orders. The situation on board deteriorated into a comic opera as frantic attempts were made to find a serviceable rubber tender. During this performance the main part of the Company were stood down, out of the cold, and the disappointed 84-mm teams ordered to unload. After much pumping and cursing, graphically audible across the icy void, an inflatable boat finally flopped into the water. Energetic attempts to start a small outboard failed, despite further verbal abuse. Eventually the boat made erratic progress ashore under oar power. A fairly disjointed interview then revealed that the tug had been despatched to South Georgia to stand by for salvage operations. An indignant RNR Lieutenant-Commander complained that the Captain had been disorientated after being hit on the head by a piece of debris when the illumination rounds burst over his ship. Chris Nunn's reaction was unsympathetic. He pointed out that if they had announced their arrival no one would have been surprised, so no illumination would have been necessary. He conceded, however, that this had been a realistic test in which the standard of shooting had proved excellent. Honour was satisfied on both sides. It was the first of several alarms and excursions, none of which ever amounted to a genuine confrontation.

As time went by the peculiarities of the weather increasingly manifested themselves. Patterns varied by the day, sometimes within the hour. Without warning, extremes of conditions and temperatures would sweep over the island. A change from pleasant calm to ferocious winds in excess of 70 miles an hour might be accompanied by white-out blizzard conditions.

On one such occasion, the barometer had actually registered its highest reading since their arrival, 1026 millibars. Chris had set out with a party to view the awe-inspiring Nordenskold Glacier, across Cumberland Bay, using the MV *Albert Ross*. The clear weather deteriorated dramatically. Dense low stratus came scudding in from the south, bringing with it thick snow in squalls. The effect was dramatic and very sinister. Small icebergs, called 'growlers', had often been seen close inshore, but now they saw an unforgettable spectacle. Complete icebergs came into being, each crashing from the glacial ice-cliffs into the water to emerge as huge, incandescent masses. The size of cathedrals, they drifted off into the Antarctic ocean. Later, there were even more fantastic sights, as icebergs whose centre of gravity had changed with erosion turned turtle, exposing their water-sculptured undersides.

On 25 May, the cable ship *Iris* rounded Hope Point into King Edward's Bay. She brought back the Royal Marine detachment from HMS *Endurance*. They were returning to the scene of their spirited action, in which they had inflicted disproportionate losses on Argentine men and equipment before being captured. Chris Nunn and his officers walked with Lieutenant Keith Mills, the detachment's commander, around King Edward Point. With difficulty they extracted from this young subaltern a modest account of the action for which he had subsequently been awarded the Distinguished Service Cross. Soon afterwards, boats from *Endurance* came ashore for the newly arrived marines. Captain Nick Barker had a soft spot for his 'Booties', and was not slow to reclaim them. On board they received a tumultuous welcome from their shipmates, who had not seen them since their capture and subsequent repatriation.

Some time later, word came from *Endurance* to expect large ships in the vicinity. These turned out to be the *Queen Elizabeth 2*, *Canberra*, *Norland* and RFA *Stromness*. *QE2* was to transfer 5 Brigade, which was on its way to reinforce 3 Commando Brigade in the Falklands. Cumberland Bay became more crowded than it must have been in the whaling days. Once again it proved a haven from the South Atlantic weather and, to a lesser extent, a refuge from the Argentine Air Force. By now, the men on South Georgia were aware that the main landings had taken place and a beach-head established. Almost all their sketchy knowledge had been gleaned from monitoring the intermittent news broadcasts they could pick up. There was a virtual black-out on naval signals for security reasons. Because of that, Chris had not received our 'situation report', sent to them as soon as we were established ashore.

Real news was on hand, however, in the welcome presence of Robert Ward, the Royal Marines Major who had been Ship's Adjutant of *Canberra* since her amphibious adventures began. He was able to bring them up to date on the successful landings, the air attacks, the protracted logistic build-up, the consequences this had had for subsequent operations. Before *Canberra* sailed for South Georgia, however, all units had still been within the beach-head, so he had no news of developments inland. With him came the sad figure of another old friend, Alan West, Captain of HMS *Ardent*. During the winter exercises in Norway 'M' Company had been crowded into his cheerful ship for an amphibious raid. Many firm friendships had been formed between 'Jack' and 'Royal' as a result. The stark realization that *Ardent*, with some of their friends, now lay at the bottom of San Carlos Bay shocked the marines. For Chris, there was the tragic revelation that two helicopters from the Brigade Air Squadron had been shot down on 'D'-day. He knew all who had been killed or wounded, as well as their families. Even more harrowing was this brutal reminder of how vulnerable his brother Richard would be in the fighting to come.

How demoralizing it felt to have to stay whilst others, obviously less prepared, sailed on to war! That was something many marines now questioned bitterly. Their attention was diverted, however, by a revised intelligence assessment passed through *Endurance*. Because of all this maritime activity around South Georgia, the likelihood of enemy air attack there had become much greater. For 'M' Company, improvisation with their own and captured automatic weapons to repel air attacks was given urgent incentive. The graphic descriptions of events on 'D'-day in San Carlos emphasized their vulnerability in so similar a situation. The Argentine air capability might seem reduced by South Georgia's greater distance from the mainland, but carrier-borne fighters remained a threat which could not be discounted at that stage of the war.

Chris Nunn had his own additional worries, which he kept to himself:

We managed to pick up the BBC World Service that evening and I heard with awful dread that during a large land battle a

Scout helicopter had been shot down. I knew all the pilots as friends, but with a selfish callousness I could only think: 'Please God, I don't care who, but not Richard'. The following day was my mother's birthday. She was obviously in my thoughts more than ever. I held the anti-aircraft trial firing. It was not a success so I rebriefed those concerned for a re-run. I then flew by Wasp to *Endurance* to express to the Captain my concern at the effect lack of news of the land battle would have on my men. Those fighting were our friends and probably our own unit, and so we had a right to know what was going on.

Endurance had gleaned more from the news the night before. The battle was for a place called Goose Green. After fierce fighting it had been taken by the Second Battalion, The Parachute Regiment, but casualties were unknown. David, my brother-in-law, was with 2 Para. My heart sank further. Yes, a Scout had been shot down and the pilot killed. Captain Nick Barker, as usual, fully understood my point of view and gave his assurance that he would endeavour to obtain more and regular news. From him that promise was good enough for me.

On Tuesday 1 June I recorded that we were five months into the year. Where had it gone and where was it going? I, along with many others, had hardly seen my family in that time. We left for Norway late in December and after our brief and interrupted return had departed again. My journal records the amount I was missing my wife, Siobhan, and two small sons Adam and Rory.

Heavy snow fell continuously that day precluding any re-run of the anti-aircraft trial. Despite fierce winds and drifting snow I walked, or rather staggered, to the Gull Lake observation-post with the Sergeant-Major. Although there had been continuous snow, ski-ing was rarely possible, because the wind caused so much drifting that the bare surface was so often exposed. We returned to base as the weather deteriorated further. Throughout the night I received radio reports that all three OPs were suffering from the wind and snow. They spent the night continuously digging themselves out. Snippets of news that evening were that Mounts Kent and Challenger had been taken.

Two days later, Friday 4 June, the snow was thick. The OPs had, after a terrible blizzard two nights before, fully re-established themselves, which was a credit to the corporals and marines concerned. I decided to spend the day writing some of the confidential reports on members of the Company which I knew, come hell or high water, would be called for on our return to Plymouth. Come deployment or conflict the paperwork must go on! At about 1030 hours I heard a Wasp helicopter, one of the two from HMS *Endurance*, land and close down. Two or three minutes later I saw the figure of Lientenant-Commander Tony Ellabeck, who was the ship's Flight Commander, walking past my window, obviously coming into the Post Office. I stood and gave him a mock salute. The outside door opened and I heard him talk briefly to Mr. Juleff, the Sergeant-Major. My greetings were cut short by his words, 'I'm sorry, I have a letter for you from the Captain.' I looked back and said, 'It's Richard, isn't it?' 'Yes,' he replied. I said, 'He's dead.' 'Yes, I'm sorry,' he responded. No more was said. I sat and despite my efforts broke down ...

'M' Company endured blizzard conditions throughout most of June, with a windchill on one occasion of around minus 45 degrees centigrade. Too cold for any activity other than basic survival! At one time heavy snow showers alternated with torrential rain. This is the most nightmarish combination of the elements, known as 'cold-wet' in the arctic warfare jargon. The three forward observation-posts bore the brunt of these atrocious conditions. On 9 June the Gull Lake OP had to be temporarily evacuated when its tents were destroyed. Moving about in these conditions was extremely hazardous and a section commander, Corporal Carter, was injured and had to be evacuated. There was no doubt that the Company's cold-weather expertise, as well as their specialist clothing, were vital.

The mood of the Company remained one of restlessness and frustration. News that 'J' Company had been formed before the main landings undermined the justification for 'M' to rejoin 'Four-Two'. Marines became bored and depressed. It was a testing time for leadership at every level. Any constructive activity which would maintain interest was seized upon.

Events passed routinely until Monday 14 June. At 2000 hrs that evening they heard on the World Service that a cease-fire had been called in the Falklands. Chris immediately 'cleared lower deck' to pass the news. The Operations room was told to inform the Troop HQ in Grytviken and the three OPs by radio. There was no indication of how the victory had been achieved, nor of what part 'Four-Two' had played. But lack of detailed information did not matter. The end was in sight.

The sense of excitement was tremendous, and it seemed entirely appropriate there should be a celebration. Despite his own grief,

Chris Nunn joined in as someone produced a battered recording of The Last Night at The Proms. 'Rule, Britannia!' and 'Pomp and Circumstance' blared out. Chris wrote:

> It was a pleasure to mingle among the marines. I had not enjoyed the more difficult aspects of command our time on South Georgia had demanded. I realize in retrospect I had, even before Richard's death, been under a certain amount of strain, but in circumstances I had never before imagined. Because of this I made an initial decision to distance myself and implement the full chain of command which, I still believe, was the correct one. It increasingly certainly proved so as life and morale became more difficult to maintain while our stay lengthened and the sense of purpose diminished.
>
> I went into the room which had been given over as the Corporals' Mess and invited them into the Officers' and Senior NCOs' Mess. In the past few weeks I had demanded a lot of them, because on their leadership had rested the day-to-day drive necessary to keep their sections fully motivated, whether in the OPs room, on guard, or carrying out the mundane administrative duties which kept the base running and hygienic ...

On the morning of 15 June the Company awoke to blizzard conditions. A huge iceberg had blown inshore and was looming close in off King Edward Point. This foul weather continued throughout the day. Captain Barker of HMS *Endurance* had often spoken to Chris about repossessing Southern Thule, one of the South Sandwich Islands which lie off the Antarctic coast. Some six years before the war in the Falklands a party of Argentines had landed on Thule to establish a base. There was still a presence there now. Although diplomatic protests had been made, the UK seemed tacitly to have acquiesced to the argument that this was simply a scientific survey location. But Nick Barker had long since detected that it was a radio intercept station, gleaning intelligence from the important international radio traffic around the South Pole. Even before the war, it had rankled with him that the island should continue to be usurped. Now he was seeking permission to repossess this barren, ice-covered volcano.

On the following day, at a meeting on board *Endurance*, Nick Barker confirmed that the Thule option had been approved. Barker had spoken to the enemy in their base camp, inviting them to surrender, but they had refused, declaring that they had been ordered to fight to the death. Chris Nunn briefed him that, if the reported group of around one hundred troops and scientists resisted, then there was no option but to mount a proper operation. He represented strongly that it would be an unjustifiable risk to mount such an operation without naval gunfire support. Northwood grudgingly accepted this, and HMS *Yarmouth*, with the RFA *Olmeda*, were despatched from the Total Exclusion Zone surrounding the Falkland Islands. Their passage would take several days.

With the detachments from HMSS *Endurance* and *Antrim*, there were sufficient marines to assemble a reasonable force. But security would still have to be maintained on South Georgia. Time was critical as the seasonal pack ice was already beginning to isolate Thule. *Endurance* and the ocean-going tug *Salvageman* therefore sailed in advance of the reinforcing ships, with Tac HQ and reconnaissance elements of 'M' Company embarked. *Salvageman* was the nearest equivalent to an ice-breaker that Nick Barker could hope for. There were two light helicopters and one Wessex for troop lift available. Chris Nunn described the scene when the advanced force arrived:

At 0700 hrs on 19 June we arrived off Thule in nasty weather. The sea was rough. There was very low stratus and the upper decking was always iced with freezing spray. We had seen numerous icebergs during our passage but no sign of the actual pack ice we feared. Southern Thule itself had to be seen to be believed. Against the grey sea and leaden sky it rose up, a mass of snow and ice, shaped in a pyramid typical of volcanoes. Its top was lost in the clouds. There was no coast-line, the ice cliffs dropped straight into the icy sea. There were some big bergs in the vicinity. One I remember was huge and flat, it reminded me of a vast floating airfield. The base itself was out of sight. Barker had told the Argentines we were coming but there was no need to advertise exactly when, particularly before the other two ships joined us.

As with South Georgia we lacked accurate intelligence. Recent British Arctic Survey reports gave indications that extensive building had been in progress and it was confirmed, by contacting their base in Cambridge, that one very large hangar was being constructed. Military intelligence indicated that the base was garrisoned by approximately 110 men and it was highly likely that they had helicopter support in the form of a winterized Chinook or Puma, probably one of either type.

This was a worry. I knew that a recce in force was necessary and had anticipated the requirement by embarking a section of the Recce Troop, of which half the men had served in the Mountain and Arctic Warfare Cadre. I gave a warning order to their leader, Sergeant Napier, to expect to mount a full ten-man patrol at mid-afternoon that day. The problem was how to insert them? Boats were out! It had to be by helicopter, despite the risk of detection through noise ...

Chris Nunn now decided that he and Sergeant Napier must fly over the ground to identify routes and a landing point. The hydrographers found a map somewhere in the bowels of *Endurance*. This provided at least some geographical data. Southern Thule is 5 kilometres long north-east to south-west, and 4 kilometres wide west to east. It rises 2,300 feet to the top of Mount Larsen, on which is an active volcanic crater. The only flat ground is a spit of land at the south-eastern tip. Here the enemy base had been established.

By 1300 hours Sergeant Napier and his patrol had been successfully dropped off. Each marine had experience of alpine snow and ice climbing, and their equipment included axes, crampons and ropes. One of the most demanding and specialized roles within the Royal Marines was about to be searchingly tested. The lengthy and hazardous training would at last be evaluated on an operation in arctic conditions. After the earlier disaster on South Georgia's glacier, both Nick Barker and Chris Nunn were keeping fingers tightly crossed.

The insertion went well. But conditions were certainly dangerous. Each man fitted twelve-point crampons in the hovering aircraft, before jumping one by one onto the icy slope. The crampons and ice-axes gave them purchase while they grouped together. As if to emphasize the penalty for carelessness, one rucksack was dislodged. It tumbled sickeningly down the mountainside and into the sea below. Fortunately the contents were equipment, rather than personal clothing. That would make the difference between life and death should a blizzard sweep over them.

On board *Endurance* there came confirmation of what had always been a concern. The aircraft insertion had been detected by the Argentines. It was 1500 hours. HMS *Yarmouth* and the *Olmeda* were not expected to rendezvous before 0400 hours the next morning. The reconnaissance group was clearly vulnerable to enemy reaction, probably in the form of a heliborne force that would outnumber them heavily. Then, perversely, communications between Napier and the ship suddenly broke down. There was no means of establishing whether the patrol realized that they had been detected. Several hours of daylight remained.

It was decided to bluff it out. Helicopters began to fly around transmitting spurious radio traffic, as if a major operation was taking place elsewhere on the island. At one stage Chris Nunn's helicopter flew close enough to the Argentine base camp for him to photograph their impressive facilities. There appeared to be little evidence of external defences, or even activity within the base. But, an aviator himself, Chris knew how vulnerable the helicopter was to hand-held weapons, and was none too keen to linger. Attempts to express this point of view to the pilot were temporarily hindered as the latter's head-set became unplugged from the intercom. Chris ended up taking many more pictures than he considered prudent in the circumstances.

As darkness fell the enemy threat against Napier and his patrol was temporarily lifted. Radio communications were still very bad, however. Although the ship had now managed to warn the patrol that they had been detected, their transmissions back were indecipherable. The weather deteriorated sharply as the long night began.

Sergeant Napier had divided his patrol into two groups, one commanded by himself, the other by Sergeant Mac McLeman. After their precarious insertion, they found that the crevassing around them was very severe. Napier decided that the patrol had to climb nearer to the fracture line from which the crevasses spread. In his report, he described the ground as 'hard packed wind-driven snow with large ice fields and crevassing, especially on the convex spurs. Route-finding was extremely dangerous. Several members of the patrol broke through snow bridges at different times'.

Previous training led Napier to think about roping the men together – experience and common sense caused him to discount the idea. He believed that, with the loads they were carrying, if one man fell he would certainly pull a small group of others with him. During the tortuous trek to the observation point the patrol moved in to the face of fierce south-west winds. Napier, leading both groups, then fell into a crevasse. The others managed to pull him back out. According to plan, despite the appalling conditions, he finally brought his patrol to the vicinity of the base camp. A stealthy stalk showed that the best OP site was on a forward slope, so it could not be occupied before dusk. Just after last light Sergeant McLeman and his team moved into position overlooking the base. Sergeant Napier and his group were in the rear to provide protection against a flanking patrol that might be searching for them. Surveillance of the enemy had been achieved.

During the night, driving wind and snow produced white-out conditions. In windchill temperatures of minus 50 degrees, Napier withdrew the forward OP to his own location. There they established a continual sentry routine and concentrated on surviving the night. Throughout their ordeal the group had continually to dig their tents free of spindrift. Napier recalled that they were covered every thirty-five minutes. By first light the OP was back in position, but the appalling weather prevented them observing any activity at the base. HMS *Yarmouth* and the RFA *Olmeda* were now on station. The decisive advantage of naval gunfire support directed by this patrol, should prove overwhelming once the visibility lifted.

During the night, *Endurance* had intercepted the BBC World Service. They were already reporting that Southern Thule had been retaken. Once again, the BBC had irresponsibly anticipated the outcome of an operation before it had been achieved. Buenos Aires separately reported that the scientists on the island had been instructed to surrender; but only because British helicopters had strafed the base with rockets and machine-gunfire. Each newscast was as inaccurate as the other!

The weather began to clear soon after first light. The OP was able to scan the base again, but could see no activity. The orange semi-spherical buildings seemed like frozen tombs. Captain Barker declared on the radio that if the Argentines did not surrender, offensive action would follow. He set the deadline at 1130 hours. H-hour approached, while tension mounted ashore and at sea. Eventually, at 1128 hours, HMS *Endurance* was radioed from the base and told that the garrison would surrender. There was just time for *Yarmouth* to be told to hold her fire. Shortly afterwards Sergeant McLeman radioed that a single man had walked from the buildings with a white flag. Captain Barker told Chris Nunn to fly ashore and take the surrender. The Wasp helicopter landed close to where McLeman and his team were covering an Argentine sub-lieutenant. He was clearly very frightened by the appearance of these camouflaged warriors from the frozen wastes.

He revealed that there were only nine other people on Southern Thule. Somehow the intelligence reports had rather over-estimated the opposition!

The state of the base was chaotic, because it had been systematically ransacked. Lavishly equipped for a sizeable garrison, its facilities included a surgery and dental departments. However, when the presence of Sergeant Napier's patrol had become known, the occupants had run amok. Almost all the fittings and equipment were smashed. They had even despoiled their own food supply. Then, throughout the long night, the apprehensive defenders awaited attack from the troops which they knew had been landed. The suspense had obviously had a profound psychological effect on them. They admitted to having been armed with a variety of weapons, but these had all been dumped in the sea the previous evening. Which would have made the exhortations from the mainland difficult to carry out ...

A day of searching and examining the base culminated with an official surrender ceremony in the wardroom of HMS *Endurance*. There was also well deserved champagne in Chris Nunn's cabin for Sergeant Napier and his nine Royal Marines. Despite the privations they had endured the previous night, satisfaction in their achievement kept spirits high.

This had been one of the most difficult but successful special operations in the whole war. Although there were no casualties on either side, the potential for disaster had been ever-present. Less specialized troops would certainly have frozen to death, or required a hazardous recovery operation. At any time the demoralized enemy could have revived a will to resist, had the marines' ability to operate ashore in those conditions seemed in doubt. Instead, Operation 'Keyhole' ended the Falklands war with another amphibious success. The Royal Navy and 'M' Company, 42 Commando, had performed the finale, having originally raised the curtain in this area of the South Atlantic. For many marines of 'M' Company, however, there was the frustration, for the second time, of not going into action. Their satisfaction was that neither Operation 'Paraquat' nor 'Keyhole' would have been feasible without them in support.

For all of them, the return home now loomed larger than anything else. But, before departing from South Georgia, there was one more event to be staged:

On 25 June we had our Christmas celebration. The guys entered into the spirit completely. They decorated their accommodation with paper-chains and other home-made ideas. The two wooden Christmas trees and lights, last used so long ago by the residents of Grytviken, were brought carefully from the church and set up. *Endurance* had returned on 24 June and tied up alongside the whaling station. We were then given our share of captured Argentine red and white wine from Southern Thule. On the evening of the 24th I, along with all the officers and SNCOs, put lighted candles in jam-jars and trudged our way through the snow, singing carols outside the troop accommodation. We finished on the jetty by *Endurance*, serenading a very bemused Officer of the Watch! Captain Barker came to the ship's side and we were invited to respective messes for 'Christmas' drinks. On the evening of the 25th celebrations began in earnest. The chefs, Corporal Smith and Marine Mellor, had managed extremely well. Captain Ian Grant had, over the weeks, hoarded various foodstuffs from passing ships. The fruits of his efforts were presented in the form of a full Christmas dinner of soup, roast turkey and pork with all the trimmings, and a full spread of vegetables. This was followed by Christmas pudding. Captured wine was served throughout the meal by the officers and SNCOs. When all the guys had eaten we had our own celebration in our mess room. The evening was rounded off by a mock trial of Marine Boswell. He was charged with having been in the Army before joining the Corps. After much hilarity and costume drama, he was found guilty and sentenced by the jury to be dyed green. This was duly done and for some days afterwards he had a very sickly tinge to his skin – it would be fair to say that he was not the only one!

Three weeks later, 'M' Company, 42 Commando, Royal Marines, handed over South Georgia to a relief garrison from the Scots Guards. They then set sail for Ascension Island and a flight to RAF St Mawgan in Cornwall.

16

COMPLETION

Fortunately, salvation for the POWs at Stanley Airport was not long delayed. Conditions in the airfield encampment became increasingly unhygienic, while the spartan circumstances weakened the will to survive. The Argentine officers somehow still remained better off than the conscripts. They had to be allowed to retain their pistols for 'self-defence', and guard dogs protected their food supplies. On 18 June it was announced that the majority of the prisoners would soon be repatriated in *Canberra*. However, a selected group of commanders and specialists were retained as hostages against mainland aggression. Our own feelings were mixed. Clearly at least some of us must stay until the 10,000 or so captives had left. Eventually it would have to be *Canberra* that carried the majority of us back to UK: her diversion postponed our repatriation. Those closely associated with the 'Great White Whale' also felt it highly distasteful that she should be made to return these invaders to their homeland. It was, however, obvious that the Argentine propaganda apparatus would exploit a mass return in their own vessels. In the end we were just relieved to see them go. It meant our own departure must be closer. By now boredom and uncertainty were being aggravated by the discomforts of camping in the festering outskirts of Stanley. There was no electric light or running water, trench foot remained an insidious problem, and diarrhoea was ominously taking hold again.

When there was time to do so, I sent letters or signals to those who depended upon us. At last I could write home. They seem such uninformative letters now. But we were exhausted, and circumstances felt so unreal:

18 Jun.

Hallo darling. Well, as you know by now we won and I survived, which seems a pretty satisfactory conclusion all round? Now we are into the frustration of post-war reorganization ...

Our pleasant duty at the moment is to be the unit which disarms the Argies as they shamble disconsolately onto the airfield – tell Tara she was correct, 'The Argies are tragic!'

21 Jun.

Basically 42 Cdo are knee-deep in mud (or worse) on the outskirts of Stanley, which is the most desolate dump you ever did see. The 'town' is actually worse, overcrowded, filthy, wreathed in smoke, ravaged by looters. All in all a typical 'end of war' scene which I am determined to keep the unit away from ... an increasingly squalid and frustrating situation which hopefully will conclude soon, before cholera or dysentery, or both, sweep through us to take the toll the enemy couldn't.

Regular sitreps were also signalled back to our Rear Party in Bickleigh and, of course, to 'Munch' Company, to whom we listed the casualties:

FROM CO 42 CDORM

1. FOL UNCONDITIONAL SURRENDER OF EN LAST NI WE ARE REGPING IN STANLEY AT SEVERAL LOCS INCL A VERY BATTERED MOODY BROOK. EARLY INDICATIONS ARE THAT WE MAY REMAIN A WEEK OR TWO SO CONSTANT LOBBYING WILL BE DONE CONCERNING YOUR EARLY RELIEF.
2. DURING LAST WEEK 42 CDORM ENGAGED IN SEVERAL OPS CULMINATING IN A UNIT NI ATTACK ON MT HARRIET. THIS WAS HEAVILY DEFENDED BUT AFTER FIERCE FIGHTING FELL BEFORE FIRST LT. BY MIDDAY WE HAD TAKEN OVER 300 POW. THE SURRENDER FOL A DAY LATER
3. SADLY THIS SUCCESS COULD NOT BE ACHIEVED WITHOUT COST BUT OUR LOSSES ARE HEARTEN-INGLY SMALL COMPARED TO OTHER LESS FOR-TUNATE UNITS. THE CAS LIST IS AT PARA 4. OTHERWISE WE ARE ALL IN HIGH MORALE ALTHOUGH TIRED AND SOMEWHAT WORN BY

MORE THAN 14 DAYS IN THE MOUNTAINS DURING
MOSTLY SEVERE WEATHER. IT HAS BEEN A LONG
WINTER EXCLAM. WE ALL LOOK FWD TO SEEING M
COY AGAIN AND SOON ...

When the 'Argies' left I went down to the jetty to watch their
embarkation. Boats packed with elated POWs were heading for
Canberra. It was a time for reflection, at the end of a remarkable
experience. We had just heard of Galtieri's resignation, which
seemed a symbolically satisfying conclusion. I had also been tipped
off that we would return in *Canberra* as soon as she was available. If
only 'M' Company could rejoin and return with us, our
satisfaction would be complete. But there was no chance of that,
although Brigade HQ was mounting a vigorous campaign to have
them relieved and brought back as soon as possible.

A blue-clad, woolly islander sidled up beside me. 'Good
riddance to the Dago bastards, I say. You sure taught them a
lesson they won't forget! We can sleep easy at nights again now.' I
asked him if he thought we would return again to eject subsequent
invaders. ''Course you would! We're British, aren't we?' There
was no refuting that, so I returned to my thoughts. In contrast,
Max Hastings wrote in the *Daily Express* of another rare exchange
with a local:

> Lieutenant-Colonel Nick Vaux ... CO of 42 Commando, was
> commiserating with an old shepherd whose horse had just died,
> and whose house had been thoroughly vandalised by the
> Argentinians.
>   Surely he could put it all together again, he said
> encouragingly to the Falklander. 'I don't know,' said the old
> man doubtfully. 'Just tell me – are you all going to come down
> here and do this for all of us again?'

It had been an unexpectedly simple, almost chivalrous conflict.
Atrocities on either side were unknown. Enemy wounded
invariably shared medical attention. Prisoners were looked after
before being swiftly repatriated. Although invaders, they had
conducted themselves more or less in accordance with the Geneva
Convention. As warriors, however, they had not done so well.
'Military pygmies' is how Peter Babbington dismissed them.
Perhaps that was rather harsh. Apart from their courageous pilots,
some Argentines, notably the marines, fought tenaciously under
heavy fire before defeat. However, they were completely out of

To all the military forces & crew aboard this ship. We are sorry for all the troubles we may have caused you during this trip, and we are greatly grateful to you for your kind treatement to us — Thank you

Four Argentine soldiers

This message – handed to the RSM on our re-embarkation in *Canberra* – was scrawled on a menu card, the ribbon of which can be discerned on the edge.

their depth, outclassed in experience, initiative and fitness. In particular, their conscripts had none of the self-confidence and high morale which our own troops possessed. This was because leadership at every level was generally abysmal.

But why had we prevailed? How had outnumbered, exhausted, British infantry so easily driven the enemy from his mountain strongholds? Where did this apparent invincibility come from?

In 'Four-Two', the average age of marines was less than twenty. They were 'teenagers'. By all modern criteria their youth and inexperience should have been highly susceptible to insecurity or depression. For weeks they had remained afloat, exposed in the glare of uncertain publicity. Finally, they were precariously disembarked under air attack. But amongst today's youth is an awareness of the media, and the discernment to scrutinize politics or strategy. Many of them had realized the risks of this venture long before the air attacks in San Carlos. Afterwards they had never faltered once. At no time was there the slightest indication that resolve was diminishing; indeed, during their ordeal in the mountains they had positively rejected any suggestion of a respite. The only times morale became a worry were when we waited impatiently for the breakout at San Carlos. Or now, here in Stanley, while we anticipated repatriation.

Leadership, of course, was the key. This began at the level of section commander, and was most prominent within the companies. That was why so many of our casualties had been young officers or NCOs. It was the explanation for the concentration of decorations between captain and corporal. Team spirit came next: the cohesive thread of military history; the *raison d'être* of Special Forces. The section, platoon, or company forms a separate identity, while their parent unit provides security in exchange for commitment, pride as the reward for loyalty. Last, but never least, came the peculiarly British, sardonic humour. An instinctive inheritance from one generation of servicemen to the next, we could not have won without it. Forgiving mistakes, dispelling frustration, mocking at fear, it eased our burden, made light of adversity. In the turn of a phrase, the roll of an eye, disaster could be mocked, misery uplifted.

Retrospectively, there was one other important influence. Through radio, newspapers, video and letters, we had always sensed approval and encouragement from home. Naively, almost undeservedly, we took it for granted. Even when the tears were slipping unashamedly on *Canberra*, as she steamed triumphantly up the Solent to a welcome few in history have been privileged to receive. Even then, I don't believe we knew how fortunate we were! Six months later, on a lecture tour of USMC establishments, I sat in the audience after speaking. My front seat was between two imposing, crew-cut 'Bird' colonels. Our presentations always ended with video of those emotional scenes in Southampton. On this occasion I noted with surprise that it was one of my neighbours who had been reduced to tears. As the lights went up I began some distracting remark, but was cut short: 'Colonel. You should know that I was not so moved at British triumph. My emotion was for the welcome home you enjoyed from the Falklands, which we did not after Vietnam!' We were indeed fortunate. Who can say how long resolve could have been maintained without support from the nation?

On 24 June we embarked back in our beloved *Canberra*. From all sides came greetings, smiles, handshakes, and words of welcome. It was the next best thing to coming home. As I trod gingerly across the gleaming lobby floor a fresh, scented Miss Mulberry came out from behind her counter and gave me a warm embrace, despite my grimy condition. In the stateroom were flowers, cards and champagne. One simple greeting said 'I prayed for you every day. Welcome Back! Geoffrey.' Uncorking the Veuve Clicquot I shed my putrid garments to revel under a cascade of hot water for the first time in thirty days. There I remained until the bottle was empty, and the dirt and smell finally washed away.

Next day, *Canberra* sailed around to San Carlos. We were back where it had all begun. There was little incentive to go ashore, nor were the means to do so readily available. Almost all the helicopters and landing-craft remained in Stanley, to be used for ferrying stores on to the other ships. For various reasons it had been decided that marines and paratroops would return separately. These were largely functional: the red beret is based at Aldershot, the green in the West Country. 2 Para, with other elements of 5 Brigade, had travelled south in *Norland*. Now it had been decided that their sister battalion should return with them to Ascension Island. From there both units would fly. We were all sad not to sail home with our friends in 3 Para. We had experienced a great deal together since leaving Southampton, so returning in company seemed fitting. These sentiments were in sharp contrast to press speculation that regimental rivalry was considered uncontrollable now the war was over.

An individual absentee from the original company was 'Uncle Tom'. Soon after the surrender he had left for the UK and a course at the Royal College of Defence Studies. His ebullient presence would be sorely missed – not least by myself. The job of Military Force Commander on the return voyage now devolved upon CO, 42 Commando. Enjoying a well earned rest in the stateroom opposite mine would be Brigadier Julian Thompson.

Naturally a passage back in *Canberra* was highly sought after at every level. The control of applicants, or gate-crashers, became a major issue, calling for stringent measures. All over the Task Force groups, or unattached individuals, homed in on the 'Great White Whale'. Repelling boarders was vigorously directed by the indefatigable 'Beagle'. Fresh from his duties as the maritime commandant of a floating prison, he mercilessly banished anyone suspected of being a stowaway. Early one morning we stood on the bridge together as a series of helicopters disgorged battle-stained figures stooped beneath packs. As they stumbled off the landing-pad, heads bowed against the blast from the rotors, Chris Burne scrutinized each one piercingly. Every now and again he would rasp down an intercom to the deck below, 'Check No.4 in that stick, Master-at-Arms.' 'Aye, aye, Sir' meant that, regardless of rank or cap-badge, the individual must now justify his presence on *Canberra*. Failure to do so brought instant expulsion. Momentarily, in a swirl of movement, I glimpsed distinguished grey hair before it was furtively hooded. The crouched figure shielding itself behind the rest as they scurried away seemed suddenly familiar. 'The Beagle' quivered with excitement, like a gun-dog poised to retrieve:

'Master. That man in the hood. Check him.' Sure enough, it turned out to be Ewen Tailyour!

Without much hope, I intervened on his behalf. He had slept in a bath on *Intrepid*. During the war he had lived mostly on landing-craft. Perhaps he had nowhere else to go? 'The Beagle' remained implacable. After I had declared that Ewen could share with a 'Four-Two' officer, and had accepted responsibility for the Southby-Tailyour behaviour, Chris began to relent. Eventually he succumbed to his own sporting instincts when he discovered that Ewen was desperate to get back quickly and compete in the Round-Britain Yacht race.

On 25 June we sailed for Stanley again to pick up Brigade HQ. Afterwards, as the silhouette of Fanning Head shrank below the horizon, the real world suddenly seemed discernible. We began receiving a shower of congratulatory signals. One that was especially appropriate came from Admiral Woodward, the Task Force Commander:

To: CANBERRA
OPERATION CORPORATE – DEPARTURE. Very much regret I was unable to visit in the general exodus to say Goodbye personally. P and O Service, as an LPH [Heliborne Commando Carrier], Floating Harley Street, Maritime Wormwood Scrubs, and great survivor of San Carlos Bay was in the true style. Well done. Bon Voyage Great White Whale.

Another that seemed to make it all worthwhile quoted from a letter sent to the Ministry of Defence:

... I hope that you can find a way, with the sophisticated equipment at your disposal, to send thanks and three cheers to all members of your Task Force from this particular, most grateful family. You have been in our thoughts day and night for weeks, as we are aware of the relative luxury we live in, and the small price 'we' pay for our freedom and peace ...

On our side, one of the final messages we sent home said:

OPERATION CORPORATE – SITREP.

1. THE WHOLE UNIT LESS M COY, THE WOUNDED AND TWENTY ODD RANKS ON LSL/LPD ATTS ARE NOW EMBARKED IN CANBERRA. STAFF PLANNING CURRENTLY INCLS EARLIEST POSS RELIEF OF M COY BUT TIMINGS AND ARRANGEMENTS STILL TO BE CLARIFIED. WE HOPE TO SAIL FOR UK WITHIN A FEW DAYS AND TO ARR BEFORE MID JULY. DESTINATION THERE AND DISEMBARK ARRANGE-MENTS NOT YET KNOWN.
2. THE WAR STORIES MUST WAIT UNTIL OUR RETURN BUT ALL CONCERNED HAD THEIR SHARE OF THE ACTION AND PLAYED THEIR PART MAG-NIFICENTLY. MOST OF THE UNIT WAS IN THE FD FOR NEARLY A MONTH IN DEMANDING TERRAIN AND APPALLING WEATHER. WE ARE ALL TIRED BUT ELATED AT THE THOUGHT OF RETURNING HOME FOR SOME LONG OVERDUE LEAVE. THIS SHOULD BE AT LEAST SIX WEEKS AND CAN BE PLANNED ON DURING AUG/SEPT
3. START BAKING THE OGGIES AND RACKING THE SCRUMPI!

It was decided that the three-week voyage home would be in keeping with *Canberra*'s proper role. Only essential 'Admin or Reorg' would divert embarked troops from rest and relaxation. Eating, light exercise, eventually sunbathing, whiled away the daylight hours. In the evenings there were films, concerts and parties. The contribution of the Commando Forces Band to morale and enjoyment was inestimable. Daily they performed to several different audiences. A concert in the lounge, martial music on the upper deck, a sing-song for some unit party. As the weather improved their outdoor performances excelled. A Beat Retreat one evening, in the glow of the setting sun, can never be forgotten. Nor will the memory of 'Four-Two's' final 'smoker' fade. On this occasion, only the CO and RSM were invited as outsiders.

The theme of the evening was musical cabaret. The material for amusement was ridicule of the enemy, of the officers, and our recent experiences, all skilfully interwoven. Within a group of several hundred, the inevitable talent is usually elusive to pin down. Somehow it had all been concentrated to advantage that evening. Chisnall and I laughed without end, choking back the tears of mirth as one sketch followed another. The players' feeling for the absurd was acute, their pantomime of mannerisms hilarious. One exquisite sketch depicted a Brigade 'O' Group at which even the resemblances to Brigade staff and commanding officers was uncanny. Another was a song-and-dance routine, the chorus dressed as nervous, immaculate Argentines who 'kept movin' on'. By popular demand Marine Toombs rendered his Malvinas song once more. The evening ended with stirring martial chorus again. Finally, we both left to cheers, an expression of goodwill that was extremely moving. It was a special celebration amongst so many – never to be forgotten.

As we churned back across the vast South Atlantic, a topical subject for many was the state of our feet. The three weeks of sodden chill had affected individuals in varying ways. My feet had stood up amazingly well, without blisters or chilblains, though my toes now ached spasmodically, usually in the middle of the night. But many people suffered from painful cold sores which needed medication and fresh air. As we approached Ascension Island, a team of specialists flew on board to conduct surveys of various groups. Whether this was to assess physical capability, or to try to improve footwear for the future, seemed uncertain. Within Commando Forces there was widespread concern about the consequences of residual damage to circulation. If that was diagnosed, then we might no longer be considered fit for service in the Arctic. A statistic which needs no embellishment was revealed by this medical survey of 'K' Company. Among them a horrifying 98 per cent were suffering from some form of cold injury to their feet. Eventually the majority recovered completely, but it is an indication of how time was running out for the infantry towards the end of the campaign.

The arrangements for our reception became another preoccupation. Understandably, local opinion and family feeling held that the Royal Marines should disembark at Plymouth. After all, it was home for many, and the base for most. But this would mean diverting *Canberra* from her own home port, Southampton. What is more, the huge liner could not get alongside at Plymouth; indeed there was some doubt that she should even come inside the breakwater. Instead of a swift, controlled disembarkation into one area, there would have to be landings by boat or helicopter to separate locations. Stores and equipment would subsequently have to be fetched from Southampton.

With the consideration that we had come to know so well, Captain Dennis Scott-Masson and his crew indicated that we should decide as we judged best. But, apart from our West Country loyalties, there was one other that appeared paramount to many of *Canberra*'s passengers. The 'Great White Whale' had been our home, as well as a comfortable base. An age ago we had left together on this adventure. Through uncertainty, danger and discomfort, her civilian crew had unstintingly supported the Task Force. Without their skill and dedication the landings could not have taken place. Now we were contentedly recuperating aboard en route to a victorious reunion. Surely we should enjoy it together? An unofficial census confirmed that view overwhelmingly. The decision was made to sail straight into Southampton.

The evening before we arrived, a final concert was held on the upper deck. In the distance the soft outline of English hills confirmed that home was now very close. Recently, we had been receiving local radio as well as the BBC Overseas Service, and it was becoming clear that interest in our arrival was not confined to family and friends. After a special dinner I went aloft to join other officers above the sun deck. They were watching a substantial 'chorus' from 'Four-Two' in a sing-song on the deck below them. This was being filmed for ITN News.

It was coming to an end as I arrived, confidently directed by Jeremy Hands. A dedicated volunteer for those PT torture-sessions on the way out, Jeremy was a familiar and popular figure with the troops. At this moment he was ecstatic about their performance: 'Colonel. I'm just going down to congratulate them. Do you want to come? ...' How to communicate a lifetime of cautious instinct for these occasions? Before that was possible, it was too late! One second Jeremy appeared to be walking amongst apparently admiring disciples. The next he had disappeared beneath jubilant, whooping marines. Seconds later he reappeared – naked as the day he was born. Triumphantly they held him aloft, parading jovially to the cheers of the assembled company. The grinning camera crew recorded it all, allegedly for the ITN Christmas party.

The next morning I awoke at around 0500 hours. Anticipation had proved too disturbing. These were my last reflective moments in the luxury of surroundings I could never actually afford. What a lot of unexpected memories this stateroom held. How much worry and work, conversation and laughter had taken place here ... Suddenly, the notes of the Reveille call sounded close by. There was no such routine on *Canberra*, so I was more than a little surprised. Then came a rattle at the door before it was briskly thrown open. Preceded by a Bugle Corporal, in came two files of immaculate 42 Commando Warrant Officers.

In the centre was WO2 Cook, the Chief Clerk, bearing a salver on which were sparkling glasses of champagne. Dumbfounded, I struggled into a dressing-gown. Apparently it had been decided a few hours before that this would be an appropriate prelude to the day. I tried hard to indicate approval and adequate appreciation. While we were toasting the occasion, a bewildered Brigadier appeared from across the passage to discover what all the noise was about. Even Regimental Sergeant-Major David Chisnall sipped at a glass. There was no doubt that this was going to be a most unusual day ...

Excitement and anticipation tingled throughout the ship. Radio broadcasts revealed our arrival to be a national preoccupation, as helicopters began landing VIP visitors on board. Assorted offshore mariners cruising in company were absorbed into fleets of motor-boats and dinghies. In the haze of a summer morning 2,500 jubilant commandos jostled together on the upper decks of the 'Great White Whale'. This would be her greatest moment: 'Queen of the Seas', 'First Lady of the Merchant Navy', 'Heroine for the Day', pronounced the commentators.

As *Canberra* left the Solent and turned towards Southampton, the ship's company of 400 volunteers must have thought so too. Her towering sides were pitted with indentations, her paintwork flaked from salt, the whole hull streaked with rust. Those spacious decks were still cluttered with the paraphernalia of war, the elegant superstructure distorted in order to land-on helicopters. But, with battered majesty, she steamed imposingly towards Berth 106, to a Welcome Home no other liner can have known. Overhead, there were almost more helicopters than once we had so desperately needed. Preceding her came fire tenders cascading clouds of spray. Alongside romped ferries, tenders and yachts. Sirens sounded. Flags fluttered. Bosoms were bared. It was an incredible spectacle, a most emotional experience.

As we approached West Dock, the colourful mass of people could be seen, waiting in their thousands. The volume of noise swelled until it was deafening. On board, our Commando Forces Band stirred emotions for the last time, while, on the jetty, their Royal Marine colleagues from Portsmouth responded. Instinctively their Directors of Music began to synchronize the music, until the two bands played as one. The ship was festooned with streamers and bedecked with home-made banners. '*Canberra* Cruises where *QE2* Refuses' reflected her crew's justifiable pride in their own achievements. 'Lock up your daughters, the Bootnecks are back' revealed the optimistic intentions of unmarried marines. 'Maggie Rules OK' simply stated an overwhelming conviction; regardless of politics, we had all sensed the authority and support behind our cause.

The last fifty yards seemed to take an age, as straining tugs pushed *Canberra* broadside on to the jetty. By now individuals could recognize each other, and frenzied scenes were enacted as they attracted one another's attention. Somehow I detected my family within the surging throng, waving miniature 'Four-Two' flags. After a while they located me. In a climax of collective emotion clouds of balloons were released as the bands prompted hundreds of voices into 'Land of Hope and Glory'. It was a fairytale ending to this extraordinary adventure. But, for once, those who had born the brunt of danger and adversity shared the glory. Chris Burne, speaking in an interview for ITN, remarked perceptively that 'Each young man who fought in this war deserves every cheer here today ...'

Brigadier Julian Thompson and the commanding officers came off first. We hung back to let him be seen by the troops. He was not only 'Man of the Match'; he had tried to safeguard their interests whenever possible, and they knew it. That seems as appropriate a memory to end upon as any of the endless warm welcomes which followed. Towering above us, lining the garlanded decks, were tiers of cheering troops. Green berets, bearing Naval, Marine or Army cap-badges, intermingled as they had done in battle. Amongst them could be seen the white caps of the Royal Navy and the Merchant Service, without whom we could not have succeeded. Here and there were civilians who had chosen to come along as well.

I indulged in one final glance along the shouldered white lanyards of my own 'Four-Two'. This was the end. Their war was over. We could go home.

EPILOGUE

We were all professionals in Commando Forces. Willing recipients of the Queen's shilling, content with the conditions of service. Stimulated by the challenge, variety and comradeship. Free to retire at minimal notice. But each man was also aware that he could be called to account at any time.

Corporal Jeremy Smith lies now in the churchyard of Buckland Monachorum. Just a few miles from Bickleigh camp, it is a quiet hamlet in his home county of Devon. His comrade, Corporal Lawrence Watts, is buried in Scotland. Nearby his widow, and the daughter he never saw, have their home. For us in 'Four-Two', they both symbolize the lost opportunity of youth, and the cost in grief, paid in that war by twenty-six Royal Marines or their next of kin. Both would have resented their unlucky destiny amongst the unfortunate few. Neither would have complained that they had been unaware of the risk.

Perhaps they might have been surprised not to have remained where they had fallen. Over the centuries, our casualties have been buried by their battlefields. In every continent can be found plots that are 'for ever England'. These two corporals actually lost their lives fighting to regain British territory. But traditions overturned by technology often seem to pose new dilemmas, or to set imponderable precedents. In the Royal Navy, the issue of repatriating the bodies of those killed did not arise. Some believe that this may have been for the best.

More disconcerting for many servicemen was the creation of the South Atlantic Fund. As an expression of public appreciation towards the Task Force it was munificent. But it may be that this unique, emotional wave of public compassion could distort sacrifice in combat for the future. To other bereaved or wounded who were not eligible, the Fund was largely seen as being discriminating. At the time of the Falklands war, other servicemen and women in Northern Ireland remained at risk. Death or mutilation brought them no special compensation then; nor is that an expectation for Falklands veterans serving there now. Such anomalies can create misunderstanding and bitterness, as much as they provide solace. The spontaneous generosity of the nation could have been gratefully absorbed into established Service charities. Their role is to dispense public donation where it is most needed amongst those who have served their country. Which must be easier than, as well as preferable to, assessing what is just compensation for the cost of duty.

Astonishing demonstrations of national acclaim for those who took part in the war have not yet ceased. In 1982, contingents of the Task Force marched in triumph through the City of London, and selected people from each rank and Service banqueted together in the Guildhall. Representatives of all who had been concerned in the campaign congregated for thanksgiving at St Paul's in 1985. At other times, such ceremonies have been repeated across the country with an unusual solidarity of patriotism. Whatever the cause or motive, those who went south have been more than adequately honoured in their lifetimes.

Three years after the war, the Falkland Islands Memorial was unveiled by Her Majesty the Queen in the Crypt of St Paul's Cathedral. Beforehand a service of Remembrance had been attended by royalty, peers, politicians, members of the establishment. Some of those who had fought, and many of the next of kin, were there. Within this glorious building, where heroes have been traditionally honoured, the tombs of Wellington and Nelson stand either side of the latest memorial. Nearby, commanders with names like Gort, Ironside, Slim and Montgomery are commemorated. Everywhere previous deeds of valour in each continent, on every ocean, are recorded.

The two hundred and fifty-two names are listed on the memorial alphabetically, lettered in gold, with only their Service a distinction between individuals. Royal Navy, Royal Fleet Auxiliary, Army, Royal Air Force, Merchant Navy.

Somewhere in America, I once read these words:

They say: We were young. We have died. Remember us.
They say: Our deaths are not ours; they are yours, they will
  mean what you make them.
They say: Whether our lives and deaths were for peace and a
  new hope or for nothing we cannot say; it is you who must say
  this.
We were young, they say. We have died. Remember us.

The nation has certainly done that.

AUTHOR'S ACKNOWLEDGEMENTS

It was not long after the conflict that Max Hastings first suggested to me that I should write this book. Three years later, at a Falklands Reunion, his persistence finally prevailed when I decided to try. I owe him a very special debt of gratitude for his patience and frank advice while this account tentatively took shape, as well as for writing the Foreword.

Other long-suffering friends who provided the help aspiring authors really need include my commander throughout this adventure, Major-General Julian Thompson. Fresh from the success of his own book, he gave me generous encouragement and sound advice on how to proceed. I must also particularly mention Ian McNeill and David Chisnall, who, throughout my labours, prolonged their roles as comrades-in-arms with discerning comments and helpful suggestions. Their colleagues, the four Company Commanders and David Brown, our 'Gunner', who all feature prominently in the story, have likewise made invaluable contributions to the narrative.

Another individual to whom I owe a great deal is Shandra Keelan. Besides typing the draft immaculately, she also provided pithy and humorous comments with each chapter, before proof-reading the manuscript. My friend Brigadier Robin Ross not only found time from an important staff appointment to scrutinize the text, but also introduced me to Toby Buchan, who must be one of the nicest publishers to work with in the business. His sensitive direction and tactful encouragement were just what was required as the magnitude of the task became apparent, and frustration or dejection had to be dispelled.

Most of the photographs in this book were taken by Leading Airman Paddy Ryan, whose graphic shots of 42 Commando in this campaign have already been widely published. Both he and his professional colleague, Petty Officer Peter Holdgate, preserved for posterity much of the action and pathos of this bizarre war, gaining deserved international acclaim for doing so. I count myself fortunate to have so many of their pictures in this book.

Amongst many friends who also contributed to the enterprise I must single out Frank Allen, who advised on the maps, Patricia Roberts, who co-ordinated endless research for me, Captain Derek Oakley and Major Alistair Donald, for their regimental scrutiny, Gerald and Philippa Roberts, as well as Ian MacDonald, who provided astute and objective criticism.

Most of the actual writing was completed in London, in the privacy of the comfortable home that Louis Mazel kindly made available. There was also a crucial break for inspiration in the sun at Pam Poole's Spanish villa. They both did much to provide the peace and quiet that was needed for recollection and drafting.

Finally, I thank my stoical family, who loyally adapted to the novelty and distraction of this unexpected project which dominated our domestic world for over a year.

NICK VAUX
July 1986

APPENDIX I

42 Commando, Royal Marines

CASUALTIES IN THE FALKLANDS CAMPAIGN 1982

KILLED IN ACTION

Acting Corporal J. Smith. 11 June. Mount Wall. Chest wounds. Buried in Devon.

Corporal L.G. Watts. 12 June. Mount Harriet. Chest wounds. Buried in Scotland.

WOUNDED IN ACTION

Lieutenant I.W.H. Stafford, Argyll and Sutherland Highlanders. 12 June. Mount Harriet. Gunshot wounds to left leg. Recovered and still serving.

Lieutenant C.V. Whiteley, RM. 12 June, Mount Harriet. Shrapnel wounds to both legs. Recovered and still serving.

Acting Lieutenant J.D. Pusey, RM. 12 June. Mount Harriet. Gunshot wounds to left upper arm. Retired.

Sergeant J.F. O'Neill. 13 June. Mount Harriet. Head injuries. Recovered and still serving.

Sergeant R.G.R. Shephard. 12 June. Mount Harriet. Shrapnel wounds to buttocks. Voluntary discharge, July 1986.

Corporal S.C. Newland, MM. 12 June. Mount Harriet. Gunshot wounds to both legs. Recovered and still serving.

Corporal P.A. van Heerden. 13 June. Mount Harriet. Shrapnel wound in stomach. Recovered and still serving.

Lance-Corporal S.J. Gilroy. 12 June. Mount Harriet. Shrapnel wound to head. Recovered and still serving.

Lance-Corporal B. Lynch. 12 June. Mount Harriet. Shrapnel wound to right buttock. Recovered and still serving.
Lance-Corporal J.W. McKay. 13 June. Mount Harriet. Wounded in left leg and wrist. Recovered and still serving.
Marine G.D. Brown. 12 June. Mount Harriet. Gunshot wounds to chest. Medical discharge, April 1984.
Marine S. Chubb. 13 June. Mount Harriet. Shrapnel wounds to left shoulder and right arm. Medical discharge, May 1984.
Marine D.J. Coulthard. 12 June. Mount Harriet. Shrapnel wounds to body. Recovered and still serving.
Marine M.A. Curtis. 3 June. Patrolling from Mount Challenger. Amputation of right foot. Invalided from the Service, January 1984.
Marine M. Hagyard. 11 June. Mount Wall. Shrapnel wounds to abdomen. Voluntary discharge, March 1985.
Marine P.A. Hodges. 12 June. Mount Harriet. Gunshot wounds to left leg. Recovered and still serving.
Marine P. Hugill. 13 June. Mount Harriet. Shrapnel wound to left hip. Recovered and still serving.
Marine S. Jacques. 12 June. Mount Harriet. Blast injury. Recovered but killed in Norway, January 1983.
Marine A. Martland. 12 June. Mount Harriet. Gunshot wounds to right leg. Recovered and still serving.
Marine K.R. Patterson. 5 June. Patrolling from Mount Challenger. Amputation of left foot. Invalided from the Service, June 1983.
Marine D. Pickard. 13 June. Mount Harriet. Blast injury. Recovered and still serving.
Marine G.P. Stringman. 24 May. Port San Carlos. Gunshot wound to left leg. Recovered and still serving.
Marine I. Vincent. 12 June. Mount Harriet. Gunshot wounds to both upper legs. Recovered and still serving.
Marine M.D. Yates. 13 June. Mount Harriet. Gunshot wounds to left arm. Voluntary discharge, October 1985.

Total casualties suffered by 'Four-Two' were as follows:

Killed in action	2
Wounded in action	24
Injured in action	17
Others	5
TOTAL	48

NOTE Those listed as still serving were doing so in August 1986.

APPENDIX II

42 Commando, Royal Marines

HONOURS AND AWARDS IN THE FALKLANDS CAMPAIGN 1982

DISTINGUISHED SERVICE ORDER

Lieutenant-Colonel (now Colonel) N.F. Vaux (Campaign)

MILITARY CROSS

Captain (now Major) P.M. Babbington (Mount Harriet)

MILITARY MEDAL

Sergeant (now Colour Sergeant) M. Collins (Mount Harriet)
Corporal (now Sergeant) M. Eccles (Mount Harriet)
Corporal (now Sergeant) S.C. Newland (Mount Harriet)
Corporal (now Sergeant) C.N.H. Ward (Mount Harriet)

MENTIONED IN DESPATCHES

Captain M.J. Norman (as RM Garrison Commander)
Captain C.R. Romberg, RA (Mount Harriet)
Sergeant M. McIntyre (Mount Harriet)

Sergeant J. Napier (Southern Thule)
Sergeant B. D'Oliveira (LSL *Sir Galahad*)
Lance-Corporal P.W. Boorn (Mount Harriet)
Lance-Corporal G. Cuthell (Mount Harriet)
Marine N.J. Barnett (Mount Harriet)

OFFICER OF THE ORDER OF THE BRITISH EMPIRE

Major J.M.G. Sheridan (South Georgia)

MEMBER OF THE ORDER OF THE BRITISH EMPIRE

Captain D. Sparks (Campaign)

COMMANDER-IN-CHIEF (FLEET) COMMENDATIONS

Captain C.J. Nunn (South Georgia)
Captain M. Sturman (Campaign)
Sergeant I. Robinson (Mount Wall)
Corporal T. Sicklemore (Mount Harriet)
Lance-Corporal O. Mewes (Mount Harriet)

APPENDIX III

42 Commando Royal Marines
— UNIT CITATION

BATTLE OF MOUNT HARRIET 11-12 JUNE 1982

On the night 11/12 June 1982, as part of a night attack by 3 Commando Brigade Royal Marines to break into the Argentine positions defending Port Stanley in the Falkland Islands, 42 Commando Royal Marines assaulted and captured the key Argentine position on Mount Harriet. This night attack by 42 Commando Royal Marines had been preceded by 9 days of intensive and brilliantly conducted night patrolling over very rough ground, extensive minefields and in adverse weather conditions.

The information acquired so painstakingly by the Commando's patrols was sufficiently detailed to enable the Commanding Officer to make a bold plan to outflank the enemy positions and assault them from the rear. This attack from an unexpected direction aimed to catch the enemy, consisting of the best part of 4th Argentine Infantry Regiment and the Regimental Headquarters, by surprise. Furthermore it would avoid a frontal assault through the main minefield and the enemy's planned killing ground.

After a long approach march, the assault started about 2 hours after midnight. K Company, the leading Company, got within 150 metres of the enemy before being fired on. The battle was on; the fighting was fierce. Bold and decisive leadership, combined with great aggressiveness, established K Company on the crest of the feature and then the long process of winkling out the enemy began. L

Company then began their clearing operation through the heavily defended Western end of the enemy position. Meanwhile J Company, who had diverted the enemy's attention before the attack began, supported K and L Companies on to their objectives.

Despite the stubborn resistance by the enemy machine gunners and enemy defensive artillery fire on the objective, the attack by 42 Commando Royal Marines was a brilliant success. The battle was fought with great dash and determination by the Commando, many of whom were suffering from cold injuries sustained in the preceding 10 days of appalling weather on Mount Kent and Mount Challenger. For the loss of two killed and 26 wounded, the Commando secured this vital feature; killing at least 50 of the enemy and taking over 300 prisoners, including the Regimental Commanding Officer and great quantities of equipment.

For this great feat of arms the Commando was awarded the following decorations.

One DSO
One MC
Four MMs
One OBE
One MBE
Eight MIDs

JHA Thompson
Brigadier
Commander
3 Commando Brigade RM

APPENDIX IV

42 Commando Royal Marines
DRAMATIS PERSONAE

'FOUR-TWO'

Commanding Officer	The author
Second-in-Command	Major Guy Sheridan
Operations Officer	Captain Ian McNeill
Adjutant (later Support Company Commander)	Captain Phil Wilson
Battle Adjutant	Captain Matt Sturman
Battery Commander	Major David Brown, Royal Artillery
'K' Company Commander	Captain Peter Babbington
'L' Company Commander	Captain David Wheen
'M' Company Commander	Captain Chris Nunn
'J' Company Commander	Captain Mike Norman
Quartermaster	Captain Dennis Sparks
Assistant Quartermaster	Lieutenant Frank Allen
Regimental Sergeant-Major	WO1 David Chisnall, BEM
Provost Sergeant	Sergeant Josh Shiel
2 Troop Sergeant	Sergeant 'Jumper' Collins
CO's Radio Operator	Corporal John Adams
CO's Attendant	Marine Robert Green

DIVISIONAL HEADQUARTERS

Divisional Commander	Major-General Jeremy Moore, CB, OBE, MC (and Bar)

Staff Officer (Operations)   Lieutenant-Colonel Paul Stevenson, MBE

3 COMMANDO BRIGADE HEADQUARTERS

Brigade Commander   Brigadier Julian Thompson, OBE
Brigade Major   Major John Chester
Officer Commanding Landing-Craft   Major Ewen Southby-Tailyour
Special Forces Commander   Lieutenant-Colonel Mike Rose, OBE, QGM

SS *CANBERRA*

Captain   Captain Dennis Scott-Masson
Royal Navy Captain   Captain Christopher Burne
Military Force Commander   Colonel Tom Seccombe, OBE

'THE HACKS'

Max Hastings   *Daily Express*
Kim Sabido   IRN
John Shirley   *Sunday Times*
Patrick Bishop   *Observer*

INDEX